Perfect Day

TUSCANY

Travel with

Insider Tips

www.marco-polo.com

Contents

For chapters: see inside front cover

TOP 10

Not to be missed!
Our top hits – from the absolute No. 1 to No. 10 –
help you plan your tour of the most important sights.

1 PIAZZA DEL DUOMO (FLORENCE) ➤ 58

The square with its white and green ensemble – the cathedral, bell tower and baptistry – is one of our top attractions not least of all due to Brunelleschi's dome (ill. left).

2 PIAZZA DEL CAMPO (SIENA) ➤ 98

Thanks to the strict building regulations introduced back in the Middle Ages, nothing spoils the harmony and beauty of this shell-shaped square.

3 AREZZO ➤ 101

The fresco cycle 'Legends of the True Cross' in the Basilica of San Francesco is one of the masterpieces of the Renaissance.

4 PIAZZA DEL DUOMO (SIENA) ➤ 104

This is where the city's true importance can be seen – the breathtakingly beautiful cathedral and the extraordinary history of Santa Maria della Scala opposite.

5 PIENZA ➤ 138

Renaissance architects designed the ideal town here on the orders of Pope Pius II, displaying a sense of scale and proportion so typical of the Tuscans.

6 PISA ➤ 164

The gleaming white architectural 'miracle' – the cathedral, baptistry, the Campo Santo and the Leaning Tower – rises above the Campo dei Miracoli.

7 SAN GIMIGNANO ➤ 110

The taller the tower, the more powerful the family – this small town owes its skyline to this medieval competition in the name of vanity.

8 MONTALCINO & SANT'ANTIMO ➤ 141

The Benedictine abbey near the little Brunello-producing town is the most beautiful of the Romanesque jewels in this area.

9 SANTA CROCE (FLORENCE) ➤ 61

The hall church was built for the local populace. Because many people could not read, young, unknown artists, including a certain Giotto di Bondone, painted the Gospel on the walls.

10 LUCCA ➤ 168

The Piazza dell'Anfiteatro is like a case study in the history of urban planning – in the course of time the tiers of seats for spectators in the Roman amphitheatre were built on and turned into houses.

THAT TUSCANY

Find out what Tuscany is all about and savour its unique flair. Just like the Tuscans do.

OPEN-AIR GALLERY

"Giuliano, don't put your money in the bank!" The textile manufacturer Gori heeded this piece of advice from a friend and invested instead in art. He invited famous artists to create a work of art for the park of his Fattoria Le Celle near Montale (208 B4). Meanwhile there are more than 60 objects in the landscaped park that can be viewed in summer if you apply well in advance (www.goricoll.it, info@goricoll.it).

CULINARY TRIPS

The Tuscans like to take short weekend breaks to sample delicious culinary highlights found in the surrounding countryside. And there are plenty of these here. They travel to Marradi for the sweet chestnut festival, buy sheep's cheese in Pienza, sample the season's olive oil in Montecarlo and buy honey from beekeepers in Montalcino. The website www.vetrina.toscana.it provides some orientation, listing farm shops and where to buy regional specialities as well as local events.

FOR THE LOVE OF A FIGHT

The *calcio* tournament in historical costume in Florence (www.calciostoricofiorentino.it), that recalls an episode dating back to 1530, is not for the weak of heart. During this mixture of football and rugby, played by four teams in front of the church Santa Croce, virtually everything is allowed. The historical matches are typically Tuscan, about whom it is often said that most fun was to be had in twos – and when a third person turned up, two sides were formed straight away to make fun of the 'opponent'.

AN APÉRITIF AT DUSK

An *aperitivo* is a fixture in everyday life in Tuscany. People arrange to meet at the local bar after work, order a rather over-priced cocktail or a glass of bubbly white wine and can then help themselves to the more or less opulent fingerfood buffet free of charge.

LIKE IN THE GOOD OLD DAYS

Strade bianche, dusty unmade lanes, are just as much part of

FEELING

Culinary delights are just waiting to be discovered all over Tuscany.

Tuscany as cypresses, vineyards and olive trees. They generally used to be the only link between remote settlements. Just 20 years ago Tuscany was still criss-crossed by a network of these tracks but then the majority were sacrificed in the name of progress. However, a few do still exist to this day and these reveal the very essence of Tuscany in the hilly countryside where time has stood still. SP112 in Chianti, between Panzano and Castello Volpaia, and SP Cipressino from Murlo to Monte Antico, are just two suggested routes.

THAT TUSCAN SUMMER FEELING

Every year between June and September, the cultural calendar moves to the country. All across the region, in restored cloisters, picturesque castle ruins and on village squares masses of different events are held – from the Mercantia street performance festival in Certaldo (➤ 125) to the Teatro Povero in Monticchiello (➤ 195), to mention just two of many.

The setting sun near Castiglione della Pescaia

STESSA SPIAGGIA, STESSA MARE

The Tuscans do not simply go off to the seaside for their holidays. They carefully seek out the one place, the one beach and the neighbours under the sunshade next to them and faithfully come back year in, year out. For this reason you will find people interested in culture and the countryside in the pretty port Castiglione della Pescaia in southern Tuscany, whereas families with children are in the majority on the Etruscan coast between San Vincenzo and Cecina and the 20km (12mi)-long stretch of resorts in Versilia is popular among those whose day starts in the late afternoon.

THE CALL OF THE COUNTRYSIDE

Baroque villas near Lucca, picturesque stone cottages in the Chianti region, privately-run spas in Val di Merse – what is offered under the collective heading *agriturismo* in many places has little to do with the original idea of guaranteeing owners of small farms an additional source of income. Such places are generally only to be found in the less touristy areas. Nevertheless, the Tuscan version of 'holidaying on the farm' is still the best way to get to know the area and its people.

The Magazine

A LAND OF GENIUS

Tuscany has not just produced some of Italy's greatest writers and thinkers – Dante, Petrarch, Boccaccio and Machiavelli – but also a host of peerless artists: Giotto, Michelangelo, Donatello and Leonardo da Vinci.

Dante Alighieri

Dante Alighieri was born in Florence in 1265. He served the city as a diplomat, but in 1302 was exiled – on trumped-up charges – and spent the years before his death drifting between cities across northern Italy. He died in 1321 in Ravenna, where he is buried. He is best known for his great epic poem, *La Divina Commedia* (*The Divine Comedy*), which

Detail from *Dante and his Worlds* by Domenico di Michelino

helped secure the use of everyday Tuscan – the vernacular in which the poem is written – as a literary language. This language would eventually evolve into Italian as it is spoken today.

Francesco Petrarch

Francesco Petrarch, or Petrarca, was born in Arezzo in 1304 and died in 1375. A traveller and diplomat, he attended the papal court in Avignon, France, where he probably met Laura de Noves, the romantic inspiration for his *Canzoniere*, some of the finest sonnets ever written. Like his predecessor Dante and contemporary Boccaccio, Petrarch often wrote in Italian, but was also a member of the vanguard of writers who sought to revive Greek and Latin as literary languages, thus forming part of the upsurge in Classical scholarship that helped pave the way for the Renaissance.

Giovanni Boccaccio

Giovanni Boccaccio (1313–75) was probably born in Paris, the illegitimate son of an Italian merchant. He spent his formative years in Tuscany and Naples, settling in Florence in 1340. Here he met fellow writer Petrarch, with whom he shared an interest in reviving Greek and Latin as literary languages. His most famous work is *Il Decamerone* (*The Decameron*), which was written (in Italian) after the Black Death of 1348. It consists of 100 tales told by 10 people over 10 days as they seek to escape the pestilence raging in Florence.

Portrait of Nicolò Machiavelli, painted by Santi di Tito in 1527

Nicolò Machiavelli

Nicolò Machiavelli (1469–1527) has always had a bad press. The term 'Machiavellian', suggesting cunning and treachery, was actually coined by the French to denigrate all things Italian. Machiavelli himself was a Florentine diplomat, politician and bureaucrat. His book *Il Principe* (*The Prince*) was a masterpiece of political analysis, combining the study of historical cycles, political science and human nature, things which Machiavelli himself held to be immutable throughout history.

Giotto di Bondone

Much about Giotto's life is a mystery, including the place and date of his birth (probably Vespignano, in 1266). What is beyond doubt is the fact that his iconoclastic approach to painting, along with the work of contemporaries such as Cimabue and Pietro Cavallini, would alter the course of Western culture. Before Giotto, religious art was a simple act of devotion, usually presented in the form of a Byzantine *Madonna and Child*, its flat, stilted and stylised form unchanged for centuries. Giotto swept away convention, introducing narrative incident, emotion, buildings, spatial depth, realistic figures and more. Much of his major work is outside Tuscany, in Padua (in the Arena chapel) and Assisi (the Basilica di San Francesco), but glimpses of his genius can also be seen in Florence in the *Maestà* in the Uffizi and both the Bardi and Peruzzi chapels in Santa Croce.

Marriage at Cana **by Giotto**

Donatello

Donatello (*c.* 1386–1466) may not enjoy the reputation of Michelangelo or Leonardo, but in the field of sculpture he was as great a pioneer as either of his successors. The bronze *David*, for example, now in Florence's Bargello, was one of the first nude statues of the Renaissance; the figure of St George for Orsanmichele, also in Florence, has a relief that represents the first rigorous use of perspective in Western art; and the mounted figure of the mercenary, *Gattamelata*, in Padua, was the first equestrian bronze created since Roman times. His most extraordinary work, however, is the *Mary Magdalene* in Florence's Museo dell'Opera, a figure so strange and haunting that it seems almost contemporary.

Leonardo da Vinci

The polymath Leonardo (1452–1519) was born in Vinci (► 182), a small village in the hills just to the west of Florence. In early life he trained under Andrea del Verrocchio, who is said to have become so disillusioned at the paucity of his own talent compared to his pupil, that he gave up painting. Leonardo's first completed work that survives, an *Annunciation* from 1481, still hangs in Florence (in the Uffizi), but much of the artist's life was spent outside Tuscany. From 1483 he worked in Milan, where he remained for 16 years, painting, among other things, the *Last Supper*. He returned to Florence in 1499, spending much of his time on anatomical research, and working on a fresco cycle in the Palazzo Vecchio (now lost), as well as works such as the *Mona Lisa*. He left for Milan again in 1506, before moving to Rome and, finally, France.

Michelangelo

The sublime painter, sculptor, architect – and sometime poet – Michelangelo (1475–1564) was born in Caprese, in eastern Tuscany, but moved to Florence with his family when he was a month old. At 13 he was apprenticed to the painter Domenico Ghirlandaio, but where or how he learned to sculpt is unknown: Michelangelo himself always insisted he was self-taught. In 1496 he arrived in Rome, where, by 1499, he had carved the *Pietà* in St Peter's. In 1501 he returned to Florence and was working on *David*, and by 1503 he had begun the *Doni Tondo* (now in the Uffizi). He continued to move back and forth between the two cities, working on the Sistine Chapel in Rome, with the odd project in Florence (such as the Biblioteca Laurentiana) before leaving the city for the last time in 1534. He would return only after his death, to be buried in Santa Croce.

Michelangelo's *Tondo Doni*

GREEN POTENTIAL

Tuscany is predominantly visited because of its artistic connections and rich history, but the region has a few image-blowing surprises up its sleeve. Pull yourself away from the undoubtedly unmissable 'mother lode' of culture for a while, and you'll be rewarded by amazing sights that are not manmade. You'll also discover that Tuscany is doing it's part to save the planet, with modern scientific breakthroughs that even da Vinci would have been proud of.

Natural Tuscany

Tuscany has a wealth of natural environments to explore. Specialist flora and fauna colonise habitats from below sea level to the top of snow-capped mountain peaks. A quarter of the region is hilly – it is the most forested area in Italy – and is less densely populated compared to the Italian average, offering some exceptional places to escape the tour groups and immerse yourself in natural surroundings.

Of Italy's 22 National Parks, three are in Tuscany and they showcase the range of landscapes and environments exceptionally well. The Parco Nazionale dell'Appennino Tosco-Emiliano, founded in 2001, straddles the border with neighbouring Emilia-Romagna. The park is characterised by true mountain environments with a range of peaks over 2,000m (6,560ft), many of them inaccessible but offering magnificent vistas.

Parco Nazionale dell'Arcipelago Toscano is currently the largest marine park in Europe, covering 56,766ha (219mi²) of sea and 17,887ha (69mi²) of land, comprising seven islands and a stretch of coastline. The park protects habitats ranging from craggy cliffs and sandy beaches, to tidal flats and deep water, and has large expanses of *Posidonia oceanica*, a sea grass that's a key marine plant species for ecosystem stability.

Parco Nazionale delle Foreste Casentinesi, Monte Falterona, Campigna, in the far east of Tuscany, also shares borders with the neighbouring region of Emilia-Romagna. Here you'll find the largest and best-preserved mixed woodlands in Italy, which are also some of the oldest in Europe – perfect for that family day out.

The autumn mood in Tuscany

Green Tuscany

The world's first geothermal power generator was developed at Larderello, south of Volterra, in 1904, and the first power station was opened here in 1911. The site continues to be at the forefront of technological developments and today produces 10 per cent of the total geothermal energy output on the planet. There are 33 geothermal plants in operation in Tuscany, producing enough power for 2 million households and saving 3.8 million tonnes of carbon dioxide emissions annually.

TUSCANY IN CONTEXT

Tuscany is an administrative region of modern Italy located at the north-eastern corner of the Italian or Apennine Peninsula. Hemmed in by the Tyrrhenian Sea (part of the Mediterranean) in the west and the Apennine Mountains in the north and west, it covers an area of almost 24,000sq km (9,260sqmi), and its administrative capital is Florence. The name Tuscany comes from 'Tuscia', the name given to the region by the Etruscans who settled here from around 800 B.C. and who were swallowed by the Roman Empire in around 300 B.C. A papal bull of 1569 issued by Pius V raised the status of Tuscany to a Grand Duchy which later became part of the Kingdom of Italy, founded in 1861.

Tuscany's LEATHER DISTRICT

Italy is renowned worldwide for the excellent quality of its leather goods and Tuscany has always played an important role in this industry. Even the famous Gucci haute couture empire began in a small shop in Florence.

If you choose to buy a pair of genuine Italian-made shoes, a handbag, luggage or a briefcase as a souvenir of your visit, you can be fairly sure tha the leather you are buying was tanned and treated just a few kilometres from the boutique where you bought it.

Artisan tanning developed in Tuscany during the medieval era and was transformed into a full-scale industry in the 18th century when the region cemented its monopoly. Today, the area between Florence and Pisa is sti known as the Leather District, centred on the small town of Santa Croce sull'Arno and its surrounding communities. There are around 400 factorie taking raw hide in and delivering finished leather, and the industry employ some 10,000 people.

Quality Leather

98 per cent of Italy's thick leather for shoe soles – *cuoio* in Italian – is processed here which basiclly amounts to most of that produced in Europe as a whole. In addition, 35 per cent of all Italian softer leather hides – *pelli* in Italian – comes from Tuscan tanneries. In total, the indust generates 2 billion euros in revenue every year for the region.

Most tanneries now use modern synthetic chemicals and dyes to achie their results. This allows the leather to be produced in a consistent qualit and allows the *pelli* to be dyed in whatever colours designers deem fashio able for that season.

Traditional Methods

But a few still keep to traditional methods. Consorzio Vera Pelle Italiana Conciata al Vegetale (The Genuine Italian Vegetable-Tanned Leather Consortium; www.pellealvegetale.it) was founded in 1994 to promote those business still practising the traditional methods of using only

Above and left: Tuscany's leather goods are sold all over the country

natural products in their tanning and curing processes.

All the 26 tanneries that form part of the consortium are located in the Leather District of Tuscany, and they use natural tannin to dye the leather, a process that takes around 40 days. Tannin can come from the bark of trees or the leaves of plants, including the chestnut that grows so prevalently in the Tuscan hills and mountains. This means that naturally dyed leathers can never be gold or purple or lime green, only colours produced by nature, such as rich tan or deep russet. Natural tannins don't contain any toxic substances so they are much better for the environment, and the leather produced this way is more appropriate for people with skin conditions and allergies because it doesn't contain residues of artificial dyes and chemicals. Consortium members also recycle many by-products from the tanning process, such as animal hair for agricultural fertiliser, and salt, which is used to treat icy roads in the winter.

> "Even the famous Gucci haute couture empire began in a shop in Florence"

Look for The Genuine Italian Vegetable-Tanned Leather Consortium quality trademark, with the slogan *Pelle Conciata al Vegetale in Toscana* incorporated into a handprint symbol, to ensure it's genuine natural-dyed leather from Tuscany.

HOW TO PAINT A FRESCO

Painting in medieval Tuscany was not easy. As well as talent and inspiration, you had to have technical know-how and the ability to work at speed. You also had to employ staff, satisfy patrons – and avoid falling off your scaffolding.

Most wall paintings in Tuscany from the 13th century onwards were frescoes, so-called because they were painted onto wet, or fresh *(fresco)* plaster. Oil painting, a medium which allowed greater range of colour and effect, was practised in the 15th century but not fully mastered until the 16th century.

First Steps

To paint a fresco, an artist would first look for a suitable wall, best of all in a church, villa or palace. Money from a patron such as the Church or a wealthy banker was always welcome. Assistants then also had to be paid for carrying out peripheral chores such as putting up a scaffold from which the artist could work. That this profession was anything but safe can be seen from accounts of accidents that have been passed down through time. Michelangelo was injured when he fell off a platform in Rome's Sistine Chapel and the Tuscan painter Barna da Siena died after falling from his scaffold.

> "... only the smallest of areas can be worked in a day ..."

Assistants applied the first of several layers of plaster to the wall: a layer known as the *arichio,* or *aricciato,* a rough coat of lime and sand. Then it was the artist's turn to incise the painting's basic composition and principal divisions into the plaster.

A more detailed drawing was made at the next stage using a red-earth pigment known as *sinopia,* named after Sinope, the Greek city in Asia Minor which was believed to produce the finest quality pigment in the Middle Ages. Such sketches have often been revealed during restoration work in many Tuscan churches.

Speed is of the essence

Now the real problems begin. As damp plaster is essential for fresco painting, only the smallest of areas can be worked on in a day before the plaster dries. A fresco is therefore divided into *giornate,* from the Italian *giorno,* meaning day, and each morning or evening an assistant would apply a thin coat of wet finishing plaster *(intonaco)* to the *arichio* for the day's painting ahead. Once work on a fresco had been started, things had to be done quickly. If an artist hesitated too long or even worse, made a mistake, the dried *intonaco* had to be hacked off and a fresh layer applied.

At the end of each session the edge of the *intonaco* needed to be bevelled to prevent it from crumbling and provide a clean edge for the following morning's work. Thanks to these edges, art historians can determine how many *giornate* an artist needed to paint any particular fresco. Most Tuscan painters could create a figure in two days – the first day for the body and the second for the head and shoulders. Masaccio completed his *Expulsion of Adam and Eve* fresco in the Brancacci Chapel in just four days (►80).

Selecting colours was particulary difficult when using this technique as the pigments used for fresco painting were not easy to mix. The limited palette of colours made it virtually impossible to achieve effects of light and shade. Short cuts taken can also be spotted easily as poor or unsuitable pigments fade or change colour over time. Paint applied to a dry wall flakes off almost immediately too. Not that this puts any artist in bad company. Even Leonardo da Vinci, frustrated by the limitations of fresco painting, completed most of his *Last Supper* in Milan on dry plaster with pigments of his own invention – with disastrous results for those trying to restore the original version after it had been virtually completely lost.

Albrecht Dürer is visited by the emperor Maximilian while painting a fresco

FOUR GREAT FLORENTINE FRESCO CYCLES ...

Palazzo Medici-Riccardi, Cappella dei Magi

The Journey of the Magi by Benozzo Gozzoli (➤ 77).

Santa Croce, Cappella Bardi and Cappella Peruzzi

Scenes from the Life of St Francis, and *Scenes from the Life of St John and St John the Baptist* by Giotto (➤ 62).

Santa Maria del Carmine, Cappella Brancacci

Scenes from the Life of St Peter by Masaccio, Masolino da Panicale and Filippino Lippi (➤ 80).

Santa Maria Novella

Chancel frescoes by Domenico Ghirlandaio of the Virgin and St John the Baptist (➤ 67).

Gozzoli's masterpiece in the Palazzo Medici-Riccardi

Sodoma and Luca Signorelli's *Scenes from the Life of St Benedict*

How Fresco Works

A fresco relies for its longevity on a complex chemical reaction and, in particular, the drying qualities of plaster, a mixture of lime, water and sand. As plaster dries, carbon dioxide is absorbed from the air, converting the lime (calcium hydroxide) to calcium carbonate. This crystallizes around the sand particles, binding them to the wall.

If you add powdered and water soluble pigments to the wet plaster, the crystallization process also fixes the pigments and makes them resistant to further action by water. Thereafter, only the crumbling of the plaster or the deterioration of the pigments will affect a fresco's appearance.

...AND FOUR GREAT TUSCAN FRESCO CYCLES

Arezzo, San Francesco

The Legend of the True Cross by Piero della Francesca (➤ 101).

Monte Oliveto Maggiore

Scenes from the Life of St Benedict by Sodoma and Luca Signorelli (➤ 145).

San Gimignano, Collegiata

Scenes from the Old and New Testaments by Bartolo di Fredi and Lippo Memmi (➤ 112).

Siena, Palazzo Pubblico

Allegories of Good and Bad Government by Ambrogio Lorenzetti (➤ 100).

A day at THE RACES

Twice a year, Siena's Piazza del Campo is the stage for a bareback horse race. The prize is modest and the race short. Yet the Palio is one of the most vivid and fiercely contested sporting events in Europe.

The race, which has been run every year almost without interruption for 700 years, involves representatives of Siena's *contrade,* the medieval parishes into which the city has been divided since the 13th century. Once there were 42 such parishes, today there are just 17, but only 10 are chosen by lot each year to enter the race. Once the event was held throughout the whole city, but since 1656 it has followed a three-lap circuit of the Piazza del Campo. The prize has always been the same,

however – the embroidered banner *(pallium)* which gives the race its name. The contest is dedicated to the Holy Virgin and held on or around feast days associated with the Madonna – 2 July (the Feast of the Visitation) and 16 August (the day following the Feast of the Assumption).

Preparations go on for months beforehand. Deals are often made during this period. Divine assistance is sought, horses being marched up the aisles of *contrade* churches to be blessed.

Stable hands in medieval costume lead the *contrade* into the arena. National television broadcasts the event, while the Campo in Siena is filled to bursting. The race is hectic and often dangerous – and obstructing the opposition is expressly permitted.

> "Preparations go on for months beforehand. Deals are often made."

Victory is tasty: the winning *contrada* celebrates with a vast banquet and revels in its triumph for weeks.

Watching the Palio first hand is an experience not to be forgotten

TUSCANY AND THE ARTS

Tuscany and the arts go together. Whether it's as a setting for a film or an outdoor concert, the region's landscapes provide a sublime backdrop, while opera and many other events give voice to a heritage stretching back centuries.

The Perfect Stage

Tuscany may not have yielded any great film directors, but its historic towns and countryside have provided the locations for any number of well-known movies. The films that started the industry's Tuscan love affair were Merchant Ivory's *A Room with a View* in 1985, filmed in and around Florence, and Tarkovsky's *Nostalgia* (1983), which included the ruined abbey of San Galgano, among other locations. Since then, other films with Tuscan settings include: Kenneth Branagh's *Much Ado About*

A scene in *Under the Tuscan Sun*

Musicians at the Medici Court **by Antonio Domenico Gabbiani (1652–1726)**

Nothing (1993); Bernardo Bertolucci's *Stealing Beauty* (1995); Anthony Minghella's *The English Patient* (1996); Jane Campion's *The Portrait of a Lady* (1996); and Franco Zeffirelli's *Tea with Mussolini* (1998). Anthony Hopkins came to town for the filming of *Hannibal* (2001). In 2003, *Under the Tuscan Sun*, adapted from Frances Mayes' novel of a writer's new life in Italy, was shot in various Tuscan locations, including Florence. James Bond, 007, fought the bad guys in Siena in *Quantum of Solace* (2008), while in 2009, Spike Lee's *Miracle at St Anna* and *New Moon* were filmed around the region.

Where Opera was Born

One thing cannot be dismissed for certain – opera was invented in Florence. The story starts with high-society Florentine weddings, which often included *intermedii*, or tableaux involving singing and dancing. Into the mix were thrown the extravagant pageants held by the Medici in the gardens of the Palazzo Pitti, which at the end of the 16th century inspired a city academy, the Camerata Fiorentina, to mix aspects of Greek drama with semi-musical declamation. Two of the academy's members, Jacopo Peri and Ottavio Rinucci, wrote the first recognizable opera, *Dafne*, in 1597, while the first opera to have survived in its entirety – written by the same pair – was *Euridice*, first performed in the Palazzo Pitti to celebrate the marriage of Henri IV of France to Maria de'Medici.

Andrea Bocelli performing at the 50th Grammy Awards in 2008

ANDREA BOCELLI

Andrea Bocelli is one of the world's best-known operatic tenors. Born in Lajatico, Tuscany, in 1958, he first started singing in public in 1980, to help pay his way through the University at Pisa, where he studied law. He achieved wider fame after 1992, when he was championed by Luciano Pavarotti and the Italian rock singer, Zucchero. In 1994, he won the Newcomers prize at the Sanremo Music Festival and made his operatic debut (as Macduff in Verdi's *Macbeth*) in the same year. Since then he has recorded numerous crossover songs and other pieces of music, selling over 60 million CDs worldwide. The albums *Cieli di Toscana* (*Tuscan Skies*, 2001), *Viaggio Italiano* (*Italian Journey*, 2003) and *Amore* (2006) are three of the best.

Musical Heritage

Opera's origins may have been obscure, but not so the region's later musical greats. The name of Florence-born Luigi Cherubini (1760–1842) may not resonate today, but no less an authority than Beethoven considered him the greatest of his contemporaries – the *Requiem in C minor* is his most celebrated work. And the opera *Cavalleria rusticana* by Pietro Mascagni (1863–1945), who was born in Livorno on the Tuscan coast, caused a sensation on its premiere in 1890, ushering in the verismo (realism) movement in Italian dramatic music. But the most famous Tuscan composer was Giacomo Puccini (1858–1924), who was born in Lucca and composed *La Bohème,* one of his most popular operas, at Torre del Lago, nearby on the Tuscan coast.

A Feast of Festivals

Torre del Lago is the setting for an annual summer festival of Puccini's works, the Puccini Festival (July–August; www.puccinifestival.it). This is just one of many concerts and events, large and small, held across the region, from recitals in the lovely surroundings of the church of Orsanmichele in Florence (March–October; www.orcafi.it) to the Maggio Musicale (late April to early July; www.maggiofiorentino.com), Italy's foremost music festival. Smaller, but no less tempting, events include the festival in Barga, a village north of Lucca (www.barganews.com); the theatre festival in Volterra (mid/end July; www.volterrateatro.it); and the Estate Fiesolana (June–September; www.estatefiesolana.it) in Fiesole.

A performance of *La Fanciulla del West* during the Puccini Festival

TUSCAN WINES

Once upon a time Tuscan wine meant little more than Chianti, but in the last 20 years the region's viticulture has been transformed, producing an ever-increasing variety of excellent new red and white wines.

Chianti, like virtually every traditional Tuscan red wine, is made predominantly from Sangiovese – one of the most highly revered varieties of grape. Due to the traditional methods used to produce wine that remained unchanged for centuries, Chianti was often regarded as a cheap wine and sold in bottles in a wickerwork basket. In the meantime, it has regained a good reputation.

"The best ... are found in the tiny area around Montalcino"

There are hundreds of Chiantis, good and bad. Producers in the Gallo Nero (Black Cockerel) consortium make some of the better wines (including Fontodi, Felsina and Isole e Olena), and the ancient *vino nobile*, the so-called 'King of Wines', from around Montepulciano, can also be excellent.

But the best of the traditional wines are found in the tiny area around Montalcino, notably the elegant and expensive Brunello di Montalcino and its cheaper cousin, Rosso di Montalcino.

Super Tuscans

As younger, skilled and more adventurous producers emerged, a lot of them have not entered their wines for the official 'DOC' classification (Denominazione di Origine Controllata), frustrated by the many restrictions it imposes. As a result, many of the region's best wines are to be found under the most humble classifications of all: *vino da tavola* (table wine) or IGT *(Indicazione Geografica Tipica).* This is especially true of the so-called Super Tuscans, which are wines from small estates that blend traditional Sangiovese grapes with imported grapes to create 'non-Italian' varieties such as Syrah, Merlot, Cabernet franc and Cabernet Sauvignon, and have perfectly hit contemporary tastes. The first of these varieties (and often the most expensive) are Tignanello, Solaia, Sassicaia and Ornellaia. Many estates across the region are open for tours and wine-tasting, especially in Chianti.

WHITE-HOT WINES

Tuscan whites have long lagged behind the region's reds, victims of the traditional *trebbiano* grape and the bland wines it produces. Among other varieties, only Chardonnay could compete and cope with the hot Tuscan sun, but it's a capricious grape under Italian skies. Now, though, a few brave souls are experimenting with new production techniques and different grape varieties. Top tips are wines made from the Vermintino grape such as Poggio al Tesoro, or Chardonnay and Sauvignon blanc blends such as L'Anima, from Livernano.

Insider Tip

THE MEDICI BANK

Without the Medici family it is arguable whether the Renaissance as we know it would have taken place. The Medici's funded the design of cutting-edge buildings and commissioned original paintings that revolutionised our view of the arts, allowing some of the greatest architects and artists ever known to flourish. They were the dynasty that set the mould for what we can now marvel at today in major museums around the world.

The Medicis found themselves in a position to spend the modern equivalent of billions of their own cash on the rebirth of the arts due to the fortune they made as the most important bankers of the late medieval period. Although the family had been involved in banking for some decades in partnership with others, the independent Medici Bank was founded in 1397 by Giovanni di Bicci de Medici. The Medici held most of the big money accounts, starting with the most lucrative of them all – the Vatican coffers – and several royal households across Europe also used the bank. At it's height, under Cosimo de' Medici (1389–1464), the bank had six branches around western Europe, plus a mobile branch that formed part of the papal court entourage.

Above: Cosimo de' Medici, known as 'Il Vecchio' (The Elder)

From Strength to Strength

The bank expanded the use of Bills of Exchange across western Europe making the movement of monies more secure, simple and effective than it had ever been. A client could deposit a sum at a Medici bank and receive a Bill of Exchange from the manager. This Bill of Exchange could then be presented at another Medici bank in another country and the sum could be retrieved, minus a fee. Medici Bills of Exchange were so popular and secure that they were bought and sold as a commodity on the open market.

> "The bank had six branches around western Europe, plus a mobile branch"

However, the banking system in the Middle Ages differed in one major way from the systems we use today. Since usury (taking money as a fee for money lent) was a heinous sin punishable by excommunication, bankers could not charge interest on the money they lent out. Instead, the family used funds they held in their reserves to finance Medici commercial activity, such as merchant shipping or the production of high-value goods like silk and wool. Controlling these activities from source produced almost immeasurable wealth for the family.

Death of the Bank

Despite the seemingly limitless profits to be made, the history of the Medici Bank does not have a happy ending. As generations went on, the Medici became much more interested in patronizing the arts, playing politics and monopolizing the upper ranks of the Catholic Church, to pay much attention to the 'core business' that had once been the dynasty's mainstay. A series of managers began to mishandle affairs and branches began to fail.

Though the cancer of mismanagement had rotted the structure, it was political upheaval that brought about the death of the bank. The Medici suffered a humiliating loss of face at the hands of the French when they invaded Tuscany in 1494 and they were thrown out of Florence in the wake of a popular revolt led by a Catholic priest and itinerant preacher with a message of repentance, Girolamo Savonarola. Bank assets were seized and the pro-Savonarola crowds rampaged through the bank headquarters at Palazzo Medici-Riccardi, burning documents and ledgers. The Medicis returned from exile in 1512 to rule Florence as Grand Dukes once again, but their bank did not rise from the ashes.

The Tuscan Garden

Tuscany contains Italy's loveliest gardens, ranging from grandiose city gardens to beautiful villa gardens in some of the region's most scenic rural retreats.

Urban Gardens

Where you have a garden in Tuscany you usually have a rural villa, but some of the region's earliest and most popular gardens are in towns or cities. The most-visited garden in Italy, for example, is the Giardino di Boboli, in the heart of Florence (➤ 80). In Lucca you can enjoy the Giardino Botanico (➤ 173), while in San Quirico d'Orcia, near Pienza, the Horti Leonini offer a wonderful but little-known retreat (➤ 151).

Garden Philosophy

Pienza has one of Tuscany's earliest surviving urban gardens in the Palazzo Piccolomini (➤ 139), created as part of Pope Pius II's attempt to convert the village of his birth into a model Renaissance town. Begun in 1458, it exemplifies the Renaissance ideas of this art-historical period that would dominate Tuscan garden design for centuries. Chief of these was the notion that the wider landscape should influence a garden, a marked shift from the medieval belief that gardens should tame or exclude nature. The garden has a modest, domestic air and scale – illustrating the idea that a garden should be a 'room' and an extension of the house to which it is attached.

The Medici Villas

Several major gardens dot the Florentine hills, where the Medici built a series of grand villas, many of them now open to the public. The best is the Villa Medicea di Castello, about 8km (5mi) north of the city, built for Lorenzo the Magnificent. Although much has been altered or lost, the effect is still wonderful – highlights include the grotto and the *limonaia*, with more than 600 different varieties of citrus trees. Other fine Medici gardens open to the public can be seen in Fiesole at the Villa Medici; Poggio a Caiano, 18km (11mi) northwest of Florence; and the Villa La Petraia, close to the Villa Medicea di Castello.

The Lucchese Villas

A second cluster of villas can be found in the countryside around Lucca, notably the Villa Garzoni, Villa Torrigiani, Villa Mansi and Villa Reale (➤ 180). Elsewhere, foreign owners have either restored or created some delightful gardens, notably the Villa La Pietra in Pietra, whose theatrical appearance owes much to the English Acton family, who bought it in 1907. Or Villa La Foce in the Val d'Orcia, transformed in the 1920s and 1930s by English landscape artist Cecil Pinsent, who used classical Italian gardens as his inspiration.

The formal gardens at Villa Garzoni

The marvel of MARBLE

The creamy-grey marble of Carrara is the world's most famous, used for everything from London's Marble Arch to Michelangelo's *David*. Not to mention also a million bath-rooms worldwide.

Marble is a metamorphic form of limestone, hardened by colossal heat and pressure, and comes in a multitude of colours – Carrara's version is prized for its pure colour and near flawless lustre. It's popularity has come at a price, however, and today, whether you're coming in to land at nearby Pisa airport, or travelling by car or train along the coast north of Viareggio, you can't fail to notice the vast scars of the quarries that have eaten away entire mountainsides around Carrara and the nearby town of Massa.

From Wood to Diamond

Marble has been mined in the region for millennia: the name Carrara probably derived from 'kar', an ancient Indo-European word meaning 'stone'. In pre-Roman times, miners extracted the stone by driving pegs made of fig wood into natural flaws in the rock. Water was then poured on to the wood and as the pegs expanded they split the marble. The Romans introduced the use of iron pegs, which they hammered into shallow scored lines, creating blocks of around 2.7m^3 (95ft^3), which is still the standard measure today. The Romans' methods prevailed until the end of the 19th century, when the use of steel and, more recently, diamond-edged wire, revolutionised the extraction and cutting process. Even so, working marble is still a painstaking affair – the finest saws can still only cut 20cm (8in) of stone an hour.

Big Business

As you travel around the region, where there are around 200 marble works, you will often hear the whine of machinery, a whine that continues 24 hours a day, 365 days a year. Around 750,000 tonnes of stone is extracted annually, making this vast area the world's biggest marble-producing region.

Strong horizontal and vertical lines in one of Carrara's marble quarries

MARBLE AND SCULPTURE

Roman sculptors used Carrara marble extensively, but it then fell into decline for a thousand years, enjoying a revival in the 11th century during the great era of Romanesque church-building. Nicola and Giovanni Pisano pioneered its resurgence as a stone for sculpture in the 13th century, creating Gothic masterpieces in Pisa and beyond. Later, Michelangelo liked to say that his skill and destiny as a sculptor came from the fact that his wet-nurse hailed from Carrara, and that he ingested the region's marble dust – and thus his prowess – through her milk. Much later, Mussolini's architects made great use of marble, one reason why it was shunned in the post-war years. Latterly, many sculptors, with Henry Moore among the most famous, have used the marble, often travelling to the region to select pieces of stone personally.

LIQUID GOLD

The olive is as much a part of Tuscany as its art, the familiar silvery-grey trees a timeless feature of the landscape, the mild, unctuous oil a cornerstone of its cooking.

The Tree

Most of the world's estimated 750 million olive trees (95 per cent of which are found in the Mediterranean) are cultivated, descendants of wild members of the *Oleaceae* family – which also contains lilac, ash and jasmine trees – that originated in present-day Anatolia in Turkey. Hardy and resistant to drought, the tree can live for hundreds of years but requires warmth – anything below –12°C (10°F) is fatal – which is why most Italian olives are found in southern Italy. Tuscany is close to their natural northern limit, but the region's more temperate climes actually result in the best olive oil.

The Harvest

One of the secrets of good olive oil is choosing the right time to harvest – usually some time between late October and early January. If they are picked too early, when the olives are pale, then the acidity will be low – a good thing – but the yields of oil will be low and the taste

bitter. Pick them too late, when the olives are dark – having changed from green through pink, violet and black – and the yields will be high, but so will the acidity, rendering the oil rancid.

A Gentle Hand

Pick by hand and you'll be able to select the best olives and return to individual trees again and again, as olives on the same tree ripen at different times. Hand-picking also prevents bruising, which affects the quality of the oil. But it's a slow business, and over the centuries the traditional method has been to surround trees with nets and beat the branches with poles. Latterly, farmers have turned to tractors with mechanical claws, which vibrate to dislodge the fruit.

> "The region's more temperate climes actually result in the best olive oil."

Crushing

Once picked, olives are washed to remove twigs, leaves and other debris and then stored, ideally for no more than 36 hours. If left for longer, olives produce heat, leading to fermentation and oxidization, both of which impair the taste of the eventual oil. The olives, including the stones, are then crushed (or finely chopped in more modern processing plants), traditionally between water- or mule-driven millstones, but today more usually with mechanical metal grinders.

Olives ripening in the sun

Above: Olives for sale in Lucca

Pressing

The resulting paste must then be pressed to remove the oil from the solids. Traditionally, this was achieved by covering hemp mats with the paste and placing them in layers in a column, which was then compressed using weights or a wooden 'lever' or screw press. Today, fibre mats and a hydraulic press are used, usually in combination with a centrifuge, which separates out the paste's natural water content.

More oil can be extracted from the paste if it is heated, if the paste is repressed or if chemicals are added, but this has an adverse effect on the flavour. As a result, the best oils come from the first 'natural' pressing and are 'cold pressed' – EU regulations state that only oils extracted at temperatures below 27°C (80°F) are allowed to be labelled 'cold pressed'.

Quality

Low acidity is important in olive oil, and Tuscan oils have some of the lowest levels – under 1 per cent, virtually unheard of elsewhere in the olive-growing world. 'Extra-virgin' oils should have acidity levels of below 0.8 per cent and 'virgin' olive oil below 2 per cent. However, bear in mind that acidity is not all, and low levels do not guarantee quality – tiny differences will be imperceptible to most palates.

Look for cold-pressed oils from small producers, and don't be fooled by deep-green oils – they are not necessarily better than the amber or light-gold oils from around Lucca, for example, which are some of the best in the world.v

Finding Your Feet

First Two Hours

Tuscany's main airport at Pisa welcomes some European flights, and nearby Bologna has connections with major European cities, however, most international and intercontinental flights land in Rome. From here there are internal flight connections to Florence, Pisa or Bologna, or good rail and road links north to Tuscany.

Arriving By Air

There are four options if you are flying to Italy for a Tuscan holiday.

- **Rome** has the most international connections, but is approximately a three-hour drive to Florence or Pisa from the Italian capital.
- **Pisa** is served by major European airlines and lies about an hour by road or train from Florence; it also leaves you well placed for Siena, Chianti and the west and north of the region.
- **Bologna**, in the region of Emilia-Romagna to the north of Tuscany, also has an international airport. It is about 80 minutes by road or rail to Florence.
- **Florence** has a small airport which makes the most convenient entry point for the Tuscan capital and the central and eastern parts of the region, although at present its modest size means it is only served by a handful of small international airlines.

From Rome

Rome's airport is officially called **Aeroporto di Roma-Fiumicino 'Leonardo da Vinci'** (tel: 06 6595 1; www.adr.it).

- **Car rental** desks lie within walking distance of the main arrivals terminal, near the airport railway station for trains to central Rome (➤ 44). Take the underpass or the raised, covered walkway across the parking area outside the main terminal towards the railway station and follow the appropriate signs.
- **By car from Rome Airport** Follow signs for 'Roma' (Rome) and, after 11km (6.5mi), watch for signs to 'Firenze' (Florence) and the Grande Raccordo Anulare (GRA), the main Rome ring road: be prepared, as the junction comes suddenly. Follow the GRA clockwise for about 35 to 45 minutes to junction 10 (Firenze-A1); from here it is 240km (149mi) to Florence on the A1 toll motorway. If you are heading for western Tuscany, leave the airport's motorway spur earlier, following signs for Civitavecchia and the SS1 Via Aurelia, the main west-coast route to Grosseto and Pisa.
- **For trains from Rome Airport** to Florence, Pisa or Arezzo, first take the **airport shuttle train to Stazione Centrale Giovanni Paolo II** (still commonly known by its former name 'Termini'), Rome's main railway station. Shuttles leave roughly every 30 minutes and the journey takes 30 minutes. Buy tickets for the shuttle from the office to the right of the station concourse as you face the platforms. You can also buy tickets here for the main leg of your journey, which avoids long queues at Termini.
- **Trains for Florence** leave at least every hour from the main station in Rome. The quickest trains (Eurostar and InterCity services) make the journey in less than two hours – the slowest take up to four hours. Remember you will need to pay supplements for InterCity and Eurostar trains, and don't forget to validate your tickets before travelling (➤ 44)!

From Pisa

Pisa's **Galileo Galilei Airport** (tel: 050 84 93 00 for flight information or 050 84 91 11 for the switchboard; www.pisa-airport.com) lies about 83km (52mi) west of Florence. It is served by many **European airlines**. The arrivals area has a small tourist office, a desk for bus connections to Florence (➤ below) and a ticket office for Tren-italia (FS) trains (➤ below). Car rental desks are located about 300m (330 yards) from the forecourt outside Arrivals. A shuttle bus is available, but queues are often long – it's probably quicker to walk.

- **By car from Pisa** The airport lies close to major dual-carriageway and motorway links to Livorno (the A12 south), Viareggio and Lucca (the A12 north), and the A11 to Florence by way of Empoli (connections to Siena). The network of roads is confusing, however, so pay careful attention to the signs outside the airport.
- **By train from Pisa** About six **direct train services** daily link Pisa Aeroporto (Pisa Airport) with Florence's main railway station, Santa Maria Novella. Journey time is about 1 hour. Most trains stop at Empoli for connections to Siena. A shuttle train runs two or three times hourly from the airport station to Pisa Centrale, Pisa's main station, where you can connect with more services to Florence (and other Tuscan towns). Buy through tickets to Florence's main station at the airport ticket office, located just outside the customs area.
- **By bus** Terravision buses (tel: 050 26 00 80; www.terravision.eu) run to Florence's Santa Maria Novella station. Buses meet incoming flights 8:40am–00:20am. The journey time is around 70 minutes. Tickets cost €10 (€16 return) and can be bought online or at the Terravision desk in Arrivals or (returning from Florence) at seven outlets in Florence, including the hotel reservations desk near Platform 16 in the main station. Buses leave from in front of the station for Pisa airport 3:35am–7:10pm.

From Florence

Florence airport is officially called **Aeroporto Firenze-Peretola 'Amerigo Vespucci'** (tel: 055 30 61 13 00, 6am–11pm for information; www.aeroporto.firenze.it),. It lies just 4km (2.5mi) northwest of central Florence. Several **small scheduled** and **charter companies** have direct flights from European cities, including Meridiana (tel: 087 12 22 93 19 in the UK, 89 29 28 within Italy; www.meridiana.it) from London Gatwick (two to three flights daily). The tiny arrivals area has a small visitor information desk (tel: 055 31 58 74; daily 8:30am–6:30pm) and a handful of desks for the major **car rental firms**.

- **Taxi to Florence** Taxis (**white** in Florence) are the **most expensive** but most convenient way to reach central Florence from the airport. Journey time is about 15 minutes in light traffic. Cabs wait outside the airport's small arrivals area and by the almost adjacent departure terminal. Expect to pay in the region of €18–€20, plus surcharges for any baggage in the boot, travel on Sundays or public holidays, and travel between 10pm and 6am.
- **By bus to Florence** Take the **ATAF-SITA 'Vola in bus' service**. Tickets can be bought on board and cost €6 (single) or €10 (return). There are departures daily every 30 minutes between 6am and 8:30pm, and hourly after 8:30pm to 11:30pm. Buses depart from outside the arrivals area and arrive at the city's main bus terminal on Via Santa Caterina da Siena, three minutes' walk west of Santa Maria Novella railway station. For information, contact ATAF (tel: 800 42 45 00; www.ataf.net) or SITA (tel: 800 37 37 60; www.sitabus.it).

- **By car to Tuscany airport** lies alongside a 10km (6-mile) spur of the A11 motorway, which runs west to link with the main A11–A1 motorway junction between Prato and Florence. From here there are onward links to north, west and south Tuscany.

From Bologna

Bologna's **Guglielmo Marconi Airport** (tel: 05 16 47 96 15; www.bologna-airport.it) lies 105km (65mi) northeast of Florence and caters for both **scheduled services** (Alitalia, Air France, British Airways, SAS, Lufthansa) and **charter** and **low-cost airlines**. All major **car rental firms** have booths inside Terminal A (Arrivals).

- **By car from Bologna** The main route to Tuscany is the A1 motorway south, which crosses the A11 Lucca–Florence motorway between Prato and Florence. Note that the A1 is a **busy road** and has many twists and tunnels along its route over the Apennine mountains between Bologna and Florence.
- **By train from Bologna** For trains from Bologna Centrale, the main railway station, you need to take a taxi or the 'Aerobus' **shuttle bus** (tel: 0 51 29 02 90; www.atc.bo.it) from the airport. Aerobus services leave roughly every 20 minutes (6:30am–00:15am) from outside Terminal A. Journey time to the station is about 25 minutes and tickets cost €5 and can be purchased on the bus. **Express trains** (two to three every hour) run from Bologna Centrale straight to Florence. The journey takes 30 minutes. Again, you must remember to validate tickets before travelling (➤ 44).

Arriving By Train

- Florence is one of the **main arrival points** for trains from Europe, and has direct links with Paris, Frankfurt and other major European cities. The city's main station, Santa Maria Novella, is located close to the heart of the Tuscan capital, within easy walking distance of the Piazza del Duomo (➤ 58) and Piazza della Signoria (➤ 70).
- Some **international train links** to Rome also follow Italy's main coast route, stopping at Pisa.
- For information on **Italian train services** contact the state railway, Trenitalia, or FS (tel: 1 99 89 20 21; www.trenitalia.it; open daily 24 hours).

Getting Around in Tuscany

The ideal way to explore Tuscany is by car, but it is also possible to see virtually all of the region's main highlights by bus or train. Cars can be rented at Rome, Pisa, Florence and Bologna airports (➤ 40), other companies can be found in the cities. Parking, however, can be difficult as many city centres have restricted vehicular access or have been completely pedestrianised.

By Car

Drivers need a **full driver's licence** and must have the vehicle registration papers and an international green insurance card with them.

- **Car rental** To rent a car in Italy you must be over 21 and possess a full valid driver's licence. It is often **cheaper** to rent a car when you book your holiday as part of a 'fly-drive' package to the region – ask for details from your travel agent or holiday company. Cars can also be booked through the central telephone numbers or websites of the major rental companies in your country of origin before leaving. In Tuscany, ask for details of local companies at tourist offices or look in the *Pagine Gialle* (Yellow Pages; www.paginegialle.it) under *Autonoleggio* (car rental).

Driving Essentials

- Driving is **on the right** and you should give way to traffic from the right unless there are signs to the contrary.
- Road signs are **blue**, but **green** on motorways *(autostrade)*.
- The wearing of seat belts is **compulsory** in front and back seats.
- Unless indicated otherwise, the **speed limit** is 50kph (31mph) in urban areas, 90kph (56mph) outside urban areas on secondary roads, which are known and signed as *nazionale* (N) or *strada statale* (SS), 110kph (68mph) on dual-carriageways *(superstrade)* and 130kph (80mph) on motorways *(autostrade)*. Dipped headlights should be used on motorways.
- Many historic towns and villages are creating **traffic-limited zones (ZTL Zona Traffico Limitato)** that are under electronic surveillance. Any unauthorised vehicles entering the zone, even to check baggage into a hotel, will be automatically issued with a fine.
- **Tolls** are payable on motorways *(autostrade)*. Collect a ticket from the automated machines at your entry junction and present the ticket at the manned booths at your departure junction. Some booths, however, are automatic and do not accept cash, so make sure you choose the correct lane as you approach the payment area.
- In rural areas in Tuscany you will also often encounter hard-packed **gravel roads** known as *strade bianche* (white roads). These are marked on maps and are intended (and suitable) for cars.
- **Petrol** is *benzina*, diesel is *gasolio*. Petrol stations follow shop hours (closed daily 1–3:30pm) and many close all day on Sunday. Motorway petrol stations, however, are open all day, seven days a week. Smaller rural petrol stations may not accept payment by credit card. Many stations have automatic dispensers for use in closed periods which take euro notes.
- The best Tuscan **map** is the green Touring Club of Italy (TCI) 1:200,000 Toscana sheet (No. D39), widely available in local Tuscan bookshops or in larger bookshops in the UK and abroad.
- It is often difficult to find a **car park** *(parcheggio)* or parking place in Tuscany's towns and cities. This is especially true of Florence and Siena. **Metered parking** *(parcometro)* is now common. It is often wiser to park on the outskirts and take a local bus to the centre, or to make day-trips to Florence by train. Never leave luggage or valuables unattended in cars. If your car breaks down, switch on the hazard warning lights and place a red warning triangle (provided with rental cars) about 50m (55 yards) behind your vehicle. Call the **emergency breakdown number** (tel: 116) and give the operator your location and the car's make and registration number. Many car rental companies often have their own arrangements in the event of vehicle breakdown; enquire at the time of booking. In the event of an **accident**, place a red warning triangle 50m (55 yards) behind the car. Call the police (tel: 113) or breakdown services (tel: 116). Do not admit liability or make potentially incriminating statements. Ask witnesses to remain on the scene, exchange names, addresses and insurance details with any other drivers involved, and make a statement to the police.

By Train

Trains provide **quick and efficient links** to a large number of Tuscan towns and cities. Connections south from Florence's Santa Maria Novella station run to Arezzo and Cortona, with a branch line link from Arezzo to Poppi and Stia in the heart of the Casentino region. Connections west from Florence link to Prato, Pistoia, Lucca and Viareggio, with a scenic branch line from Lucca running north through the Garfagnana region to Aulla. Another line west from Florence runs to Empoli (with connections to Pisa) and then south to Siena, continuing through beautiful countryside to Buonconvento and Grosseto near the coast. Italy's main **west-coast line** runs from Rome to Genoa, linking Pisa and other minor centres.

- Italy has several types of trains. The fastest are **InterCity** and **Eurostar**. The latter needs to be booked in advance (a reservation is *una prenotazione*). Seats can however be reserved until a few minutes before departure. Both types of trains generally run only on major routes such as Florence–Rome, Rome–Bologna or Rome–Pisa–Genoa. Slower trains which stop at more stations are known as *espressi* (ES), *diretti* (Dir), *regionali* (Reg) or *inter-regionali* (IR).
- **Rail tickets***(biglietti)* can be bought online (www.trenitalia.it), at stations, some travel agents and – for some shorter journeys – newspaper kiosks. They are issued in first- *(prima)* and second- *(seconda)* class categories. A single ticket is *andato*, a return is *andato e ritorno*.
- On key fast trains such as InterCity (IC) or Eurostar (► above) a **supplement** *(supplemento)* is payable on each fare. These should be bought at the same time as buying a ticket as they are more expensive if you buy them on the train.
- Whatever type of train you take, it is absolutely essential to **validate your ticket** by inserting it immediately before travel into one of the small machines (usually yellow or gold in colour) in ticket halls and on platforms. Failure to do so will result in a large on-the-spot **fine** from ticket inspectors.
- **Rail passes** are available for non-resident visitors, but are not really cost-effective over the short distances you'll travel in Tuscany.
- Ticket offices and platforms always have two **timetables**: *Arrivi* (Arrivals), which are usually white, and *Partenze* (Departures), which are usually yellow: be sure to consult the right one. If you intend to use trains extensively, the small *Pozzorario* timetable is invaluable: it is available to buy from most newspaper kiosks.

By Bus

Town and city buses are known as ***autobus***, while long-distance inter-town buses are known as ***pullman*** or ***corriere***. Inter-town buses link main centres such as Florence, Pisa, Lucca and Siena to a large number of out-of-the-way towns and villages. Services are reliable and inexpensive. Services to smaller places, however, are rare. Train journey (► above) are usually faster.

- **City buses** Most Tuscan towns and cities are small enough to negotiate on foot. The only place where you might need to take a bus is Florence. Its distinctive orange buses are run by **ATAF** (tel: 800 42 45 00; daily 7:30–7:30; www.ataf.net). Buy tickets before boarding the bus from shops and bars displaying ATAF stickers, from automated machines, or from the ATAF office near the east entrance to Santa Maria Novella railway station. Depending on price, tickets are valid for 90 minutes (€1.20 pre-bought, €2 bought on board) from when you validate them by stamping them in the small machines on board. You can also buy **one-** and **three-day passes** (€5/€12), which are validated in a similar way. An electronic Carta Agile (€10 or €20) offers 10 or 20 90-minute tickets. It can be used for one or more people and must be swiped as many times as there are passengers. Special small **electric buses**, which run on four loop routes (C1, C2, C3 and D; Mon–Sat 7:30am–8:30pm), can be most useful for exploring the city.

- **Inter-town buses** (almost always blue)Towns and cities rarely have a special bus terminal. Instead, buses often leave from a town's main or other large square, a major street or from the local railway station. Ask at tourist offices if in doubt. Tickets must generally be bought before boarding the bus and, in larger towns such as Siena or Lucca, can be obtained from dedicated ticket offices. Elsewhere, **tickets** are usually available from the railway station bar or newspaper kiosk or a shop or major bar on or near the square or street used by departing buses.

Tourist Information Centres

Arezzo
Piazza della Repubblica, 28 ☎ 05 75 40 19 45; www.arezzoturismo.it
Mon–Fri 10–1, 1:30–5:30, Sat, Sun 10–6
Emiciclo Giovanni Paolo II – next to the escalator ☎ 0 57 51 82 27 70 daily 9–7

Cortona
Piazza Signorelli, 9 ☎ 05 75 63 72 23
Summer: Mon–Sat 9–1, 3–6, Sun 9–1; Winter: Mon–Fri 9–1, 3–6, Sat 9–1

Florence
Via Cavour, 1r ☎ 055 29 08 32; www.firenzeturismo.it Mon–Sat 8:30–6:30
Infopoint Stazione, Piazza Stazione, 4 055 21 22 45 Mon–Sat 9–7, Sun 9–2
Infopoint Bigallo, Piazza San Giovanni, 1 ☎ 055 28 84 96 Mon–Sat 9–7, So 9–2

Lucca
Piazzale Verdi & Vecchia Porta San Donato
☎ 05 83 58 31 50; www.luccaitinera.it Winter: 9–5, Summer: 9–7

Montepulciano
Piazza Don Minzoni, 1
☎ 05 78 75 73 41; www.comune.montepulciano.si.it oder www.prolocomontepulciano.it
April–July, Sept–Oct daily 10–1, 3–7, Aug 10–7, Nov–March 10–1, 3–6

Pienza
Corso Rossellino, 30 ☎ 07 58 74 97 96; www.comunedipienza.it
mid-March to Oct Wed–Mon 10:30–1:30, 2:30–6, Nov to mid-March Sat, Sun 10–4

Pisa
Piazza Vittorio Emanuele II, 6 ☎ 05 04 22 91; www.pisaunicaterra.it
daily 9:30–4:30 (subject to changes)
Piazza Arcivescovile, 8 (Campo dei Miracoli) ☎ 05 04 22 91; www.pisaturismo.it Daily 10–7

San Gimignano
Piazza del Duomo, 1 ☎ 05 77 94 00 08; www.sangimignano.com
March–Oct daily 9–1, 3–7, Nov–Feb 9–1, 2–6

Siena
Piazza del Campo, 56 ☎ 05 77 28 05 51; www.terresiena.it Daily 9–7

Accommodation

Tuscan towns and villages generally have a wide range of accommodation, but prices in main centres such as Florence and Siena are higher than in much of Italy. You'll need to book well in advance in the main centres, especially between June and September, but in the countryside you also have access to less busy farm-stay and other rural accommodation known as *agriturismo*. It is also worth noting that many hotels, particularly in smaller towns, close in January, February and August.

Grading

- Every Italian hotel *(albergo)* is graded by the state from **1- to 5-star** (5 being luxury). The old *pensione(locanda)* classification, which referred to a simple hotel or set of rooms, sometimes with a restaurant, no longer exists, but you may still see 1-star hotels calling themselves *pensione*.
- The criteria used to award stars are usually based on the **number of facilities** offered rather than the standard of those facilities, the service or other qualitative aspects. Invariably, 1-star hotels are budget options, and often have shared bathrooms or only a handful of rooms with private bathrooms; 2-star hotels have private bathrooms; and rooms in 3-star hotels usually have telephones and TVs. Most 4-star hotels represent a jump in price and quality – you should expect something a little special in such establishments, both in the presentation of the rooms and the public areas. Luxury 5-star hotels are a class apart. New bed-and-breakfast establishments outside these classifications are increasingly common.

Agriturismo

- *Agriturismo* is the name given to **rural accommodation** in Italy. It is becoming very popular, with much choice in many parts of rural Tuscany. Occasionally the accommodation may be part of a working farm, estate or vineyard, though often the rooms or apartments are purpose-built and away from the main property. Many offer activities, notably horse-riding, and many – unlike town hotels – have swimming pools.
- Prices are competitive when compared with most hotels, and though rooms are usually simple, they are invariably clean and modern. Some places, however, require a **minimum stay** of two or more days in high season, though many offer discounted rates for longer stays. Many also have multi-room accommodation, making them ideal for families.
- Listings of such properties are still rather haphazard, but most **local tourist offices** have details of *agriturismo* accommodation in their immediate vicinity. Often, though, you will stumble across such places by chance while touring the countryside – most are signposted using a standardised yellow sign.

Location

- It pays to stay in the (historical) **centre** *(centro)* of Tuscan towns and cities. You will be close to all the sights; on the **outskirts***(la periferia)*, you will invariably be in less characterful hotels and more modern surroundings. This said, parking can be a real problem in larger and busie towns, especially Florence and Siena, where a peripheral hotel – or one in the countryside nearby – can be an advantage. Some town hotels will have **private parking** *(parcheggio privato)*, but it is likely to have limited spaces.

- In **Florence**, the main concentrations of inexpensive hotels are in the streets east of the station – Via Faenza, Via Nazionale and Via Fiume – and the far less convenient streets around the Piazza della Libertà on the northeast edge of the city centre. You'll need to take a bus or taxi into the centre if you're staying in the latter. The former are far more convenient but, as in most cities, the railway station district is relatively unappealing (though rarely dangerous).

Noise

- This **can be a problem** in Tuscan towns, even in smart hotels, and it can be worth asking for a room at the back of a hotel or looking onto a central courtyard or garden, as on summer nights, unless there's air-conditioning, you'll need to have windows open.
- Visitors are often surprised at how noisy it can be in the Tuscan countryside and its small villages: church bells, busy main squares or streets, barking dogs, cockerels crowing, teenagers revving scooters and the like, can all be a problem. **Ear plugs** are the perfect solution.

Prices

- Prices for each room *(camera)* in a hotel are **fixed by law** and must be displayed in the reception area and in bedrooms. They may **vary within a hotel**, so look at a selection of rooms.
- Prices should also include any **taxes**, but watch out for **surcharges**, notably over-priced breakfasts *(prima colazione)*, which may or may not be included in the room rate: where it's optional, it's invariably cheaper and more fun to have breakfast in a bar. Good buffet-style **breakfasts** are becoming more widespread in better hotels, but a Tuscan hotel breakfast generally still means just a bread roll, jam and coffee.
- Hotels may also add surcharges for **air-conditioning** *(aria condizionata)* and garage facilities.

Accommodation Prices

Expect to pay per double room per night:

€ under €125 **€€** €125–€200 **€€€** over €200

Booking Accommodation

- Book all hotels **in advance** year-round in Florence and Siena. Neither city has a low season to speak of, though the quietest months are November, January and February. The high season at Easter and June to September is always busy.
- Book well ahead in smaller towns if you are visiting at a time that coincides with a **major festival or cultural event**.
- **Reservations** should be made by phone and followed by a faxed or email confirmation. It is also an idea to reconfirm bookings a couple of days before arrival. A double room with twin beds is *una doppia*, and *una matrimoniale* for a double bed. A single room is *una singola*.
- Hoteliers are **obliged to Index** guests, so on checking in you must hand in your passport.
- **Check-out times** range from around 10am to noon.

Villas and Apartments

Several companies offer villas and apartments to rent throughout Tuscany. The following give you some idea of what is on offer:

- **Traditional Tuscany**, interesting and good-value properties from apartments to palaces (tel: 01945430055; www.traditionaltuscany.co.uk).
- **www.ownersdirect.co.uk/italy-florence-and-tuscany.htm**
- **www.tuscanyvillasandapartments.com/**

Food and Drink

Sampling culinary delights in Tuscany can easily turn into a memorable experience. Restaurants range from Michelin star gourmet establishments to small, rustic *trattorie* where *mamma* herself still guards the stove. There are also cafés and bars almost everywhere, offering everything from a *cappuccino* for breakfast to a snack lunch, or a hunk of bread and cheese washed down with a glass of wine in the evening.

Eating Places

The differences between the types of restaurant are becoming increasingly blurred. Some years ago a *ristorante (*restaurant) used to refer to somewhere smart and expensive; a *trattoria* was simple and cheap; an *osteria* even more so; and a *pizzeria* a no-frills place to fill up on pizza and little more.

- The old-fashioned ***trattoria***, at least in cities and larger towns, is fast disappearing, to be replaced by a more modern and informal type of eating venue (often called an ***osteria***) with young owners and younger attitudes to style and cuisine. The term ***ristorante*** can now be applied to just about any eating establishment, and ***pizzerias*** – while often still fairly utilitarian – now usually also serve a range of pastas, salads and other main courses.
- These changes are also true of restaurants in the more popular Tuscan towns and villages, where the influx of visitors has led to a proliferation of eating establishments. **Quality**, however, can be poor in some of the more obvious tourist traps – set 'tourist menus', for example, are invariably bad value. But wherever you are, price and appearance are no guarantee of quality – smart interiors often mean nothing in Florence and Siena, and you can frequently eat excellent food at fair prices in humble-looking places in cities or in the countryside.
- An ***enoteca***, a wine bar, usually indicates a place to buy wine by the glass or bottle and the chance to eat a limited selection of light meals or snacks. A ***fiaschetteria*** or ***vinaio*** is similar, but often much simpler; these establishments were once found in many Tuscan towns, but today they're a dying breed. The same cannot be said of the ***gelateria***, or ice-cream parlour, a mainstay of just about every Italian town and city.

Eating Hours

- **Bars** open from 7am or earlier for breakfast *(colazione* or *prima colazione),* which generally consists of coffee *(cappuccino* or *caffelatte)* and a plain or filled sweet croissant *(brioche).*
- **Lunch** *(pranzo)* starts around 12:30pm and finishes at about 2pm, although most restaurants stay open a little later.
- **Dinner** *(cena)* begins at about 8pm, although many restaurants open before this to cater for tourists used to dining earlier. Bars that are busy in the day usually close at around 8 or 9pm, but in larger towns there

are often late bars aimed more at the nocturnal visitor. An *enoteca* usually follows bar opening times, but some may close in the afternoon.

Meals

- Italian meals start with hors d'oeuvres or ***antipasti*** (literally 'before the meal') and are followed by a **first course** *(il primo)* of pasta, soup or rice.
- The main or **second course** *(il secondo)* is the meat *(carne)* or fish *(pesce)* course, and is accompanied by vegetables *(contorni)* or salad *(insalata)* which are usually served (or eaten) separately.
- **Desserts** are *dolci*, and may be accompanied by, or offered as an alternative to, fruit *(frutta)* and cheese *(formaggio)*. Ice-cream *(gelato)* from a *gelateria* makes a good alternative to desserts, which are often uninspiring.
- Meals are **accompanied** by bread *(pane)* and mineral water *(acqua minerale)*, for which you sometimes pay extra. Ask for mineral water to be fizzy *(gassata)* or still *(non gassata)*.
- Meals can be **followed** by *grappa*, a bitter digestif such as *amaro*, an *espresso* coffee, or an infusion tea such as camomile. Note that Italians *never* drink *cappuccino* after dinner.
- At lunch and in all but the grandest restaurants it is acceptable to **order a pasta and salad** and little more. More expensive and popular restaurants, however, may take a dim view of this in the evening.

Cafés and Snack-bars

- In cafés and bars it costs less to **stand at the bar** *(al banco)* than sit at a table. Pay for what you want first at the separate cash desk *(cassa)* and then take your receipt *(scontrino)* to the bar and repeat your order. You cannot pay at the bar.
- If you **sit at a table**, a waiter will take your order. Meals and drinks ordered at the bar cannot be eaten here.
- Cafés and bars are excellent sources of **sandwiches** *(tramezzini)*, filled rolls *(panini)* and light meals. Also look out for small shops or bakeries selling **pizza by the slice** *(pizza al taglio)*.

Set Menus

- If possible, steer clear of restaurants full of foreigners and those that offer a ***menù turistico*** (tourist menu). Portions are often meagre, wine (if offered) unexceptional, dishes plain – usually a pasta with simple tomato sauce and grilled chicken with a salad or single side dish.
- In more expensive restaurants, a ***menù degustazione*** or ***menù gastronomico*** provides a selection of the restaurant's best dishes – a good option if you can't decide what to choose from the à la carte menu.

Paying and Tipping

- The **bill** *(il conto)* must be a formal itemised receipt – if it appears on a scrawled piece of paper the restaurateur is breaking the law and you are entitled to demand a proper receipt *(ricevuta)*.
- Most eating places charge *pane e coperto*, a **cover charge**; if it is included you must pay it.

Restaurant Prices

Expect to pay for a three-course meal for one with wine:

€ under €26 **€€** €26–€52 **€€€** over €52

Etiquette and Smoking

- Italians generally make more of an effort – **'smart casual'** is a good rule of thumb, though aim to be more elegant (jacket and tie for men) in top restaurants.
- Smoking is **banned** in public places, including the interior of bars and restaurants.

Shopping

All across Tuscany you'll find a wide variety of shops selling mouth-watering food, wine and local craft objects, while Florence and Pisa have numerous luxury and other shops selling top designer clothes, exquisite shoes, fine leatherware, jewellery, rich fabrics, artisan and craft items, and a host of paintings, prints and antiques.

Florence

Florence is the place to go for serious shopping. A wealthy city, its chief strengths for shoppers are luxury goods, especially leather and high-quality shoes and clothes. Much the same goes for other large Tuscan towns, notably Pisa and Lucca, but none have quite the choice and variety of the region's capital.

- The main **designer shops** lie in the west of the city on Via de' Tornabuoni and nearby streets such as Via della Vigna Nuova.
- **Leather shops** are found across the city, but the most popular area is in the Santa Croce district.
- **Jewellers** occupy the Ponte Vecchio, their traditional home since the 16th century, though you'll also find jewellery stores on most busy city streets.
- The same is true of **craft** workshops and shops selling everything from furniture to beautiful marbled paper. There is a concentration of such shops in Oltrarno, especially on or near Via Maggio, on Via del Porcellana and around Borgo degli Albizi.
- Via Maggio and its surrounding streets also contain many of Florence's leading **antiques shops** and commercial **art galleries**, though such shops are also dotted elsewhere across the city centre.
- The city centre is also where you'll find the majority of kitchenware and household goods shops – with wonderful designer gadgets – bookshops and **department stores**, of which COIN is the best (➤ 89).

Tuscany

Food and wine are good buys across the region, but check import **restrictions** on meat and other products if you wish to take purchases home: safe items include pasta, wine, olive oils and most cheeses.

- **Specialities** of the region include the wines of Chianti, Montalcino and Montepulciano, the oils of Lucca, Pienza's sheep's milk cheese *(pecorino)*, the honey of Montalcino and spicy *panforte* cake from Siena.
- Other notable buys are **craft items**, such as the alabaster ware of Volterra, glassware from Colle di Val d'Elsa and the marble artefacts of Carrara.

Markets

You can buy perfectly good produce in most neighbourhood food stores (known as *alimentari*), but for the best selection of gourmet and other provisions, and for plenty of local colour, head for town markets.

- In **Florence** the best market for food is the wonderful Mercato Centrale near San Lorenzo (➤ 77). The streets around San Lorenzo are also filled with a general market, a good place to buy inexpensive clothes, bags and souvenirs. Other less well-known markets include Sant'Ambrogio, northeast of Santa Croce, and the small flea market, or Mercato dei Pulci, in the Piazza dei Ciompi.
- Most smaller towns hold markets **once a week**, which tend to be general markets – Florence's biggest such market is held in the Parco delle Cascine near the River Arno to the west of the city centre every Tuesday (8–1). Few visitors come here, and prices for goods of all descriptions are highly competitive.

Opening Times

- Most stores in smaller towns and villages are traditionally open **Tuesday to Saturday** about 8 or 9 to 1 and 3:30 or 4 to 8. Most stores close on Monday morning or one other half-day a week.
- Many of Florence's shops, however, are beginning to **open all day** (known as *orario continuato*), which means Monday or Tuesday to Saturday 9 or 10 to 7:30 or 8. Some shops, notably the city's major department stores, also open on Sunday.

Credit Cards

Credit cards are accepted in most large shops, but cash is still preferred in smaller stores: check before making any major purchases. Note that non-European Union visitors can take advantage of tax-free shopping on a variety of goods: many shops are members of the **Tax-Free Shopping System** (keep an eye out for the respective symbol).

Entertainment

Tuscany offers a broad spectrum of entertainment, from the music and cultural festivals of Florence and other large towns to the plethora of smaller pageants and festivities *(festa* or *sagra)* held across the region to celebrate a local saint's day, a prized local delicacy or a historical event from a town or village's past. Nightlife in the conventional sense – clubs, bars, live music and such like – is mostly restricted to Florence, though larger cities such as Pisa, Lucca and Siena also have a smattering of late-night entertainment. Most of the region's cultural entertainment is easily accessible to visitors, except for theatre and cinema, where most presentations and productions are in Italian.

Information

Your first ports of call for information on cultural events should be the internet (➤ 201), or tourist offices in individual towns.

- Tourist offices in larger places such as Florence and Siena (➤ 45) generally have details of all **major cultural festivals** in the region, and may be able to provide programmes and advice on how to book tickets or obtain further information. They may also have details of the region's smaller festivals, though often you stumble across these almost by accident: most *feste* or *sagre* are advertised in advance on **posters** in and around the villages in which they are to take place.

- Consult visitor centres too for details of **local nightlife**. This way you will find out what new club has opened where or which is the place to be at the moment.
- Alternatively, consult the **listings section** of Florence and Tuscany's main daily newspaper, *La Nazione* (www.lanazione.it), which has listings of numerous events and festivals: scan its different regional sections for details of events in your area.
- In Florence you can also buy the monthly city magazine ***Firenze Spettacolo*** (www.firenzespettacolo.it), a detailed listings magazine. It contains a section in English, but the layout is such that you should be able to understand the information even if you don't speak Italian. The magazine is available from many newsstands and bookshops such as Feltrinelli (➤88).
- The online English-language newspaper www.florencenewspaper.it is also useful.

Tickets

Tickets for events in Florence can be obtained from individual box offices or through **Box Office**, the city's central ticket agency at Via Alamanni 39 (tel: 055 21 08 04; www.boxofficetoscana.it or www.boxol.it). Open Mon–Fri 9:30–7, Sat 9:30–2.

Festivals

The key festivals in Florence and Tuscany are detailed below, but there are many minor and more specialised events celebrating religious holidays, the arts and gastronomic delicacies, information on which can be obtained from visitor centres.

- The **Scoppio del Carro** concludes Florence's Easter Sunday ceremonies, when a cart of flowers and fireworks is lit at noon by a mechanical dove that 'flies' along a wire from the altar of the cathedral to the piazza.
- May and June see the prestigious **Maggio Musicale** arts and music festival in Florence, with concerts, and dance and drama performances.
- Key summer events in **Pisa** are the Regatta di San Ranieri, a costumed boat race and colourful procession (16–17 June), and the Gioco del Ponte, a mock battle in period costume on the last Sunday of June.
- **Arezzo's** main events are called the Giostro del Saracino which are held in mid-June and on the first Sunday of September. These jousting contests have been held as celebrations since the Middle Ages and commemorate the success of the Crusader forces against the Moors.
- The most vivid of Florence's city festivals is the **Calcio Storico**, consisting of three fast and furious football games played in traditional medieval dress; the first takes place on the day commemorating Florence's patron saint (24 June), and other dates are picked from a hat on Easter Sunday. The games take place in Piazza Santa Croce.
- The most famous event in Tuscany is Siena's **Palio** horse race, which takes place twice-yearly on 2 July and 16 August (➤22).
- **Lucca** has medieval pageants on 11–12 July (the Festa di San Paolino) and on 14 September (the Festa della Croce), when the *Volto Santo* relic is paraded through town by torchlight.
- **Montepulciano** hosts a Baccanale festival of wine, food and song on the next to last Saturday in August, to celebrate the grape harvest for the local Vino Nobile wine.

Florence

Little Treats

Small but exquisite

Inconspicuous and yet the symbol of the Golden Age in Florence – the gold florin on the first floor of the **Bargello** (➤ 68).

Not everyone's cup of tea

Pluck up some courage and give it a try: when freshly served, *trippa alla fiorentina* (tripe), e.g. at **Mario** (➤ 85), is far better than its reputation.

A treat on Thursdays

Art followed by a glass of *prosecco* – at the **Uffizi Gallery** (➤ 74; tel. 0 55 29 48 83).

Getting Your Bearings

Florence is one of Europe's greatest art centres. The city on the Arno epitomises the Renaissance, one of history's most dramatic periods of creative endeavour, and today is still home to magnificent paintings, sculptures and architecture spanning almost 1,000 years. The Marco Polo Spiral Guide on Florence provides more detailed information.

To suggest that you can see the best of Tuscany's capital in two days may sound far-fetched, but it can be done. Ideally you would stay in the city overnight, although if you are visiting between Easter and October accommodation needs to be booked well in advance. Because parking is difficult, the best way to visit Florence is by train – most Tuscan centres are linked to the regional capital by rail (➤ 44).

Florence is a city of art and architecture. Some of the best is in Piazza del Duomo, one of two main squares: here you'll find the Cathedral, Baptistry and Campanile (bell-tower), while nearby are two major museums, the Museo dell'Opera del Duomo and the Museo Nazionale del Bargello.

A short walk away lies Piazza della Signoria, Florence's second square, dominated by the Palazzo Vecchio, the seat of government. Nearby is the Galleria degli Uffizi, home to many of the

TOP 10

Don't Miss

At Your Leisure

world's most important Renaissance paintings. East of Piazza della Signoria stands Santa Croce, the most compelling of Florence's many churches, narrowly outranking Santa Maria Novella, a church in the west of the city crammed with frescoes.

Two Michelangelo highlights north of the Cathedral are his statue of David in the Galleria dell' Accademia and a series of sculptures on display in the Cappelle Medicee. In the Oltrarno area, reached via the celebrated Ponte Vecchio, are the paintings and frescoes of the Palazzo Pitti and Cappella Brancacci.

This said, not all your time need be spent admiring art. Florence has superb shopping, from designer names to lively markets (➤ 89), and there are excellent bars, cafés and restaurants. You can also enjoy gardens, notably the Giardino di Boboli, and the simple charm of medieval and Renaissance streets.

The River Arno and its bridges, including the famous Ponte Vecchio

Two Perfect Days

If you're not quite sure where to begin your travels, this itinerary recommends two practical and enjoyable days out in Florence, taking in some of the best places to see. For more information see the main entries (➤ 58–81).

Day 1

Morning

If you haven't booked online, start the day reserving tickets for the next day for the Galleria degli Uffizi, then go to the **17 Museo di San Marco** (➤ 77) for paintings by Fra Angelico (above).

Stroll to the **11 Galleria dell'Accademia** (➤ 63) to see Michelangelo's famous *David*. Then go to the **18 Palazzo Medici-Riccardi** (➤ 77) for superb frescoes by Benozzo Gozzoli. If you have time, quickly visit the **12 Cappelle Medicee** (➤ 64), which close at 1:50pm (last ticket 1:20pm).

Lunch

On the way to the Mercato Centrale, stop off at **Mario** for lunch (➤ 85) or have a picnic.

Afternoon

Explore the **19 Mercato Centrale** (➤ 77) before visiting the San Lorenzo area (➤ 65). Then pay a visit to the superb church of **13 Santa Maria Novella** (➤ 66) for some quiet time before heading back to your hotel.

Day 2

Morning

Make your way to the 1 **Piazza del Duomo** (➤ 58) and climb the Campanile or cathedral dome for some great views. Then see the cathedral – it opens later than the Campanile and dome – but note that the Baptistry is closed in the morning, so return later in the day.
Then go to the 20 **Museo dell'Opera del Duomo** (➤ 77) and the 14 **Museo Nazionale del Bargello** (➤ 68).

Museo di San Marco 17
Mercato Centrale 19
Palazzo Medici-Riccardi 18
Galleria dell' Accademia 11
21 Museo Archeologico Nazionale
Santa Maria Novella 13
12 Cappelle Medicee
Museo dell' Opera 20 del Duomo
1 Piazza del Duomo
Palazzo Davanzati 23
Orsanmichele 22
Santa Trinita 24
14 Museo Naz. del Bargello
15 Piazza della Signoria
26 Cappella Brancacci
Ponte Vecchio 25
16 Galleria degli Uffizi
9 Santa Croce
Palazzo Pitti 28
San Miniato al Monte 29
Giardino di Boboli 27

Lunch

Walk to 15 **Piazza della Signoria** (bottom, ➤ 70) to have lunch (below), which you might take as a snack in Rivoire (➤ 87) – expensive for a café. Or you could try the more reasonable Cantinetta del Verrazzano (➤ 84) nearby.

Afternoon

Devote most of the afternoon to the 16 **Galleria degli Uffizi** (➤ 74), but also take time to see 9 **Santa Croce** (➤ 61), being sure to leave enough time to see the church and Cappella dei Pazzi before they close. Treat yourself to a delicious *gelato* from Vivoli (➤ 87): Baldovino (➤ 84) is a good choice for dinner close to Santa Croce, but you'll need to book ahead.

1 Piazza del Duomo

Piazza del Duomo forms a magnificent stage for the Duomo (cathedral), the Baptistry and the Campanile, the cathedral's bell-tower. On its eastern flank it also plays host to the Museo dell'Opera del Duomo, a museum of impressive paintings and sculptures collected over the centuries from the piazza's principal buildings.

Santa Maria del Fiore (Duomo)

Florence's majestic and multicoloured Duomo was begun in 1296, when it replaced an earlier seventh-century church, Santa Reparata, on the same site. Its construction, however, has been an on-going process: Filippo Brunelleschi's magnificent **dome**, one of the miracles of medieval engineering, was only completed in the late 1460s, while the richly embellished façade was added as recently as 1887.

The highlight of the visit is the dome, which you can reach from a separate entrance midway down the right (south) side of the nave. It's a long and rather claustrophobic ascent of more than 400 steps, but the views of Florence are breathtaking. Inside, the cathedral's **interior** appears austere at first glance, but hidden in the

The intricate walls are as impressive as the dome itself

Spectacular mosaic images of Christ keep watch over the Baptistry's interior

half-gloom are several outstanding paintings and works of art. Key paintings are all on the left (north) wall: *Dante with the Divine Comedy* (1465) by Domenico di Michelino and, to its left, two equestrian portraits: *Sir John Hawkwood* by Paolo Uccello (1436) and *Niccolò da Tolentino* by Andrea del Castagno (1456).

The Battistero San Giovanni

Piazza del Duomo's second major set piece is the **Baptistry** (**Battistero**), Florence's oldest surviving building. No one is sure of its precise origins – ancient chroniclers believed it was a first-century Roman temple to Mars. It probably dates from the eighth or ninth century, while the exterior's striking marble decoration was added between 1059 and 1128.

The Baptistry's **exterior** highlights are three sets of doors: the south doors (1330–36) were designed by the Pisan sculptor Andrea Pisano; the north doors (1403–24) by the Florentine Lorenzo Ghiberti, who also crafted the beautiful **Gates of Paradise** (Porta del Paradiso; 1426–52).

The Baptistry's **interior** is equally captivating. A glance upward from the comparatively plain walls, ringed by granite columns removed from Florence's ancient Roman Capitol, reveals a glorious 13th-century mosaic ceiling decorated with episodes from the lives of Christ, Joseph and St John the Baptist. To the right of the distinctive apse *(scarsella)* on the north wall lies the **Tomb of Baldassare Cossa**, the work of Donatello and his pupil Michelozzo. Its incumbent was the 'antipope' John XXIII and a friend of the Medici family, who died in Florence in 1419.

The Campanile

It is unlikely you'll have the legs to climb both the cathedral dome and the 85m (278ft) Campanile, built between 1334 and 1359. However, the **views** from the top of the latter's 414 steps are as good, if not better than those from the cathedral dome, if only because they include views of the dome itself and the Baptistry's distinctive octagon way below. The bell-tower was designed by Giotto, and adorned with 14th- and 15th-century reliefs by Andrea Pisano, Luca della Robbia, Donatello and assistants.

TAKING A BREAK

Insider Tip Away from the piazza, try Caffetteria delle Oblate, Via dell'Oriuolo 26.

Duomo
213 D4 Piazza del Duomo
05 52 30 28 85; www.ilgrandemuseodelduomo.it
Mon–Wed, Fri 10–5, Thu 10–4:30, Sat 10–4:45, Sun 1:30–4:45 14, 23; Electric bus C1 close by Free

Dome
213 D4 Piazza del Duomo
05 52 30 28 85 Mon–Fri 11:15–7, Sun and 1st Sat of the month 8:30–2, Summer: Thu–Sat 8:30–11pm
14, 23; Electric bus C1 close by €10

Baptistry
212 C4 Piazza del Duomo–Piazza di San Giovanni
05 52 30 28 85 Mon–Fri 11:15–7, Sun and 1st Sat of the month 8:30–2, Summer: Thu–Sat 8:30–11pm 14, 23; Electric bus C1 close by €10

Campanile
213 D4 Piazza del Duomo 05 52 30 28 85 Daily 8:30–7:30 (last ticket 6:40) 14, 23; electric bus C1 nearby €10

You can climb the Campanile to photograph views over the city

INSIDER INFO

- Avoid the often considerable **crowds and queues** for the dome and Campanile by visiting them as early as possible. The **Campanile** and **dome** open earlier than the main body of the cathedral, so save time by climbing one or the other (or both) before visiting the Duomo.
- The restoration of **Ghiberti's Gates of Paradise** has finally been completed. The originals can be found in the Museo dell'Opera del Duomo (► 77).

In more depth The cathedral restoration workshop is located at Via dello Studio 23, near the cathedral itself. This is where damaged elements of the building's fabric are still repaired or copies made by hand.

9 Santa Croce

Santa Croce is arguably Florence's most important church. It is noted both for its many outstanding works of art, including spectacular fresco cycles by Giotto and other medieval masters, as well as for the fact that many of the city's most illustrious citizens, including Michelangelo, Galileo and Machiavelli, lie buried within its walls. It was built for the Franciscans and intended as a riposte to Santa Maria Novella, the church of the Dominican order, the Franciscans' rivals.

Santa Croce was probably designed around 1294 by Arnolfo di Cambio, the architect responsible for Florence's cathedral and Palazzo Vecchio. Much of the money for the church's many tombs and decorated chapels came from wealthy Florentines, bankers in particular. They were eager to be buried alongside the humble Franciscans to assuage the stigma associated with usury, or lending money with interest, a practice then considered a sin by the Church.

Famous tombs

It was not only bankers who were buried here, however: the first tomb on the right (south) wall as you enter belongs to **Michelangelo**. He is buried close to the entrance at his own request, apparently so that the first thing he would glimpse when he rose from his tomb on the Day of Judgement would be Brunelleschi's cathedral dome. Almost alongside it is a memorial to **Dante**, the Florentine poet who died and is buried in Ravenna on Italy's Adriatic coast. A short distance away is the tomb of **Machiavelli**,

Detail from Michelangelo's sarcophagus

INSIDER INFO

- The Scuola del Cuoio (www.scuoladelcuoio.com) can be reached down the left-hand side of the church. The leather workshop founded by Franciscan monks manufactures exclusive accessories.
- To the right of Santa Croce is the entrance to the **Museo dell'Opera di Santa Croce** (church museum) and Cappella dei Pazzi (1429–70), the church's former chapter house. The museum has works of art by Donatello and Cimabue, while the Cappella is one of the finest small architectural and decorative ensembles of the early Renaissance. It was designed by Brunelleschi, architect of the cathedral dome, and decorated by Luca della Robbia, Desiderio da Settignano and others.

while the tomb of scientist **Galileo** lies on the opposite wall, again close to the church entrance.

Frescoes and Tombs

The church's key works of art are two **fresco cycles by Giotto** in the two chapels to the right of the high altar: the Cappella Bardi, which is adorned with *Scenes from the Life of St Francis* (1315–20), and to its right, the Cappella Peruzzi, with *Scenes from the Life of St John and St John the Baptist* (1326–30). Other major **14th-century cycles** by Taddeo and Agnolo Gaddi grace the Cappella Castellani and Cappella Baroncelli, adjacent chapels in the right (south) transept.

Don't miss some of the other **14th-century frescoes** around the chancel and in the rooms off the right transept, or the two influential **Renaissance tombs** that stand on opposite sides of the church close to the top of the nave. The first of these, on the right (south) side, belongs to the humanist scholar Leonardi Bruni (1146–47), and is the work of Bernardo Rossellino (1445–1450); the second (1453) by Desiderio da Settignano contains another eminent humanist scholar, Carlo Marsuppini. They are in the left and right aisles respectively.

TAKING A BREAK

Piazza Santa Croce has plenty of cafés, but **Baldovino** (► 84) is a far more distinctive place for a pizza or light meal. **Lo SchiacciaVino** (Via Verdi, 6r), which serves top-quality wine with its *panino*, is very popular. Or else you can treat yourself to an ice cream at the **Gelateria Vivoli.** (► 87).

Santa Croce
213 E3 Piazza Santa Croce 05 52 46 61 05; www.santacroceopera.it
Mon–Sat 9:30–5:30, Sun 2–5, (8am–1pm for worship only)
23; Electric bus: C1, C3 €6 (includes Museo dell'Opera di Santa Croce)

Museo dell'Opera di Santa Croce – Cappella dei Pazzi
213 E3/F3 Piazza Santa Croce, 16 05 52 46 61 05
Opening times as for Santa Croce above 23; Electric bus: C1, C3
€6 (includes church of Santa Croce)

11 Galleria dell'Accademia

Tucked away in the north of the city, the Galleria dell' Accademia, or simply Accademia, as it is more commonly known, is slightly off the city's main tourist track. Yet a visit here is unmissable, if only to see one of Florence's finest artistic treasures – the original of Michelangelo's famous statue of David.

As you enter the Accademia you are greeted by Italy's most celebrated statue – Michelangelo's ***David***, commissioned in 1501 by the Opera del Duomo, responsible for the upkeep of the cathedral. Several artists, including Leonardo da Vinci, had already tried to work with the same block of marble – a thin and cracked piece of stone believed to be of too poor a quality for sculpture, which had been quarried from the Apuan mountains north of Pisa some 40 years earlier.

The 26-year-old Michelangelo managed to confound his contemporaries by transforming the stone in just three years. After months of wrangling, the sculpture was eventually raised in Piazza della Signoria, where it remained until it was moved to its present home in 1873 after suffering damage from being exposed to the wind and rain. The fact that the statue was intended as an outdoor piece explains some of its deliberate distortions – the overlong arms and over-sized head and hands were designed to emphasise its monumentality.

Also in the Accademia, don't miss Michelangelo's statues of *St Matthew* (1505–06) and the *Four Slaves* (or *Prisoners*), the latter unfinished. Other rooms contain paintings by artists such as Filippino Lippi and Fra Bartolomeo.

Michelangelo's *David* greets visitors to the Accademia

Try the **Gran Caffè San Marco** in Piazza San Marco (tel: 055 21 58 33), just north of the Accademia.

---

213 D5 Via Ricasoli, 60

05 52 38 86 09; www.polomuseale.firenze.it to pre-book tickets

Tue–Sun 8:15–6:50 (last ticket 6:05)

14, 23, 71 and all bus services to Piazza San Marco; Electric bus: C1 close by

€6.50

⓬ Cappelle Medicee

The Cappelle Medicee (Medici Chapels) comprise the Medici family's mausoleum. Many of the dozens of tombs here are either insignificant or overly grandiose, but three merit special attention, thanks to the fact that they are graced by a trio of outstanding sculptures by Michelangelo.

Michelangelo's *Madonna and Child*

The chapels fall into three sections, the first of which you come to immediately beyond the ticket hall: a low, dimly lit **crypt**, the resting place of many of the less important Medicis. From here, steps lead to the **Cappella dei Principi**, a cavernous hall decorated in coloured marble that contains the tombs of the Medici's six grand dukes, the last of the Medici to rule Florence before the dynasty died out in 1743. The building was begun in 1604 and was to be the most expensive project ever undertaken by the family: it was still draining Medici coffers when Gian Gastone, the last grand duke, died.

The highlight, however, is the **Sagrestia Nuova** (New Sacristy), which was designed by Michelangelo and contains three groups of his sculpture. It was commissioned in 1520 by Pope Leo X, himself a Medici, as a mausoleum for Lorenzo the Magnificent and Lorenzo's brother, Giuliano. Ironically, their tombs were not completed and the two lie buried near Michelangelo's unfinished sculpture of *Madonna and Child* (1521). More ironic still, the tombs that were completed are those of the most feckless of the Medici: Lorenzo de' Medici (1533), grandson of Lorenzo the Magnificent, and

THE MEDICI

The Medici dominated Tuscan life for almost four centuries. Banker Giovanni di Bicci de' Medici (1360–1429) secured the lucrative papal bank account. His son, Cosimo de' Medici, the Elder, (1389–1464) consolidated the family's position and became a patron of the arts, as did his grandson, Lorenzo the Magnificent (1449–92). Two members became popes – Leo X (1475–1521) and Clement VII (1478–1534) – and the Florentine Medici became grand dukes of Tuscany. The line died out in 1743.

The Cappella dei Principi contains the tombs of six Medici grand dukes

Giuliano de' Medici, Lorenzo the Magnificent's third son. Lorenzo is shown as a man of thought, with two figures symbolizing 'Dawn' and 'Dusk'. Giuliano is posed as a man of action, accompanied by figures representing 'Day' and 'Night'.

TAKING A BREAK

The nearby **Mercato Centrale** has several small bars (➤ 77), while to the south the best bet is the **Caffè Gilli** on Piazza della Repubblica. Other nearby recommendations are **Zanobini** or the **Casa del Vino** (➤ 87).

---

212 C5 Piazza Madonna degli Aldobrandini, 6
05 52 38 86 02; www.polomuseale.firenze.it Summer: daily 8:15–1:50; Winter: 8:15–1:50; Last entry 30 mins before closing
14, 23 close by; Electric bus: C1 €6

INSIDER INFO

- The Medici Chapels quickly become crowded, so arrive early or **pre-book** by calling 055 29 48 83 or online at www.polomuseale.firenze.it. This service costs an extra €3.
- Watch out for **pickpockets** if you explore the busy general market in the streets around San Lorenzo and the Cappelle Medicee.

In more depth The Cappelle Medicee form part of the 4th-century **San Lorenzo church**, the Medici's former parish and one of Florence's most important religious buildings. The present church was designed in the 15th century by Brunelleschi. The inner courtyard in the adjoining monastery is also eye-catching, as is the **Biblioteca Medicea Laurenziana**, another of Michelangelo's works.

⓭ Santa Maria Novella

Florence's two great churches sit like sentinels on opposing sides of the city: Santa Croce (➤ 61), built by the Franciscans, in the east and Santa Maria Novella, the work of the Dominicans, in the west. Santa Maria may lack Santa Croce's hallowed tombs and monuments, but it wants for nothing in size or fresco cycles and other notable works of art.

The church was begun in 1246 and largely completed by 1360. Only its façade remained unfinished, until a textile merchant, Giovanni Ruccellaia, commissioned Leon Battisti Alberti to finish the work in 1456. The sponsor's Latin name can be seen across the façade, along with his emblem, the billowing 'Sail of Fortune'. The sun at the top is the symbol of the Dominicans.

A Trick of the Eye

Inside, the church's vast interior is given an added sense of scale by a **trick of perspective** – the pillars of the nave are set progressively closer together towards the high altar. Skilful use of perspective also accounts, at least in part, for the effect of the church's most celebrated painting, Masaccio's *Trinità* (1427), on the left-hand (north) wall between the second and third pillars. It was one of the first Renaissance paintings to demonstrate a complete mastery of the complex laws of perspective were mastered.

Santa Maria Novella's ornate 15th-century façade

Detail from Ghirlandaio's *Expulsion of Joachim from the Temple*

Further Artworks

Less well known but no less impressive paintings are found in the chapels close to the high altar. In the first, the **Cappella Filippo Strozzi** on the right as you face the altar, is a fresco cycle by Filippino Lippi on the *Life of St Philip the Apostle* (1489–1502). The **tomb** (1491–95) **of Filippo Strozzi**, who commissioned the frescoes, is by Benedetto da Maiano, to the rear of the chapel.

The chancel is swathed with even more striking **frescoes** (1485–90) by Domenico Ghirlandaio. To the left of the chancel lies the **Cappella Strozzi di Mantova.** The frescoes (1350–57) are the work of Nardo di Cione and show *Paradiso* (left) and *Inferno* (right), inspired by Dante's poem (➤ 10).

TAKING A BREAK

Try **Belle Donne** for a light lunch (www.casatrattoria.com) or **Caffè Amerini** (➤ 86).

Church and Museo Santa Maria Novella

212 B5 · Piazza Santa Maria Novella · 055 21 92 57
Mon–Thu, Sat 9–5:30, Fri 11–5:30, Sat 9–5 Sun noon–5;
Last entry 45 mins before closing
All bus services to central train station; Electric bus: C2, D · €5

INSIDER INFO

The **Fratelli Alinari Photography Museum** on the other side of the square was Italy's first photo archive and was founded by the two Alinari brothers. In addition to historical images, modern temporary exhibitions are also held here (Piazza Santa Maria Novella, 14r, tel: 055 21 63 10, www.mnaf.it; Thu–Tue 10–6:30, €9).

14 Museo Nazionale del Bargello

The Museo Nazionale del Bargello began life as a palace and prison, but today has Europe's finest collection of Italian Renaissance sculpture, with exceptional works by Donatello, Michelangelo and many others. It also has a beautiful but little-known collection of ceramics, carpets, glassware, textiles, tapestries, ivories and other decorative arts.

The building in which the museum is housed is the Palazzo del Bargello, a superb medieval palace begun in 1255 as the seat of the Podestà, Florence's chief magistrate. It took its present name in 1574, when the Medici abolished the post of Podestà and made the building over to the Bargello, or chief of police. It opened as a museum in 1865.

Museum Highlights

Immediately past the ticket office you enter a single room of sculpture that would be the envy of most entire museums. Pride of place goes to works by Michelangelo, of which the most eye-catching is the drunken figure of ***Bacchus*** (1496–97). Other works by the master include the ***Tondo Pitti*** (1504), a delicate, shallow relief

Taking time out in the Bargello's courtyard

Priceless sculptures in the *loggia* of the Bargello

showing the Madonna and Child; a figure of ***David*** or ***Apollo*** (1530–32) – critics are unsure of the intended identity; and a portrait of *Brutus* (1539–40), the only portrait bust Michelangelo completed. Look for 16th-century works by Benvenuto Cellini, a flamboyant sculptor and goldsmith, and Giambologna, in particular the latter's lithe figure of *Mercury* (1564–65).

From this first room you walk into the Bargello's central **courtyard**. Climb the courtyard staircase to a **loggia,** dotted with a menagerie of 16th-century bronze animals by the French-born sculptor Giambologna.

Turn right at the loggia and you enter the **Salone del Consiglio Maggiore**, containing the cream of Florence's early Renaissance sculpture. Insider Tip Its most celebrated works are a diverse selection of masterpieces by Donatello, notably an androgynous bronze statue of David (1430–40), an earlier marble *David* (1408), an heroic *St George* (1416–17), the Cupid-like figure *Amor-Atys* (1430–40) and a portrait bust of soldier Niccolò da Uzzano. The panels of *The Sacrifice of Isaac* were submitted by Ghiberti and Brunelleschi in the 1401 competition to design the Baptistry doors.

Other fascinating collections in the museum include fine displays of Islamic art, ivories and miniature bronzes.

TAKING A BREAK

Walk south to Piazza San Firenze and then east along Via Condotta to **La Canova di Gustavino** (► 87).

---

213 D4
Via del Proconsolo, 4
05 52 38 86 06. Advance tickets 055 29 48 83; www.polomuseale.firenze.it
Daily 8:15–5; closed 4th Mon of the month
Electric bus: C1, C2 €4

INSIDER INFO

The 10th-century **Badia Fiorentina abbey** lies directly opposite the Bargello. Although it has erratic opening hours, it is worth trying to get in to admire a painting of the *Apparition of the Virgin to St Bernard* (1485) by Filippino Lippi, 15th-century sculptures by Mino da Fiesole and a fresco cycle on the **Life of St Benedict** (by an anonymous hand) in the abbey cloister (entered by a door to the right of the high altar).

15 Piazza della Signoria

The second of Florence's great squares has long had a civic rather than religious focus. As well as being home to the impressive Palazzo Vecchio, the city's main seat of government for more than 700 years, it is notable for its range of captivating fountains and monumental sculptures.

Piazza della Signoria dates from the 13th century, when the city set aside land here for the Palazzo dei Priori (1299–1315), a council chamber which eventually became the present-day Palazzo Vecchio. The piazza was enlarged and adapted several times over the centuries, hence its irregular shape. Major changes were made in the 14th century to accommodate the Loggia dei Lanzi (also known as the Loggia dei Signori) on its southern flank, and again in 1560, when Cosimo I de' Medici created the palace which later would house the Uffizi gallery, which took its name from the offices *(uffizi)* in the building. In 1497, the leader of the Florence uprising, Fra Girolamo Savonarola, ordered a mass burning of all things 'lewd and pagan' in the square, including Renaissance artworks, along with other mundane items such as mirrors and chess sets.

Giambologna's monument to *Cosimo I de'Medici* in the Piazza della Signoria

Statues and Fountains

The square's famous **statues and fountains** run along its eastern flank. From left to right as you face them they are an equestrian monument of *Cosimo I de' Medici* (1594–98) by Giambologna and the *Fontana del Nettuno* (*Fountain of Neptune,* 1563–75) by Bartolomeo Ammanati, in which the central figure is again an idealised portrait of Cosimo I de' Medici. Then come two copies of work by Donatello: *Il Marzocco* (*the Lion,* 1418–20), a representation of Florence's heraldic symbol, and *Giuditta e Oloferne* (*Judith and Holofernes,* 1456–60). The originals of both these are in the Palazzo Vecchio. The final major sculptures are a copy of Michelangelo's *David*

(➤ 63) and the figures of *Ercole e Caco* (*Hercules and Cacus,* 1534) by Baccio Bandinelli.

Walk to your right and wander around the **Loggia dei Lanzi**, an airy arched space built in 1376 to protect the city's dignitaries from the elements during processions and ceremonials. The most outstanding of its statues are Benvenuto Cellini's bronze *Perseo che decapita la Medusa* (*Perseus with the Head of Medusa*, 1545) and Giambologna's three-figured *Ratto delle Sabine* (*The Rape of the Sabine Women*, 1583).

Part of Ammanati's *Fontana del Nettuno* (Fountain of Neptune)

Palazzo Vecchio

The Palazzo Vecchio opens with an exquisite main **courtyard** (1553–74), the work of Giorgio Vasari, followed on the first floor by the huge **Salone dei Cinquecento**, once the palace's main council chamber. The monumental battle scenes that decorate the walls are by Vasari and his school. The Salone features the *Studiolo di Francesco I* (1570–75), a study created for Cosimo I's son, and Michelangelo's ***Genio della Vittoria*** (*The Genius of Victory*, 1525). Other highlights include rooms filled with **frescoes and sculptures**, notably the Cappella di Eleonora, the Sala dell'Udienza and Sala dei Gigli.

TAKING A BREAK

Rivoire is a famous old café with outside tables on Piazza della Signoria (➤ 87) – steep prices, great outlook.

Palazzo Vecchio

213 D3 Piazza della Signoria

05 52 76 82 24; www.museicivicifiorentini.it

April–Sept Fri–Wed 9–midnight, Thu 9–2, rest of the year Fri–Wed 9–7, Thu 9–2; Tower (no admission to childen under 6 years of age); Summer: Fri–Wed 9–9, Thu 9–2; Winter: Fri–Wed 10–5, Thu 9–2, (closed when raining)

Electric bus: C1, C2 close by €18

INSIDER INFO

- Visit the **church of Orsanmichele** (➤ 78) as you walk between Piazza del Duomo and Piazza della Signoria on Via dei Calzaiuoli.
- Look for a small round marble and brass plaque set into the stone of the paving of Piazza della Signoria. This signifies the place where Girolamo Savonarola was executed by the people of the city when his rule turned sour in 1498.

In more depth Interesting **tours for children** are available around the Palazzo Vecchio – as well as the Bardini Museum, the Palazzo Davanzati, the church of Santa Maria Novella and the Brancacci Chapel (Mon–Sat 9:30–1, 2–5, Sun 9:30–12:30; information: tel: 05 52 76 85 58, www.musefirenze.it).

In the Seat of Power

This impressive square where public meetings were once held is dominated by the massive tower of the Palazzo Vecchio. The best way to soak in the atmosphere is from one of the exquisite street cafés facing the *palazzo*.

❶ **Palazzo Vecchio:** The Palazzo dei Priori was built between 1299 and 1314 and was renamed the Palazzo Vecchio when the Palazzo Pitti became the principle Medici residence.
❷ **Tower:** The seat of the city council to this day.
❸ **Loggia dei Lanzi:** Famous sculptures such as *Perseus with the Head of Medusa* by Benvenuto Cellini can be seen in the open, three-bay hall. The Mannerist marble group *The Rape of the Sabine Women* by Giambologna is under the right-hand arcade.
❹ **Fountain of Neptune:** This fountain is also known as 'Il Biancone' (The White Giant) thanks to the huge marble figure of the god of the sea, Neptune.
❺ **The 'Salone dei Cinquecento' (Hall of the Five Hundred)**, located on the first floor, was intended for use by the Grand Council that Savonarola had called into being. Its present appearance is the result of a major remodelling by Vasari and his helpers in the second half of the 16th century. The ceiling panels with allegorical scenes depicting events from the history of Florence and the Medicis are particularly noteworthy, as is Michelangelo's famous marble statue *The Genius of Victory*.

The Uffizi Gallery, shaped like an elongated 'U', opens into the Piazza della Signoria. The famous museum was erected as an office building to house the ministries of the Grand Duchy.

16 Galleria degli Uffizi

The Galleria degli Uffizi, more commonly known simply as the Uffizi, not only houses the world's greatest collection of Italian Renaissance art, but also a host of outstanding paintings from other periods and other European countries.

The immense palace housing the Uffizi art gallery was built in 1560 by Giorgio Vasari as a suite of offices *(uffizi)* for Cosimo I de' Medici. The paintings themselves formed the lion's share of the **Medici's private collection**, acquired over many centuries but bequeathed to Florence – on condition they never left the city – by Anna Maria Luisa (1667–1743), the last representative of the Medici dynasty.

One of the most famous works in the Uffizi: *The Birth of Venus* by Sandro Botticelli (1485)

The Collection

The collection ranges over 45 rooms and comprises more than 2,000 paintings on display, with some 1,800 other works of art kept in storage. Many of the most famous works – the Italian paintings of the Renaissance and medieval period – are in the first 15 or so rooms. Be prepared for throngs of people in this area, particularly around the works of **Botticelli** in Rooms 10–14. This said, you shouldn't skip some of the early masterpieces in your hurry to reach these rooms. The three pictures which open the gallery proper in Room 2 all depict the *Maestà*, or Madonna in Majesty. They are by three of the greatest

Insider Tip

painters of the 13th century: the Sienese master Duccio and the Florentine-based Giotto and Cimabue.

Highlights in Rooms 3–6 include paintings by Sienese artists, notably a sublime ***Annunciation*** (1333) by Simone Martini and works by Pietro and Ambrogio Lorenzetti, two painters who probably died in the Black Death in 1348. Also look for the intricately detailed and beautifully coloured ***Adoration of the Virgin*** by Gentile da Fabriano (1423) and ***Coronation of the Virgin*** (1413) by Lorenzo da Monaco.

Room 7 has works by early Renaissance masters such as Piero della Francesca, Masaccio and Paolo Uccello – the latter's ***Battle of San Romano*** (*c.*1456) is outstanding for its perspective. The room is outshone by Rooms 10–14, however, where you'll see Sando Botticelli's celebrated ***Primavera*** (1478) and ***The Birth of Venus*** (1485), paintings which drew on classical myth rather than religion for their themes and imagery. Room 15 has two paintings by Leonardo da Vinci – the ***Annunciation*** and ***Adoration of the Magi***. He was born in Vinci, a village in the hills west of Florence (➤ 182).

Highlights in the remaining rooms are many. Look out in particular for the ***Venus de' Medici*** (Room 18), considered one of the most erotic works of the third century; the *c.*1490 ***Sacred Allegory*** (Room 21) by the Venetian Giovanni Bellini; the *c.*1505 ***Tondo Doni*** (Room 25), the Uffizi's only painting by Michelangelo; Raphael paintings in Room 26; the ***Venus of Urbino*** (1538), an infamous nude by Titian in Room 28; and the paintings of Van Dyck, Caravaggio, Rubens, Rembrandt and others in the last six rooms. Insider Tip

TAKING A BREAK

The gallery has a good **café bar**, but you could also visit the **Rivoire** (➤ 87) on nearby Piazza della Signoria.

Pre-book your entrance tickets to the Uffizi to avoid a long wait

213 D3 ✉ Loggiata degli Uffizi, 6, off Piazza della Signoria ☎ 05 52 38 86 51; www.polomuseale.firenze.it ⏲ Tue–Sun 8:15–6:50 (last tickets 6:05). Closed Mon. Corridoio Vasariano tours: Booking obligatory (tel: 05 52 65 43 21) 🚌 23, 71; Electric bus: C1, C3, D close by €6.50; Corridoio: €85 (with guided tour)

The stunning architecture of the Uffizi's elegant salons is almost as impressive as its exhibits

INSIDER INFO

- The Uffizi will be busy whatever day or month of the year you visit. To avoid a long wait to get into the gallery **pre-book a ticket and entry time by credit card** (tel: 055 29 48 83; Mon–Fri 8–6:30, Sat 8:30–12:30 or online www.polomuseale.firenze.it or www.firenzemusei.it). You will receive a reservation number for the day and time of entry. Tickets are held at the counter for advance reservations to the left of the main gallery entrance. A small booking fee is charged. The Uffizi's pre-booked phone and online entry service is available for Florence's **state museums**, including the Cappelle Medicee, Galleria dell'Accademia, Palazzo Pitti (Galleria Palatina), Museo Nazionale del Bargello and Museo di San Marco.
- If you have enough time, take in the view of the far side of the Arno, with its medieval skyline and the church of San Miniato in the distance, when on the middle corridor.

Insider Tip

In more depth: If you take a guided tour (➤ 75) you will be able to visit the **Corridoio Vasariano**, an extraordinary secret passage almost 1km (more than ½mi) long, lined with paintings, built by Giorgio Vasari in the 16th century to link the Uffizi with the Palazzo Pitti (➤ 80). Part of its route runs over the Ponte Vecchio.

At Your Leisure

17 Museo di San Marco

This museum lies to the north of Florence's other main attractions, but of all the city's 'secondary' sights, it is the one most worth visiting. A former Dominican monastery, it is almost entirely given over to the paintings of Fra Angelico, a monk and former prior here, and one of the finest early Renaissance painters. In the main gallery off the old cloister, the **Ospizio dei Pellegrini**, the highlights are the San Marco Altarpiece (1440) and *Madonna dei Linaiuoli* (1433). Don't miss Domenico Ghirlandaio's *Last Supper* (1480) in the Refettorio Piccolo (Small Refectory). On the first floor you are greeted by Angelico's lovely *Annunciation,* a prelude to a succession of tiny monastic cells, each with a fresco by Angelico or his assistants painted as aids to devotion. Also here is a majestic library, built with funds from Cosimo de' Medici.

Insider Tip

213 D5 Piazza San Marco, 1
05 52 38 86 08; www.polomuseale.firenze.it
Tue–Fri and 1st, 3rd and 5th Mon of the month 8:15–1:50 (last ticket 1:20), Sat and 2nd and 4th Sun of the month 8:15–4:50
All bus services to Piazza San Marco, including 1, 6, 7, 10, 11, 14, 17, 23, 25, 33; Electric bus: C1 €4

18 Palazzo Medici-Riccardi

This palace belonged to the Medicis while they were at the height of their powers. Completed for Cosimo il Vecchio in 1462, it remained the family home until 1540, when Cosimo I de' Medici moved to the Palazzo Vecchio and the palace was sold to the Riccardi family.

While the palace retains its daunting exterior, only one small fragment of splendour survives inside – the tiny **Cappella dei Magi**, frescoed by Benozzo Gozzoli in 1459–60. These three vivid panels depict the procession of the three wise men. But Gozzoli provides us with an insight into then contemporary society by incorporating aspects of 15th-century Florentine life into the biblical scenes. On the east wall the Magi Casper is escorted by a medieval entourage depicting several members of the Medici clan and their friends.

213 D5 Via Cavour, 1
Pre-booked entry 05 52 76 03 40; www.palazzo-medici.it
Thu–Tue 9–6 (last ticket 5). Entrance to the Cappella dei Magi ltd. to 10 people every 7 mins
14, 23; Electric bus: C1 €7

19 Mercato Centrale

Florence's vast covered food market, the largest such market in Europe, first opened in 1874. Since then it has been beguiling Florentines and foreigners alike with its array of fruit, vegetables, hams, cheese, olive oils and other gastronomic treats. Its stalls are a wonderful source of picnic provisions or gifts, or visit simply for the sights and smells. The market is easily seen in conjunction with San Lorenzo (► 65) and the Cappelle Medicee (► 64–65).

212 C5 Piazza del Mercato Centrale
Mon–Sat 7–2 (mid-June–Sept closed Sat)
14,23; Electric bus: C1 close by Free

45 Museo dell'Opera del Duomo

The Opera del Duomo (Work of the Duomo) was founded in 1296 to look after the Duomo, Baptistry and Campanile (► 58–60). Since 1891, its headquarters east of the cathedral have provided the home for this now modern museum, filled with works of art over a period of 700 years. Its highlights are mainly medieval and Renaissance sculptures, but it also contains a wealth of paintings, gold and silverware, illustrated manuscripts and other artefacts. Its most celebrated treasure is a statue of the ***Pietà*** (1550–53) by Michelangelo, but other fine works include Donatello's *Mary Magdalene* (1453–55), Lorenzo Ghiberti's restored bronze panels from the Baptistry's east doors, and most of Andrea Pisano's and della Robbia's bas-reliefs from the Campanile.

After admiring the wealth of artistic treasures in the museum, it is also worth exploring the galleries relating to the design of the Duomo. The immense cupola was an architectural breakthrough in its time and you can see wooden models used by Brunelleschi to explore the characteristics and the aesthetics of his double vault designs, and a range of tools used in the fabrication of the structure during the early 1500s.

213 D4 Piazza del Duomo, 9 05 52 30 28 85; www.ilgrandemuseodelduomo.it Mon–Sat 9–7:30, Sun 9–1:40 Electric bus: C1, C2 €10 (including Baptistry, Campanile and Dome)

21 Museo Archeologico Nazionale

The National Archaeological Museum is a tiny, little-visited gem just a couple of minutes' walk east of San Marco. The collection of Egyptian and Etruscan art that the Medici's amassed from the 15th century onwards forms the core of the museum's holdings. The bronze Chimera (4th century B.C.) from Arezzo, a mythical figure with a lion's head, and the *Arringatore* (2nd century B.C.), a realistic sculpture of an orator who silences a crowd, are well worth seeing.

213 E5 Piazza SS Annunziata, 9b 05 52 35 75 Sat–Mon 8:30–2, Tue–Fri 8:30–7 6, 14, 23, 31 €4

Detail of the choirloft at the Museo dell'Opera del Duomo

22 Orsanmichele

The church of Orsanmichele is often missed, situated as it is on the Via dei Calzaiuoli, but it is easily visited as you walk between the Piazza del Duomo (► 58) and Piazza della Signoria (► 70). The fortress-like building takes its name from a seventh-century oratory. The oratory was replaced in 1280 by a grain market and by the present structure in 1380.

The building's artistic importance stems from the early 15th-century statues arranged around 14 exterior niches. These were commissioned by Florence's major medieval guilds – each figure represents an individual guild's patron saint. They demonstrate some of the most important sculptures of their day and were produced by many of the period's most important artists – Donatello, Ghiberti, Michelozzo, Brunelleschi and Verrocchio. Many of the works are now copies, the originals having been removed for safe-keeping to museums such as the Bargello (► 68).

Inside, the church walls are decorated with faded medieval frescoes that also depict the guilds' patron saints. The nave is dominated by a sumptuous tabernacle (1355–59) by Orcagna, which encloses a painting of the *Madonna delle Grazie* (1347) by Bernardo Daddi.

213 C4 Via dei Calzaiuoli–Via dell'Arte della Lana 055 28 49 44 Tue–Sun 10–5 Electric bus: C1, C2 Free

The Ponte Vecchio's arcaded shops are reflected in the Arno

 23 Palazzo Davanzati

For a peek into life in 14th-century Florence that is also interesting for children, step over the threshold of this mansion, built *c.* 1330 for the Davizzi family but sold to the Davanzati family, who lived there from the late 1300s until 1838. The house had it's own water supply – a well in the courtyard – which was considered a luxury in its time, and the original medieval wooden staircase is the only one remaining in the city. Visit the Sala dei Pappagalli and the Sala Pavoni on the first floor to view the **exquisite frescoes**. The kitchen lies on the upper floor (it limited the risk of damage during a domestic fire).

222 C4 Via Porta Rossa, 13
05 52 38 86 10; www.polomuseale.firenze.it
Daily 8:15–1:50. Closed 1st, 3rd, 5th Mon of the month and 2nd, 4th Sun of the month
No direct routes €2

24 Santa Trinita

The 11th-century church of Santa Trinita is relatively unassuming to look at, its late 16th-century façade concealing a mostly Gothic interior that was remodelled between 1300 and 1330. Its real worth lies in its side chapels, several of which contain compelling works of art. The **Cappella Sassetti**, the second chapel to the right of the high altar, contains a fresco cycle of *Scenes from the Life of St Francis* (1483–86) by Ghirlandaio. The same artist was responsible for the chapel's altarpiece, *The Adoration of the Shepherds* (1485), a consummate Renaissance fusion of Christian and pagan classical imagery. The fourth chapel on the right (south) side of the church contains a fresco cycle by Lorenzo Monaco of *Scenes from the Life of the Virgin* (1420–25).

212 B4 Piazza Santa Trinita
055 21 69 12
Mon–Sat 8–noon, 4–6, Sun 4–6
Electric bus: C3, D close by Free

25 Ponte Vecchio

Florence's most famous bridge has occupied its site close to the Arno's narrowest point in the city since about 1345. Earlier bridges here included a Roman bridge and two wooden medieval bridges swept away in the floods of 1117 and 1333. The present bridge only narrowly escaped a similar fate in the great flood of 1966, and in 1944 it was the only bridge in the city not blown up by the Nazis as they sought to slow the advance of the United States Fifth Army.

The Ponte Vecchio's picturesque overhanging stores and workshops date from the bridge's earliest days (previous bridges here had similar shops). They were originally the domain of butchers and fishmongers, attracted by the convenience of being able to tip their rubbish in the river – the open space that still exists at the centre of the bridge was created for this purpose. Later, the bridge was taken over by tanners, who used the river to soak their hides, and later still by jewellers and goldsmiths. Descendants of these jewellers still operate from the bridge.

212 C3 Via Por Santa Maria–Lungarno degli Acciaiuoli Daily Electric bus: C3, D Free

26 Cappella Brancacci

Florence has many fresco cycles, but two are particularly alluring. In northern Florence, Gozzoli's Palazzo Medici-Riccardi frescoes appeal for their narrative verve (► 77); in the Oltrarno district, it is the **frescoes** of the Cappella Brancacci that draw the largest crowds. Here the appeal is the paintings' innovation and the seminal place they hold in the development of Florentine Renaissance art.

The frescoes occupy part of Santa Maria del Carmine, an otherwise uninspiring church, and were commissioned in 1424 by Felice Brancacci, a wealthy diplomat and silk merchant. They were begun by Masolino da Panicale (1383–1447) and his assistant Masaccio (1401–28). Two years into the project, Masolino was called to Budapest, as official painter to the Hungarian court. In his absence, Masaccio's genius flourished. Masolino returned in 1427, but a year later was called to Rome, Masaccio died and, in 1436, Brancacci was exiled by the Medici. Work only resumed in 1480, when Filippino Lippi completed the cycle, working so closely to his predecessors' style that his contribution was only recognised in 1838. The frescoes' narrative power, perspective and realism were unlike anything seen before in Florence.

View over the Giardino di Boboli

212 A3 Piazza del Carmine 05 52 38 21 95 or 05 52 76 82 24; pre-booked entry 055 29 48 83; www.museicivicifiorentini.it Mon, Wed–Sat 10–5, Sun 1–5 37, 38, 68 close by; Electric bus: D €6

27 Giardino di Boboli

The Giardino di Boboli (Boboli Garden), is central Florence's principal garden and the only significant open space in which you can escape the hustle and bustle of the city streets. Set behind the Palazzo Pitti, it was begun in 1549 when Cosimo I de' Medici acquired the palace. It was opened to the public in 1776. In high summer it can look parched and worn, but at other times the tree-shaded walkways, formal gardens, parterres, lawns, fountains, grottoes and statues are a delight. There is a café in the garden, but this is also a pleasant place for a picnic.

212 B1 Entrances on Via Palazzo Pitti or Via San Leonardo 05 52 38 87 86; www.polomuseale.firenze.it; pre-book tickets at www.firenzemusei.it Apr–May, Sept–Oct Tue–Sun and 2nd and 3rd Mon of the month 8:15–6:30; March 8:15–5:30; June–Aug 8:15–7:30 (last ticket 6:30); Nov–Feb 8:15–4:30. 11, 36, 37 close by; Electric bus: D €7; 3-day combined ticket with Palazzo Pitti museums: €11.50

28 Palazzo Pitti

The long-forgotten Pitti family may have begun this huge Oltrarno palace in 1458, but after it was bought by Cosimo I de' Medici in

1549 it was for many years the Medici family's main Florentine home. The last member of the Medici dynasty, Anna Maria Luisa de Medici, died in 1743. The palace was later used by Napoleon during his occupation of Florence in the first decade of the 1800s, and was the official residence of the King of Italy for a short time when Florence became the capital after the unification of the country in the 1860s. The palace was donated to the people of Italy by King Emmanuel III in 1919. Today it plays host to several museums. The **Museo degli Argenti** is devoted primarily to silverware *(argento)* but also contains precious objects accumulated by the Medici family over the centuries.

The **Galleria Palatina** contains hundreds of priceless paintings from the Medici collection, making this Florence's second-ranking art gallery after the Uffizi (► 74–76). Works by Raphael and Titian are the most prized treasures, but there are also canvases by Caravaggio, Filippino Lippi and other leading names, framed and displayed together as they were during the Medici era.

212 B2 Piazza de' Pitti Galleria Palatina: 05 52 38 86 11; www.polomuseale.firenze.it Galleria Palatina: Tue–Sun 8:15–6:50 (last ticket 6:05). Closed Jan 11, 37, 38; Electric bus: C3, D 3-day combined ticket with Palazzo Pitti museums: €11.50

29 San Miniato al Monte

The church of San Miniato is the most outlying of all Florence's major sights, yet it is also one of the most beautiful. You can take a bus or follow a pretty uphill walk from close to the Ponte Vecchio, which offers memorable views.

San Miniato is one of Tuscany's finest Romanesque buildings. It was begun *c.*1090 on the site of an earlier chapel to St Minias, martyred in Florence around AD250. The façade was completed in 1207 – note the statue of an eagle clutching a bale of cloth, symbol of the Cloth Merchants' Guild, responsible for the church's upkeep. Inside, the marble pavement dates from 1207, as do the pulpit, screen and apse mosaic. Walk down to the crypt with its tiny columns and admire the fresco by Spinello Aretino of *Scenes from the Life of St Benedict* (1387) in the chapel right of the apse.

213 F1 Via del Monte alle Croci–Viale Galileo Galilei 05 52 34 27 31 Winter: daily 8–1, 3:30–7; Summer: 8–sunset. Closed for services 12 Free

The 13th-century apse mosaic is one of many outstanding works of art in San Miniato al Monte

Where to… Stay

Prices
Expect to pay per double room per night
€ under €125 | €€ €125–€200 | €€€ over €200

Brunelleschi €€€
The 4-star Brunelleschi has an excellent position in a quiet back street between the Duomo and Piazza della Signoria. A wonderful conversion of an historic site, it was designed by the star architect Italo Gamberini and is built around a Byzantine chapel and the fifth-century Torre della Pagliazza, one of the city's oldest-known structures. A small in-hotel museum is devoted to archaeological treasures unearthed during construction. Rooms and common areas combine a modern feel with features retained or copied from the original buildings, notably the exposed brickwork.

213 D4
Via dei Calzaiuoli–Piazza Santa Elisabetta, 3
05 52 73 70; www.hotelbrunelleschi.it
50

Casci €/€€
The Casci is one of the best 2-star hotels in Florence, thanks to its position (just north of Piazza del Duomo), the warm welcome of its multilingual family owners, a good buffet breakfast, the fair prices and the range of clean and pleasant rooms.

213 D5 Via Cavour, 13
055 21 16 86; www.hotelcasci.com
10, 11, 25, 31, 82; Electric bus: C1

Gallery Hotel Art €€€
This stylish 4-star hotel is unlike almost anything else in Florence. It has a sleek, minimalist look – dark wood, neutral colours and modern art displayed in the reception and the rooms. There is a small, stylish bar and a comfortable lounge area. The position is very convenient, in a small, quiet square next to the Ponte Vecchio.

212 C3 Vicolo dell'Oro, 5
055 27 26 40 00; www.lungarnocollection.com
Electric bus: D, C3

Helvetia & Bristol €€€
The 18th-century Helvetia & Bristol may have rivals for the title of 'best hotel in Florence' but none can really compete with the historic pedigree and panache of this 5-star retreat. It's located between Via de' Tornabuoni and Piazza Strozzi to the west of the city centre, and past guests have included Pirandello, Stravinsky and Bertrand Russell. The award-winning decor is mostly old-world – antiques, rich fabrics and period paintings – but the facilities and service are modern and efficient.

212 C4 Via de' Pescioni, 2
05 52 66 51; www.royaldemeure.com
6, 11; Electric bus: C2

Hotel Davanzati €€
This well-placed small hotel, just a short distance from the Piazza della Signoria, is housed in a traditional medieval Florentine mansion. The building has been renovated with 21st-century features, including internet access in every room. In fact, if anything, the rooms lack the historical touches one might expect for a building of this age, but the decor is classic without being too fussy and the price/location ratio is difficult to beat. Insider Tip

212 C4 Via Porta Rossa, 5
055 28 66 66; www.hoteldavanzati.it
Electric bus: C2 close by

Hotel David €€

In this wonderfully old-fashioned 3-star hotel on the outskirts of the Old Town you have the feeling you are staying with a close relative. The individually furnished rooms – some with their own balcony – have all modern creature comforts too, of course. Book well in advance!

203 F1 Viale Michelangelo, 1
05 56 81 16 95; www.hoteldavid.com
12,13; Electric bus: D

Hotel Hermitage €€/€€€

You need to book early to have a chance of securing a room at this 3-star boutique hotel. It owes its popularity to the amiable service, the comfortable bathrooms (some with jacuzzis) and a superb position almost overlooking the Ponte Vecchio. Not all rooms have river or bridge views, however, and those that do can be noisy: if this is a concern, request a courtyard room. In summer, you can take breakfast on the roof terrace.

212 C3 Vicolo Marzio, 1–Piazza del Pesce
055 28 72 16; www.hermitagehotel.com
Electric bus: C3, D close by

Hotel L'Orologio €€€

Nomen est omen! Everywhere you go in this boutique hotel you will come across a clock from the owner's collection. The unobtrusive ticking of an Omega timepiece in the library underlines the elegant atmosphere. A world clock is just one of several whiling away the time in the salon and each of the 58 rooms is named after award-winning wristwatches. The location, style and service in the hotel all interact harmoniously like clockwork too.

212 C4 Piazza Santa Maria Novella, 24
055 27 73 80; www.hotelorologioflorence.com
6, 11, 12, 37

Hotel Maxim €

The friendly and well-run Maxim is only 2-star, so don't expect too many frills, but its location next to the Duomo could hardly be better. The communal areas retain the character of the period property but the rooms are modern, and though lacking in character are somewhat spacious and clean. The hotel occupies the third and fourth floors of a 19th-century building, but has lift (elevator) access. Try for the quieter rooms looking onto the central courtyard.

213 D4 Via dei Calzaiuoli, 11 (with lift) and Via de' Medici, 4 (stairs)
055 21 74 74; www.hotelmaximfirenze.it
Electric bus: C2

Hotel Morandi alla Crocetta €/€€

This 3-star gem bears the cultivated stamp of its ex-pat owner, Kathleen Doyle. The hotel's rooms all have antiques, prints and polished wood floors; the best room has fragments of fresco from the monastery that once occupied the site. East of Piazza SS Annunziata, the location isn't very convenient, but you'll still have to book in advance.

213 E5 Via Laura, 50
05 52 34 47 47; www.hotelmorandi.it
6, 14, 19, 23, 31, 32 close by

La Scaletta €€

This maze of a hotel occupies part of a 16th-century palazzo between the Ponte Vecchio and Palazzo Pitti. Although the fabric of the building has been upgraded to modern standards, the rooms retain period touches. Most are quiet, the best being the three that overlook the Giardino di Boboli; **Insider Tip** those overlooking the potentially noisy Via Guicciardini have good double-glazing. A trio of garden roof terraces offer great views, and in summer there's a bar/restaurant to enjoy drinks or a meal.

212 C3 Via de' Guicciardini, 13
055 28 30 28; www.hotellascaletta.it
Electric bus: C3, D

Where to...
Eat and Drink

Prices
Expect to pay for a three-course meal for one with wine
€ under €26 **€€** €26–€52 **€€€**over €52

RESTAURANTS

Angiolino €/€€
An Oltrarno *trattoria* of the old school, Angiolino has one of Florence's prettiest interiors, though changes over the last few years have done away with some of the rustic charm of the old brick-vaulted main dining room. Red-checked tablecloths and wicker-covered wine bottles complete the picture. The food consists of simple dishes that never stray far from the Tuscan mainstream, including a great *bisteca alla fiorentina*.
212 B3 Via di Santo Spirito, 36r
05 52 39 89 76
Daily 12:30–2:30, 7:30–11
6, 11, 12, 36, 37 close by; Electric bus: C3, D

Baldovino €/€€
If you're in a dilemma over where to eat lunch or dinner close to the church of Santa Croce, look no further than Baldovino. An informal combination of modern and traditional, the restaurant has been one of Florence's great successes of recent years, if only because of its welcoming owner, Scotsman David Gardner. As a foreign restaurateur, Gardner has managed to satisfy a demanding Florentine clientele by mixing good food – Tuscan classics, Neapolitan pizzas plus innovative salads and other non-Italian novelties – with a bright decor, young staff and a convivial, cosmopolitan atmosphere. Booking is strongly advised.
213 F3 Via San Giuseppe, 22r
055 24 17 73; www.baldovino.com
Daily 11:30–2:30, 7–11:30.
Closed Mon Nov–March
23 close by; Electric bus: C2, C3 close by

Trattoria La Casalinga €/€€
At Paolo Carrai's you can find typical, plain Tuscan cooking at a reasonable price, *cucina casalinga* in fact. Word has spread around and it can well be that you will have to wait for a free table in the evening. But it's worth the wait – the *ribollita, spaghetti al coniglio, bollito misto* & co. are as good as you'll get.
212 B3 Via dei Michelozzi, 9r
055 21 86 24, www.trattorialacasalinga.it
Mon–Sat noon–2:30, 7–10
11, 36, 37; Electric bus: D

Benvenuto €/€€
Don't expect too much of this place and you won't be disappointed. This is a basic *trattoria* with an interior that eschews design flourishes to concentrate on no-nonense food. It has been serving Tuscan staples for as long as anyone can remember and is popular with everyone.
213 D4 Via della Mosca, 16r, corner Via dei Neri 055 21 48 33 Mon–Sat noon–2:30, 7–10:30 No direct routes

Cantinetta del Verrazzano €
This is a superb place for a snack or light meal, just a short distance from Via dei Calzaiuoli. All manner of sandwiches and other tasty delights (most of them baked on site) are presented under a huge display. You can buy food to take away or

have a drink or meal at the tables in the café-wine bar. The place is owned by the Castello di Verrazzano estate, one of Chianti's leading vineyards, so the wine here is also good.

213 D3 Via dei Tavolini, 18–20r 055 26 85 90 Mon–Sat 8am–9pm Electric bus: C2 close by

Cibrèo €€€

Many rate Cibrèo as Florence's best restaurant, thanks to its imaginative interpretations of traditional Florentine 'country' fare. The dining area is simple and the service and atmosphere are informal. Prices are set for each course, regardless of what you order (and include service), but be sure to leave room for one of the excellent desserts. You can eat at lower prices in the adjoining *trattoria,* the Vineria Cibreino, but the atmosphere is somewhat muted. Don't forget the other parts of the Cibrèo 'empire' – the delicatessen and café (► 80–81). Book in advance for the restaurant.

213 F4 Via Andrea del Verrocchio, 8r 05 52 34 11 00; www.cibreo.com Tue–Sun 1–2:30, 7:30–11:15 14 close by; Electric bus: C1, C2 close by

Enoteca Pinchiorri €€€

An *enoteca* is usually an inexpensive wine bar: not here, although there's plenty of wine – some 80,000 bottles of vintage quality wine, including some of the world's rarest. In fact, this is Florence's best and most expensive restaurant, award-winning for many years, owned and managed by Annie Féolde and Giorgio Pinchiorri. The prices for the refined and elaborate 3-Michelin-star Italian and international food are extremely high, while the service and surroundings are formal (men should wear a jacket and tie).

213 E3 Via Ghibellina, 87 055 24 27 77; www.enotecapinchiorri.com Dinner: Tue–Sat Lunch: reservations only 14 close by; Electric bus: C2, C3

Gustavino €€

Putting a modern slant on Tuscan cuisine and a contemporary slant on Florentine decor, this restaurant makes an interesting contrast to the many rustic *trattorie* in the city, but it's menu concentrates on local dishes made from market-fresh produce. Enjoy excellent guinea fowl or fresh pasta with sea urchin, or a mouth-watering salad drizzled with balsamic vinegar. The restaurant also offers gluten-free options. The wine list extends to 800 different wines, which can be a bit intimidating, but the staff is knowledgeable and helpful. Try La Canova di Gustavino wine bar next door for a more informal dining experience (► 87).

213 D4 Via della Condotta, 37r 05 52 39 98 06; www.gustavino.it Mon–Fri 7–11:30pm, Sat, Sun 12:30–3:30 Electric bus: C1 close by, C2

Mario €

Mario is a Florentine institution which makes few concessions to stylish dining. It's a basic eatery just north of the Mercato Centrale that provides cheap, authentic and good-quality Tuscan food (lunch only) to students, shoppers and market traders. You'll find tripe on Mondays and Thursdays, fish on Fridays and just one choice of dessert week-round – *cantucci con vin santo* (biscuits with a dessert wine). It's good in a rough-and-ready sort of way, but if you want a little more style, look into Zà-Zà, which is located a couple of doors away.

212 C5 Via Rosina, 2r–Piazza del Mercato Centrale 055 21 85 50; www.trattoria-mario.com Mon–Sat noon–3pm. Closed Aug Electric bus: C1 close by

Osteria dei Benci €€

This place epitomises Florence's new breed of bright and informal restaurants, and is distinguished by a single attractive dining room painted in warm colours and crowned by a pretty medieval brick vault. The staff are young, the service is charming and relaxed, and the Tuscan food well prepared and imaginative without being too daring. Menus change regularly to take account of seasonal availability of fresh produce.

213 E5 Via de' Benci, 13r
05 52 34 49 23
Daily 12:30–3:30, 7:30–11; closed for a period in Aug
23; Electric bus: C1, C3

Osteria del Caffè Italiano €€

Set in an old *palazzo*, the rustic dining rooms of this traditional *osteria* couldn't be more typically Italian with their wooden panelling, glass-fronted cabinets and terracotta tiles. A combination of wine bar, *trattoria* or *ristorante* means you can drop in here for a drink, a snack or a full meal throughout the day and into the evening. The air-dried ham is sliced from a huge shoulder of meat that sits on the informal bar, while the diminutive formal dining area has neat white tablecloths and silver service.

213 E3 Via Isole delle Stinche, 11–13r
055 28 93 68; www.caffeitaliano.it
Tue–Sun 12pm–1am
23, 71 close by; Electric bus: C1, C2 close by

Osteria del Cinghiale Bianco €/€€

The menu at one of the best-known family run *osterias* in town concentrates on Tuscan specialities, including *ribollita* (bean soup) – one of the reasons that the Tuscans are nicknamed *magia-fagioli* or 'bean eaters' by other Italians – and slow-cooked *cinghiale* (wild boar), which used to roam the surrounding hills in large numbers and which gave the place its name.

212 C3 Borgo San Jacopo, 43r
055 21 57 06; www.cinghialebianco.it
Mon, Tue, Thu, Fri 6:30pm–10:30pm, Sat, Sun 12–3, 6:30–10:30
11, 36, 37 close by; Electric bus: C3

Trattoria Ruggero €/€€

For the people of Florence the atmosphere is of secondary importance when choosing a restaurant. What counts is friendly service and the quality of the typically Tuscan food. The Corsi family fulfils these criteria and, as a result, has been able to count on its faithful customers for more than 25 years. Popular dishes include *crostini*, *pappa al pomodorro*, *ribollita*, roast rabbit and the classic stewed meat in a green sauce. All washed down with a good local red wine.

Insider Tip

212 A1 Via Senese, 89r 055 22 05 42
Thu–Mon 12:30–2, 7:30–10 36, 37

CAFÉS AND BARS

Caffè Amerini €

Caffè Amerini is a little different to most Florentine eating places. While it has the familiar medieval brick-arched vaults of many of the city's bars and restaurants, its paint-effect walls and oddball furniture provide a modern and slightly eccentric edge to a place that is patronised by everyone from students to genteel old ladies. It's a cosy and easy-going retreat in which you could happily spend an hour or two with a book on a rainy afternoon. It's also good for breakfast or lunch: simply point out which of the sandwiches, salads or other snacks you want from the bar just inside the door and then take a seat to be served.

212 B4 Via della Vigna Nuova, 61r
055 28 49 41 Mon–Sat 8–8
6; Electric bus: C3 close by

Caffè Cibrèo €

It's hard to think of a prettier café in Florence than Caffè Cibrèo, whose lovely wood-panelled interior dates from 1989, but could just as easily be 200 years older. Although it's some way from the centre, it's convenient if you're visiting the Sant'Ambrogio market or

church. As an added incentive, the snacks and cakes (including a famed chocolate torte) come from the celebrated kitchens of the co-owned Cibrèo restaurant nearby (➤ 85).
213 F4 Via Andrea del Verrocchio, 5r
05 52 34 58 53; www.cibreo.com
Tue–Sat 8am–1am
Electric bus: C1, C2 close by

Caffè Pitti €
Piazza Pitti in front of the Palazzo Pitti offers several café options, of which this – the southernmost in the square – with its pretty and old-fashioned interior, is the best.
212 B2 Piazza de' Pitti, 9r
05 52 39 98 63; www.caffepitti.it
Daily 11am–2am. May close Mon in winter
Electric bus: C3, D

La Canova di Gustavino €
The informal sibling of Gustavino (➤ 79), this wine bar has shared tables and a relaxed atmosphere. You can enjoy a range of wines with excellent Tuscan dishes – anything from a simple bowl of soup or a plate of charcuterie to a more full multi-course meal. There are Chianti wine tastings every Friday from 4–7pm.
213 D4 Via della Condotta, 37r
05 52 39 98 06; www.gustavino.it
Mon–Fri 7–11:30pm, Sat, Sun 12:30–3, 7:30–11:30 Electric bus: C1, C2

Casa del Vino €
Unsurprisingly, the 'House of Wine' is a place to drink or buy wine. It's often busy, due to its location close to the Mercato Centrale, but usually with locals. You can buy wine by the bottle to take out. Alternatively you can wash down *crostini* (toasts) or *panini* (rolls) at the bar with wines by the glass.
212 C5 Via dell'Ariento, 16r
055 21 56 09; www.casadelvino.it
Mon–Sat 9:30–8:30
No direct routes

INO
There is fast food and fast food. And that is shown in an inimitable way in this mixture between an *enoteca* and a lunch bar. The *panini*, for example, are filled with Tuscan brawn meat jelly, pickled rabbit or an artichoke/sardine delicacy, accompanied by top local wines.
212 C3 Via dei Georgofili, 3r
055 21 92 08 Daily 11:30–4:30
No direct routes

Rivoire €
It's hard to resist settling down at one of Rivoire's outside tables, if only because they overlook the Piazza della Signoria. When the café was founded in 1872 it specialised in hot chocolate, but these days teas, coffee and other drinks are also available. For a café, prices are high, however, and the sandwiches and other food average, but … the view!
213 D3 Piazza della Signoria, 5r
055 21 44 12; www.rivoire.it
Tue–Sun 8am–midnight
Electric bus: C1, C2 close by

Vivoli €
A Florentine institution that has been in the same hands for three generations. It once held the unofficial title of the best ice-cream in Italy and you'll still have to go a long way to find *gelati*, or sorbets quite as good. It lies just west of Piazza Santa Croce.
213 E4 Via Isole delle Stinche, 7r
055 29 23 34 Tue–Sun 9–8
23; Electric bus: C1, C2, C3 close by

Le Volpi e L'Uva €
A first-rate wine bar in a small square just across the Ponte Vecchio. Around 50 wines are sold by the glass, with many unusual vintages, which change every few days. The snack food is also good. Insider Tip
212 C2 Piazza dei Rossi, 1r, off Piazza di Santa Felicita
05 52 39 81 32; www.levolpieluva.com
Mon–Sat 11–9 Electric bus: C3, D

Where to ... Shop

BOOKS

Feltrinelli
Feltrinelli belongs to a modern, Italy-wide chain. Invariably busy, its floors are filled not only with Italian titles, but a sprinkling of English and other foreign-language books – though the sister store, Feltrinelli Internazionale at Via Cavour 12–20r, is a better bet for such titles. This branch, just west of the Duomo, has a good selection of guides and maps in English and Italian, plus a range of music CDs and international DVD titles.

212 C4
Via de' Cerretani, 30r
05 52 38 26 52; www.lafeltrinelli.it
14, 23; Electric bus: C1

CLOTHES AND ACCESSORIES

Armani
Giorgio Armani's flagship Florentine store, showcasing the current high-end, ready-to-wear collection, is on Via de' Tornabuoni. However, the cheaper Emporio Armani outlet catering for men and women in the 20–30 age range is on Piazza degli Strozzi.

212 C3
Via de' Tornabuoni, 48r
055 21 90 41; www.armani.com
6, 36, 37, 68; Electric bus: C1 close by

202 C3
Piazza degli Strozzi, 14–17r
055 28 43 15; www.armani.com
6, 11; Electric bus: C2 close by

Gucci
The world-famous Gucci label was founded at this Florentine address, which still acts as a prestigious showroom for the revitalised company's clothes, shoes and accessories. Inevitably, prices are high, but quality and cutting-edge style are assured. There is also a Gucci museum on the Piazza Signoria documenting the history of the fashion label (www.gucci museo.com).

212 C3
Via de' Tornabuoni, 73r
055 26 40 11 6, 11

Prada
Prada may have Milanese roots, but Florentines happily patronise the two shops of what is currently the most fashionable of all designer labels. There are fantastic shoes, bags and men's and women's wear for those who want to make a style statement.

212 C3
Via de' Tornabuoni, 53r–67r 055 26 74 71; www.prada.it
6, 11 close by; Electric bus: C3, D close by

Pucci
The aristocratic Marchese Emilio Pucci made his name in the 1950s and 1960s with his bright and distinctive printed silks. His star waned somewhat until the 1990s, when the same silks again became fashionable. Today, Pucci is the doyen of Florentine designers and is much fêted in the city's fashion circles. In addition to this shop in Via de' Tornabuoni, there is a showroom just north of the Duomo at Via dei Pucci 6.

212 C3 Via de' Tornabuoni, 20–22r
05 52 65 81 82; www.emiliopucci.com
6, 11 close by; Electric bus: C2 close by

Mimi Furaha
This new type of fashion shop proves that the entrepreneurial spirit in Florence is flourishing once again: 'Made in Italy' and little labels are *de rigeur*.

213 E4 Borgo degli Albizi, 35r
05 52 34 44 56; www.mimifuraha.it
E-Bus: C1, C2 in der Nähe

DEPARTMENT STORE

COIN
COIN offers the best one-stop shopping in Florence, partly because of its central location and partly because the quality of clothes, linens and other household goods is generally outstanding. Clothes include own-label and designer items, Italian classics for men and women, and younger, more modern fashion items on the ground floor. Kitchenware is in the basement. It's open on Sundays, which is useful if you are visiting Florence for a long weekend.

213 D4 ✉ Via dei Calzaiuoli, 56r
☎ 055 28 05 31; www.coin.it 🚌 Electric bus: C2

FOOD AND WINE

Dolci & Dolcezze
This is where true perfectionists can be found. The cake shop only has a small sales area and a bar which is not really suitable for drinking coffee hours on end. But you can always take a chocolate or lemon cake back to your hotel room and you'll see – the porter will treat you from then on as someone in the know.

213 F4 ✉ Piazza Beccaria, 8r
☎ 05 52 34 54 58
🚌 23, 14; Electric bus: C2, C3

Pegna
Florentines have been visiting this temple to fine food just south of the Duomo since 1860. Here you can buy tasty foods such as cheese, salami, coffee, tea, olive oil, wine, chocolates and other treats from Italy and around the world. The company has a range of packaged goods that make excellent gifts or souvenirs. It's also a great place to pick up ingredients for a picnic. **Insider Tip**

213 D4 ✉ Via dello Studio 8
☎ 055 28 27 01; www.pegna.it
🚌 Electric bus: C1, C2 close by

HOUSEHOLD GOODS

Bartolini
Founded in 1921, Bartolini has since become such a fixture that locals refer to the shop's street junction as the *angolo Bartolini* (Bartolini corner). It sells just about every item of kitchenware you could possibly wish for, including authentic Parmesan graters and spaghetti tongs, so stock up on fine china, porcelain and glassware.

213 D5 ✉ Via dei Servi, 30r
☎ 055 29 14 97; www.dinobartolini.it
🚌 14, 23, 71 close by; Electric bus: C1 close by

JEWELLERY

Lapini
This historic shop is a cut above Florence's many jewellers. The stones and metals found here are of the highest quality, and often have more unusual designs.

212 A3 ✉ Borgo San Frediano, 50r
☎ 055 21 32 76 🚌 6; Electric bus: D

Torrini
It's hard to argue with the reputation of a jeweller's shop which first Indexed its trademark (half a clover leaf) as long ago as 1369. It is still one of the best places in Florence to buy jewellery – gold in particular.

213 D4 ✉ Piazza del Duomo, 10r
☎ 05 52 30 24 01; www.torrini.it
🚌 Electric bus: C1, C2 close by

MARKETS

Mercato Centrale
Florence's vast indoor market is a wonderful place to stock up on mouthwatering picnic provisions, gifts or souvenirs (► 77).

212 C5 ✉ Piazza del Mercato Centrale
🚌 14, 23 close by; Electric bus: C1 close by

San Lorenzo
The market fills the area outside the church of San Lorenzo, as well as side streets nearby. Many stalls sell similar products – mid-price

leather jackets, shoes, ties, handbags, luggage and T-shirts. The quality of the leatherware, coats and jackets in particular, can be good, but the prices are quite high given that this is a market. You may be able to haggle, but be warned that the stallholders here are a pretty hard-nosed bunch and don't like to give much away.

213 C5 Via dell'Ariento, Piazza di San Lorenzo, Via del Canto de' Nelli
14, 23 close by; Electric bus: C1 close by

PAPER AND STATIONERY

Pineider

Pineider is probably Italy's ultimate stationers, with its range of beautifully crafted tinted papers and inks, notebooks and desk accessories. Founded in 1774, its customers over the years have included Napoleon, Stendhal, Puccini, Lord Byron, Shelley, Marlene Dietrich and Maria Callas. All have been beguiled by the exquisite pens, diaries and other associated items.

212 B4 Piazza dei Rucellai, 4–7r
055 28 46 55; www.pineider.com 6, 11

PERFUMES AND TOILETRIES

Antica Officina del Farmacista Dr Vranjes

This lovely shop located near Piazza Santa Croce sells a range of scents, essential oils and aromatherapy products. All are handmade from natural products. Try scents such as 'Tuscan Garden' or 'Fiori di Sicilia'. You can also visit Dr Vranjes' workshop (which has a small shop area) at Via San Gallo 69r.

213 F4 Borgo La Croce, 44r
055 24 17 48; www.drvranjes.it
Electric bus: C2, C3 close by

Farmacia di Santa Maria Novella

One of Italy's most famous pharmacies, this wonderful old shop occupies a 13th-century chapel in the Santa Maria Novella complex and comes complete with frescoes, old pharmacy equipment and wooden cabinets. It was created in 1612 by Dominican monks to sell the elixirs, ointments and other products that they prepared in their workshops using the plants they grew in their medicinal gardens. Most of the toiletries are still produced using traditional methods and the highest quality natural ingredients, such as the fine pot-pourris of flowers from the Florentine hills, and Aqua di Santa Maria Novella, a toilet water made from herbs and renowned for its calming properties. All the products are lovingly packaged, making this an excellent place for gifts and souvenirs to take back home.

212 B4 Via della Scala, 16
055 21 62 76; www.smnovella.it
36, 11, 12, 36, 37; Electric bus: C2 close by

PRINTS AND ENGRAVINGS

Giovanni Baccani

Many stores in Florence sell prints and engravings, but few are quite as alluring as this beautiful old shop, which first opened in 1903. There's a huge selection of framed and unframed prints at prices to suit every budget.

212 C3 Via della Vigna Nuova, 75r
055 21 44 67
6; Electric bus: C3 close by

SHOES

Ferragamo

The famous Salvatore Ferragamo was born in Naples and made his name designing shoes for Hollywood stars. His descendants still run the company, and this shop has a top range of clothes and accessories, as well as the most up-to-date collection of beautiful shoes.

212 C4 Via de' Tornabuoni 4r–14r
055 29 21 23; www.ferragamo.com 6, 11 close by; Electric bus: C2 close by

Where to . . . Go Out

TICKETS

Tickets for many musical and other events in Florence can be obtained from individual box offices or through **Box Office**, a ticket agency at Via delle Vecchie Carceri, 1 (tel: 055 21 08 04; www.boxoffice toscana.it or www.boxol.it).

INFORMATION

For details on events and entertainment listings in Florence, ➤51.

CLASSICAL MUSIC

The **Teatro Comunale** (Corso Italia, 16; tel: 05 52 77 92 54) is Florence's main theatre, and stages performances of its own and visiting companies. The main season for concerts, opera and ballet runs from January to April and September to December. The Teatro also hosts performances of the annual music festival, Maggio Musicale. Tickets and information from the box office (tel: 05 52 77 93 50; www.maggio fiorentino.com; Tue–Fri 10–4:30, Sat 10–1) or from the Box Office agency (➤above).

Tuscany's regional orchestra, the **Orchestra della Toscana** (Via Verdi, 5; tel: 05 52 34 07 10 or 05 52 34 27 22; www.orchestradellatoscana. it) usually performs during its main December to May season at the nearby **Teatro Verdi** (Via Ghibellina, 91r; tel: 055 21 34 96, www.teatro verdionline.it). Buy tickets from the Teatro Verdi box office or the Box Office agency.

Florence's city orchestra, the **Filarmonica di Firenze 'Giacchino Rossini'** (Via Villamagna, 41; tel: 05 56 53 30 84; www.filarmonica rossini.it) performs at several venues during its January to February season, but also presents a series of outdoor concerts in the Piazza della Signoria during the summer months. Consult visitor centres for further details (➤45).

The **Orchestra da Camera Fiorentina** (Via Monferrato, 2; tel: 0 55 78 33 74; www.orcafi.it) holds concerts in the church of Orsanmichele (➤78): tickets from the above number, from Box Office, or from Orsanmichele an hour before each performance.

The **Amici della Musica** music association (Via Pier Capponi, 41; tel: 055 60 84 20 or 055 60 74 40; www.amicimusica.fi.it) organises concerts at the beautiful Teatro della Pergola, northeast of the Duomo (Via della Pergola, 18; tel: 05 52 26 43 53; www.teatro dellapergola.com). Built in 1656, it is reputedly Italy's oldest surviving theatre.

Churches such as San Lorenzo and the Duomo also sometimes host concerts – for details check with visitor centres or keep a look out for posters outside the venues.

LIVE MUSIC

The **Jazz Club** (Via Nuova de'Cacciani, 3; tel: 05 54 98 07 52; www.facebook.com/jazzclub firenze.it; daily 10pm–5am) has live jazz most nights: it's in a side street a block south of Via degli Alfani at the corner of Borgo Pinti. You need to buy 'membership' as a formality to enter the club, in a medieval cellar. By contrast, the live music at the popular **Be Bop** (Via dei Servi, 28r; tel: 05 52 64 57 56; open daily 7pm–2am), just north of the Duomo, ranges from jazz, rock and blues to tribute bands and small touring international groups. There's also the occasional open-mic night.

NIGHTCLUBS

Brand new and already totally cool: **Otel Varieté** (Viale Generale Dalla Chiesa, 9, tel: 055 65 07 91, www.otelvariete.com, Fri–Sun 11pm–4am) in the south of the city has a concept that really works: you can have something to eat first of all while watching a live show and then burn off all those extra calories on the dance floor afterwards.

In the west of the city, **Space Electronic** (Via Palazzuolo, 37; tel: 055 29 30 82; www.spaceclubfirenze.com; daily 10pm–4am) is a vast disco – it claims to be Europe's largest.

Yab (Via Sassetti, 5r; tel: 055 21 51 60; www.yab.it; open daily 9pm–4am; may close June–July/Aug) generally pursues a more adventurous music policy than its rivals, but also operates an insidious card system whereby admission is usually free, but you have to spend a minimum amount on drinks (recorded on your card): fail to spend enough and you have to pay up before leaving.

Roberto Cavalli, one of Italy's most prestigious fashion designers, has turned his hand to the night scene and opened the **Cavalli Club** (Piazza del Carmine, 8r; tel: 055 21 16 50). This is exclusive, with a sprinkling of celebrity clients, so prepare to dress to impress.

Tenax (Via Pratese, 46r, Quartiere di Peretola; tel: 055 30 81 60; www.tenax.org) is Florence's 'super club', with guest DJs like Fat Boy Slim. Unfortunately it's out of the city, close to the airport. However it can be reached quite cheaply by taxi from many parts of the city.

BARS

Expensive drinks with free finger food on the side. A trend that many bars in Florence offering apéritifs between 7pm and 10pm have now picked up on. Ever-popular places include **Moba** (Costa San Giorgio, 6), and **Caffè Sant'Ambrogio** (Piazza Sant'Ambrogio, 7).

Across the city, the ever-popular **Rex Café** (Via Fiesolana, 25r; tel: 055 248 03 31; www.firenzenotte.it/rex-café; Mon–Sat 11:30am–2am) is one of the best bars in eastern Florence. The interior looks rather alarming – lots of mirrors and strange lamps – but the atmosphere and clientele are easy-going.

At the other extreme is a bar on Piazza di Santa Maria Novella: **Fiddler's Elbow** (Piazza di Santa Maria Novella, 7r; tel: 055 21 50 56; www.thefiddlerselbow.com; daily 12pm–2am), a small Irish pub.

In the Oltrarno, a bar aimed at the night-time crowd is **Dolce Vita** (Piazza del Carmine, 6; tel: 055 28 45 95; www.dolcevitaflorence.com; Sun–Thu 7:30pm–midnight, Fri, Sat until 2am). The funkier **Cabiria** (Piazza Santo Spirito, 4r; tel: 055 21 57 32; daily 8am–1:30am; closed Tue in winter) appeals to a more 'alternative' clientele – though it opens in the day, it really comes into its own in the evening. Also in Oltrarno, just east of the Museo Bardini, is **Il Rifrullo** (Via San Niccolò, 53–57r; tel: 055 234 26 21; www.ilrifrullo.com; daily 7:30am–1am; kitchen closes 11:30pm), which has been in business since the 1970s. You can hear occasional live music, but it is also a good place for a drink or light meal, especially in the summer, when you can sit outside on the terrace until late.

The hugely popular **Girasol** (Via del Romito, 1; tel: 055 47 49 48; www.girasol.it; Tue–Thu 7pm–2am, Fri, Sat until 3am) offers live Brazilian, Cuban and other Latin music. You'll need to take a taxi from the centre, as it's located north of the Fortezza da Basso.

Central Tuscany

Little Treats

Ridable sculptures

Rattle your way through the Chianti region on a Vespa, e.g. in **Colle di Val d'Elsa** (► 122).

Thrills galore!

The most in theatre company at the moment is the Compagnia della Fortezza: tough guys from the prison in **Volterra** (► 123).

Crash course on Siena

Behind the **Palazzo Pubblico** (► 98) you can learn all about Siena – the Gothic and Gothic Revival styles, the city and the country in one fell swoop.

Getting Your Bearings

Siena and Florence are old rivals. While in the past it had to do with power and influence, today it is nothing less than which is the most beautiful city in Tuscany. And quite a few think that Siena just has the edge over Florence. You should treat yourself to at least two or three days in this medieval city to be able to do justice to the many sites – its spectacular market square, its richly decorated cathedral, its fine art museum and various other important museums, not to mention the relaxed charm of its streets, small shops, cafés and restaurants. The appeal of the rest of central Tuscany is largely its landscape: lush hills and valleys, vineyards, farmland and meandering country roads.

Its own beauty aside, Siena also makes a good base for central Tuscany, although accommodation in the city is in short supply and a largely pedestrianised centre can make access by car difficult. This said, it is perfectly placed for excursions to Chianti, a region to the north whose vineyards, villa-topped hills and pretty countryside encapsulate some of the best of Tuscany's patchwork of landscapes. You could also visit the area as part of a drive between Florence and Siena.

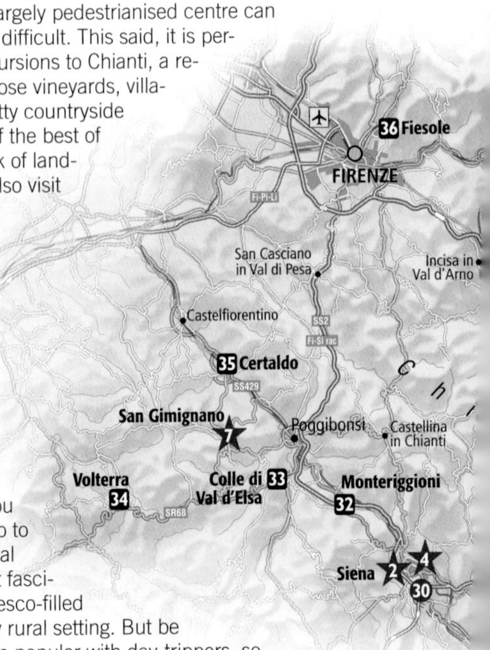

In fact, in central Tuscany almost any country road brings its scenic rewards and – invariably – leads to a town or village of interest. Make sure you go to San Gimignano to marvel at its medieval silhouette, small but fascinating museums, fresco-filled churches and pretty rural setting. But be warned: the village is popular with day-trippers, so aim to stay overnight, which also makes it easier to visit nearby medieval hill villages such as Monteriggioni and Colle di Val d'Elsa.

The area's other must-see towns, Arezzo and Cortona, are slightly less easy to incorporate into a logical Tuscan tour. Both are worth the detour, however – hilltop Cortona for its views, Arezzo for its famous Renaissance fresco cycle, and both for their well-preserved medieval architecture. Both towns lie some way from other Tuscan centres, but

Looking across the fields to San Gimignano

TOP 10

- 2 Piazza del Campo, Siena ➤ 98
- 3 Arezzo ➤ 101
- 4 Piazza del Duomo, Siena ➤ 104
- 7 San Gimignano ➤ 110

Don't Miss

- 30 Pinacoteca Nazionale & Chiese, Siena ➤ 116
- 31 Cortona ➤ 119

At Your Leisure

- 32 Monteriggioni ➤ 122
- 33 Colle di Val d'Elsa ➤ 122
- 34 Volterra ➤ 123
- 35 Certaldo ➤ 125
- 36 Fiesole ➤ 125

are linked to Siena by relatively good roads. Equally, both could be seen after visiting the Chianti region or as part of a tour of southern Tuscany after Montepulciano (➤ 147). If you need to stay in either town overnight Cortona has the better hotels.

Central Tuscany

Four Perfect Days

If you're not quite sure where to begin your travels, this itinerary recommends four practical and enjoyable days out in Central Tuscany, taking in some of the best places to see. For more information see the main entries (➤ 98–125).

Day 1

Morning

Siena is Tuscany's most perfect medieval city. The starting point for any trip must surely be the magnificent 2 **Piazza del Campo**, Italy's most majestic medieval square (➤ 98, right and below), followed by the art-filled Museo Civico und Torre del Mangia (➤ 99). Spend the rest of the morning shopping on Via di Città.

Lunch

Tasty snacks to build up your stamina for more sightseeing can be found at Gino Calcino's on the Piazza del Mercato.

Afternoon

Walk to 4 **Piazza del Duomo** (➤ 104) to see the Cathedral, Baptistry, Ospedale di Santa Maria della Scala and Museo dell'Opera del Duomo.

Day 2

Morning

Devote the morning to the 30 **Pinacoteca Nazionale** (➤ 116) and explore its collection of art by Sienese masters. For lunch, try Al Marsili (➤ 131).

Afternoon

Leave time to see some of the less well-known 30 **churches**, especially Santa Maria dei

Servi (➤ 118), and to soak up the atmosphere of the medieval streets.

Day 3

Morning

From Siena or Chianti make for 7 **San Gimignano** (➤ 110), if possible stopping off en route to spend an hour or two in 32 **Monteriggioni** (➤ 122), a perfectly preserved fortified hamlet, and in 33 **Colle di Val d'Elsa** (➤ 122), an attractive but little-visited hill town.

Lunch

Lunch at Dulcisinfundo (➤ 130).

Afternoon

Allow the rest of the day to see San Gimignano, where you should also spend the night (➤ 127). Enjoy the religious art of the Collegiata, then wander around the atmospheric streets and alleyways and treat yourself to a divine chocolate ice cream at the Gelateria Dondoli (➤ 130).

Day 4

Morning

Take the 85km (53-mile) drive east to 3 **Arezzo** (➤ 101), where two hours should be long enough to see Piero della Francesca's fresco cycle and explore the town's captivating medieval centre.

Lunch

Try Logge Vasari for a light meal.

Afternoon

Drive south to 31 **Cortona** (➤ 119) to wander in the old centre. Then visit the town's museums (Fra Angelico's *The Annunciation*, right, is in the Museo Diocesano). Stay overnight or drive to **Montalcino** (➤ 141) to continue your tour.

2 Piazza del Campo, Siena

Hilltop Siena is built on three ridges, each of which corresponds roughly to a *terzo* or 'third', one of three districts into which the medieval city was divided. Close to the point where the three ridges meet stands Siena's breath-taking Piazza del Campo (or just Campo), Europe's greatest medieval square and the city's heart.

The location of the Campo was determined as much by politics as geography, for within the ***terzi*** were – and still are – a number of smaller districts *(contrade)*. These medieval parishes commanded and continue to command fierce loyalties among their inhabitants. To avoid conflict, Siena's medieval rulers chose as the centre of the city an area that fell outside the domain of any single *contrada,* while at the same time allowing the square to be used as the stage for the Palio, a race in which the contrade's ancient rivalries are still played out (► 22).

Not that you have to be present on race day to enjoy the Campo. The distinctive scallop-shaped arena and encircling ring of **medieval palaces** is magnificent at any time. Enjoy it first from one of the many cafés on its margins – prices are high, but the view is worth it – and then head for its chief sight, the vast Palazzo Pubblico.

Medieval buildings surround the Piazza del Campo which is reminiscent of a Roman amphitheatre

Palazzo Pubblico

This palace has served as Siena's main council building for many centuries, but today also houses two important

The views of the city from the Torre del Mangia are as striking as the structure itself

sights: the **Torre del Mangia** (1325–48), a 102m (334ft) tower on its eastern side, and the **Museo Civico**, which occupies the palace's upper floors. You can climb the tower's 360 steps for staggering views, but visit the museum first so that you're fresh for its star attractions.

You enter the museum to the right off a small inner courtyard – the tower entrance is to the left – having passed the Gothic **Cappella di Piazza** (1352–1468), a distinctive arched porch at the base of the tower, begun by the city in 1352 to mark the passing of the Black Death four years earlier.

The museum's first few rooms are unremarkable, but you soon enter a succession of salons and chambers crammed with frescoes and other works of art. The most beautiful is the **Sala del Mappamondo**, which contains two sensational paintings: on the left (with your back to the entrance) is a *Maestà* (*Madonna Enthroned*, 1315) by Simone Martini, one of the greatest of the Sienese School of painters; on the opposite wall is the courtly *Equestrian Portrait of Guidoriccio da Fogliano,* which for years was also attributed to Martini but is now the subject of a

A portrait of Guidoriccio da Fogliano in the Museo Civico

controversial attribution debate among scholars. No controversy surrounds the adjoining room, the **Sala della Pace**, which features one of Europe's finest early medieval secular fresco cycles, Ambrogio Lorenzetti's *Allegories of Good and Bad Government* (1338). It illustrates the effects of good and bad civic rule on a city clearly modelled on Siena.

TAKING A BREAK

The **Bar Il Palio** (Thu–Tue 8am–2am) on the Campo is the most popular vantage point for locals to congregate.

Gelateria **Caraibi**, on the corner of Via Porrione/Via Rinaldini, sells delicious ice cream – which you can enjoy while taking a gentle stroll around the *piazza*.

214

Museo Civico
Piazza del Campo · 05 77 29 22 32 · Mid-March to Oct daily 10–7; Nov to mid-March 10–6 · €8 Joint ticket with the Torre del Mangia: €13

Torre del Mangia
Piazza del Campo · 05 77 29 22 32 · March to mid-Oct daily 10–7; mid-Oct to Feb 10–4 · €8 Joint ticket with the Museo Civico: €13

INSIDER INFO

- **Parking** is difficult in central Siena, where most roads are closed to traffic. Use peripheral car parks and walk or catch a bus to the centre. Siena's **historic centre** is small and easily explored on foot. The station is about 2km (1.2mi) from the Campo, a strenuous uphill walk, but buses for the centre leave from the far side of the station forecourt.
- Tickets and information are available from a bus ticket office in the station ticket hall.
- Siena is built on a series of hills and its medieval streets are – not surprisingly – very uneven, so wear **comfortable shoes** when exploring the city on foot.

3 Arezzo

Arezzo is best known for a fresco cycle by Piero della Francesca, but the importance of this Renaissance master-piece often overshadows the town's historic centre, an evocative medley of churches, squares, medieval streets and small museums that is as alluring as any in Tuscany.

Arezzo was first an Etruscan and then a Roman centre of some importance, and continued to thrive during the Middle Ages, when its position on vital trade routes across the Apennine mountains brought it great prosperity. Among other things, it developed as a major goldware and jewellery centre – industries that still thrive today – though the town suffered for its economic and strategic prominence when it was bombed during World War II. As a result, much of the town's outskirts are modern and unprepossessing, making the almost pristine medieval enclave at its heart all the more delightful.

The Legend of the True Cross

Much of this enclave can wait, however, until you have paid homage to **Piero della Francesca's fresco cycle** in San Francesco, an otherwise unremarkable 14th-century Gothic church. The cycle, which is painted on the walls around the high altar, portrays ***The Legend of the True Cross*** (1452–66), a complicated story which derived from the *Legenda Aurea(Golden Legend)*, a 13th-century compen-dium of apocryphal tales. In essence, the paintings follow the history of the cross on which Christ was crucified, tracing

A scene from Piero della Francesca's *Legend of the True Cross* in the church of San Francesco

the wood from the tree which grew from Adam's grave through to its use during the Crucifixion and subsequent burial and rediscovery by Helena, mother of the Roman Emperor Constantine. But while Piero della Francesca pays heed to his story, he was also concerned to explore the artistic possibilities of symmetry, space and perspective. This is one reason for the mysterious, almost unsettling quality of his paintings, and one reason why the narrative of the cycle does not follow the chronological narrative of his story. You'll notice, for example, that Piero paints two major battle scenes so that they face each other symmetrically – the large lower panels on the right and left walls.

Churches, Palaces and Gardens

After seeing the frescoes, walk the short distance to Arezzo's main central square, the steeply sloping **Piazza Grande**, filled with an eclectic mixture of buildings from different eras. The square is dominated on the left (west) side by the semicircular and arched apse of **Santa Maria della Pieve**, a fine 12th-century Romanesque church whose entrance lies around the corner on Corso Italia.

Look inside, for the interior boasts an important high altarpiece of the *Madonna and Saints* (1320) by the Sienese artist Pietro Lorenzetti. In the square's northwest corner stands the **Fraternità dei Laici**, a 15th-century palace celebrated for its Gothic door and its beautiful lunette sculptures (1434) by Bernardo Rossellino. At the top (north) side of the piazza is the **Palazzo delle Logge** (1573), dominated by a loggia designed by Giorgio Vasari, a noted painter, architect and art historian who was born in Arezzo. His former home, the **Casa Vasari** near San Domenico (► below), is worth a quick visit to admire its beautifully decorated rooms.

Continue north from Piazza Grande on Corso Italia and, in a side street to the left, you'll pass a house at 28 Via dell'Orto, reputed to have been the **birthplace** of another

Arezzo's impressive medieval Piazza Grande

eminent Arezzo citizen, the poet and scholar **Petrarch**. Continuing north, you come to the town's **Duomo**, whose interior has a handful of treasures: a small fresco of ***Mary Magdalene*** by Piero della Francesca (north aisle), the adjacent Tomb of Guido Tarlati (1330), some accomplished stained glass (1523) and sculpture (1334), and 15th-century frescoes by unknown artists in the Cappella Tarlati (last chapel off the south wall before the altar).

To the east of the Duomo stretches the Passeggio del Prato, an attractive area of parkland crowned by the **Fortezzo Medicea** (1538–60), a pentagonal castle built by the town's Medici rulers (the town fell to Florence in 1384). In the other direction, west of the Duomo, the Gothic **church of San Domenico** (begun in 1275) has a rare altarpiece (*c.*1260) by Cimabue, the teacher of Giotto. To its south in Via Garibaldi stands **Santissima Annunziata**, a church that was extensively remodelled after 1460 following the miraculous tears wept by a statue of the Virgin Mary in the oratory that previously occupied the site. The museum almost on its doorstep, the **Museo Statale d'Arte Medievale e Moderna** (Via San Lorentino 8; open Tue–Sun 8:30–7), has a disappointing collection of artefacts from a variety of eras, although there is fine majolica and terracotta pottery.

TAKING A BREAK

Caffè dei Constanti, outside San Francesco, is a good place for lunch, and Passeggio del Prato has **picnic** possibilities.

San Francesco

209 E2 Piazza San Francesco 05 75 35 27 27
Apr–Oct Mon–Fri 9–6:30, Sat 9–5:30, Sun 1–5:30; Nov–March Mon–Fri 9–5:30, Sat 9–5, Sun 1–5 Church: free; frescoes: €8

Pieve di Santa Maria

209 E2 Corso Italia 0 57 52 26 29
Daily 8–12:30, 3:30–7:30 Free

Casa Vasari

209 E2 Via XX Settembre, 55 05 75 40 90 40
Mo, Wed–Sat 8:30–7:30, Sun 8:30–1:30 €4

INSIDER INFO

- The best place to park is **Via Petri 37**. An escalator takes you up to the cathedral, from where you can reach the church San Francesco down the Corso Italia or Via Andrea Cesalpino.
- Arezzo is one of the best places in Tuscany to buy **gold jewellery**. Consult the tourist office for details of shops, workshops or factory outlets.
- You must **book ahead** to see the San Francesco frescoes (tel: 05 75 35 27 27; www.pierodellafrancesca.it; ticket office Mon–Fri 9–6:30, Sat 9–5:30, Sun 1–5:30; (30 mins earlier in winter). Visits last 30 minutes and are limited to groups of 25.

4 Piazza del Duomo, Siena

Piazza del Duomo cannot rival the Campo for scale or spectacle, but in the cathedral (Duomo), the Museo dell'Opera del Duomo and the Ospedale di Santa Maria della Scala complex it has three of the city's most interesting and beautiful buildings, together with the cream of its many artistic treasures.

Siena began life as an Etruscan settlement and then became a Roman colony, Saena Julia. Little remains of the Roman city, though the site of the present cathedral, close to the city's highest point, was almost certainly the site of a Roman temple dedicated to the goddess Minerva.

The Duomo

Work on the cathedral began in about 1179 and was largely completed by 1296, but in 1339 Siena's considerable medieval wealth – the result of banking and mercantile prowess – led the city to start a rebuilding project that would have made the church the largest in Europe. The

A queue forms at the entrance to the Duomo

The *Three Graces* in the Libreria Piccolomini is a Roman copy of a Greek original

Black Death of 1348, which brought economic ruin to the city, marked the end of the scheme, though you can still clearly see parts of the 'new' building in the area to the right (east) of the cathedral.

The cathedral's magnificent **façade** was largely overseen by the sculptor Giovanni Pisano, and stands out even in a region where the cathedrals of Florence, Pisa and Lucca are some of the most striking in Italy. The splendour continues **inside**, starting with the floor, which consists of 56 *graffito* (incised) marble panels designed by 40 of Siena's finest artists between 1369 and 1547. Above, the many sculpted heads around the nave represent 172 popes and 36 Holy Roman emperors.

At the top of the left (north) side of the nave is the entrance to the **Libreria Piccolomini** (library), decorated with glorious frescoes portraying *Scenes from the Life of Pope Pius II* (1502–09) by Umbrian artist Pinturicchio. Pius, otherwise known as Enea Silvio Piccolomini, was born in Pienza (► 138). To the left of the Libreria's entrance is the sculpted *Altre Piccolomini* (1501–04), four statues of which – saints Gregory and Paul on the right, Peter and Pius on the left – are by the young Michelangelo.

At the crossing in the centre is the cathedral's unmissable carved **pulpit** (1266–68), the work of Nicola Pisano and one of the greatest pieces of Italian medieval sculpture. In the left corner of the north transept, the **Cappella di San Giovanni Battista** contains more frescoes (1504) by Pinturicchio and a statue of John the Baptist (1457) by Donatello.

You can see more work by Donatello to the rear of the cathedral in the **Battistero di San Giovanni** (Baptistry). To get there, leave the cathedral and take the steps down to the Piazza San Giovanni. The font (1417–30) includes fine bronze panels by Donatello, Lorenzo Ghiberti – Florentines both – and the leading Sienese sculptor of his day, Jacopo della Quercia. There is also an array of 15th-century frescoes by Vecchietta.

Ospedale di Santa Maria della Scala

The unexceptional-looking building opposite the cathedral was Siena's main hospital for almost a thousand years,

Duomo Santa Maria

The magnificent cathedral of Santa Maria, boasting Romanesque and Gothic elements in its façade, stands proudly on the highest point in the city. San Giovanni baptistry is directly adjoining, located beneath the choir and, to one side, remains of the 'New Cathedral' extension can be seen which the Sienese wanted to build in the 14th century.

❶ **Marble façade:** Inspired by the French Gothic style, Giovanni Pisano designed the cathedral's façade at the end of the 13th century.
❷ **Libreria Piccolomini:** The Piccolomini Library was founded by Cardinal Francesco Piccolomini (later Pius III) to honour his uncle Pius II. This is where the famous frescos by Pinturicchio with scenes from the life of Pius II can be found.
❸ **Capella di San Giovanni:** A fresco cycle by Pinturicchio and a bronze statue of John the Baptist by Donatello (1457) are to be seen in the Renaissance chapel.
❹ **Pulpit by Nicola Pisano:** The octagonal pulpit by Nicola Pisano (13th century) rests on columns supported by lions.
❺ **Battistero di San Giovanni:** When the cathedral choir was extended in 1316, a lower church (the baptistry) was built.
❻ **Museo dell'Opera del Duomo:** Among other treasures, the original, larger-than-life sized sculptures from the façade made by Pisano and his workers can be seen on the ground floor of the cathedral museum. In the course of time these have been replaced by copies.
❼ **Il Facciatone:** The plans of the City Fathers of Siena to extend the cathedral were halted by the lack of funds and technical problems, as well as the outbreak of the Black Death in 1348. The partially completed exterior wall – called Il Facciatone (the great façade) – still reminds us today of these ambitious plans.
❽ **Crypt:** The entrance to the crypt from the 13th century is behind the cathedral. It was only rediscovered in 1999, 700 years later. Its walls are covered with well-preserved frescos from the 13th century, painted by artists of the Sienese School.

The façade of coloured marble with three portals and elaborate sculptural decoration is the work of Giovanni Pisano

Frescoes and bronze panels in the cathedral baptistry

until it closed as a medical centre in the 1990s. Today, its medieval interior, with entire 15th-century fresco cycles and other works of art, is open to the public. It was founded in the 11th century to offer rest and hospitality to pilgrims. Later it served many charitable functions, including looking after the city's orphans. Bequests made to the hospital enabled it to fund works of art.

The most impressive of these is found in the **Sala del Pellegrinaio**, covered in a fresco cycle (*c.* 1440) by Vecchietta, Domenico di Bartolo and other Sienese artists portraying aspects of the hospital's history. In the **Sagrestia Vecchia** is another fresco cycle by Vecchietta illustrating the *Articles of the Creed* (1446–49) and an altarpiece of the *Madonna della Misericordia* (1444) by Domenico di Bartolo.

Museo dell'Opera del Duomo

The first major room of this fine museum is the **Sala delle Statue**, where the walls are dotted with sculpted figures (1284–96) from the Workshop of Giovanni Pisano, removed from the cathedral façade. The room's masterpieces, however, are an ethereal relief of the *Madonna and Child* (1456–59) by Donatello (from one of the cathedral's doors) and a second relief of the *Madonna and Child with St Giralmo*

INSIDER INFO

- You can save money on admission to several sights by purchasing one of **three combined tickets**, valid for two to seven days, giving entry to a variety of sights in the city, including the Libreria Piccolomini, Baptistry, Museo dell'Opera del Duomo, Oratorio di San Bernardino, Museo Diocesano and church of Sant' Agostino.
- 

If possible, time your visit to Siena to fall between 21 August and 21 October. The **cathedral floor** can only be viewed in all its splendour at this time. For the rest of the year it is hidden under wooden boards.

(*c.*1430–35) by Jacopo della Quercia. On the first floor, La Sala di Duccio is dominated by Duccio's vast ***Maestà*** (1308–11), one of the greatest Italian medieval paintings.

TAKING A BREAK

Try **Le Logge** (➤ 129), just off the Campo, for lunch.

Duomo
214 Piazza del Duomo 05 77 28 63 00; www.operaduomo.siena.it
March–Oct Mon–Sat 10:30–7, Sun 1:30–6, Nov–Feb Mon–Sat 10:30–5:30, Sun 1:30–5:30, 26 Dec to 6 Jan Mon–Sat 10:30–7, Sun 1:30–5:30 €4 (includes Liberia Piccolomini)

Libreria Piccolomini
214 Piazza del Duomo 05 77 28 63 00 Hours as for Duomo
Free with ticket to the Duomo

Battistero di San Giovanni
214 Piazza San Giovanni 05 77 28 63 00
March–May, 26 Dec to 6 Jan 10:30–7; Nov–Feb 10:30–5:30 €4

Ospedale di Santa Maria della Scala
214 Piazza del Duomo, 2 05 77 53 45 71
Mid–June to Nov 10:30–7; Variable opening times during winter €6

Museo dell'Opera del Duomo
214 Piazza del Duomo, 8 05 77 28 30 48
March–May, 26 Dec to 6 Jan 10:30–7; Nov–Feb 10:30–5:30
€7 (incl. admission to the viewing terrace Panorama del Facciatone)

There are 56 marble panels in the floor of the Duomo

7 San Gimignano

San Gimignano is the very picture of a medieval Italian village, thanks to its crop of ancient towers – the village famously resembles a 'medieval Manhattan' – and to its unspoiled streets and beautiful hilltop setting. Appearances aside, it also boasts a superb art gallery, far-reaching views and two lovely fresco-swathed churches.

The Central Squares

The best way to see the village is to start close to its southern gateway, the **Porta San Giovanni**, then walk up its main street, Via San Giovanni, to its pair of linked central squares: Piazza della Cisterna and Piazza del Duomo. The village is tiny – around 750m (half a mile) from end to end – and everything worth seeing is within easy walking distance.

A short distance up Via San Giovanni on the right you come to **San Francesco**, a deconsecrated 13th-century

church that is now a food and wine shop aimed at visitors. Whether or not you want to browse, walk through to the terrace at the rear, from where there are glorious views over the countryside.

At the top of Via San Giovanni you come to the **Arco dei Becci**, a medieval arch that stands in the village's original set of walls – a second outer set of walls, incorporating the **Porta San Giovanni**, was added in the 13th century as the village grew in size. The arch opens into Piazza della Cisterna, which takes its name from the medieval well -***(cisterna)*** at its heart. Two of the town's major hotels are here (► 127), along with several good cafés and ***gelaterie*** (ice-cream parlours).

Adjoining the square to the north is **Piazza del Duomo**, home to the best of the village's historic sights. On its western flank stands the **Collegiata**, which served as San Gimignano's cathedral until the village lost its status as a bishopric. To its left rises the **Palazzo del Popolo** (1288), which houses the tourist office and the Museo Civico (► 113).

San Gimignano's ancient towers have earned it the title of 'medieval Manhattan'

Collegiata

The Collegiata probably dates from around 1056, but was altered in 1239 and then remodelled further by the architect and sculptor Giuliano da Maiano between 1460 and 1468. Little on its rather plain façade prepares you for the interior, which is almost completely covered in eye-catching frescoes. These divide into three main cycles. The rear (entrance) wall has a ***Last Judgement*** (1410) by the Sienese painter Taddeo di Bartolo, with ***Inferno*** and ***Paradiso*** painted on protruding walls to the left and right. Between these walls is a fresco by Benozzo Gozzoli of St Sebastian (1465), a saint often invoked during plague epidemics – one such epidemic had ravaged San Gimignano a year before the painting was commissioned.

The **second cycle** (*c.* 1333) on the right (south) wall is the work of either Lippo Memmi or Barna da Siena, both Sienese painters. The three tiers of paintings, some of which are damaged, portray episodes from the *New Testament*. The **cycle** (1356–67) on the opposite wall is the work of another Sienese artist, Bartolo di Fredi. Here the scenes portrayed are from the *Old Testament,* with episodes from the story of Creation depicted in the lunettes above the main wall.

Elsewhere in the church are two more artistic treasures: the **Cappella di San Gimignano** (left of the high altar), graced by an altar carved by Benedetto da Maiano (brother of Giuliano), and the **Cappella di Santa Fina**, a chapel on the right (south) side of the nave, with a lovely altar, marble shrine and bas-reliefs (1475) also by Benedetto da Maiano, and two frescoes on the life of Santa Fina, a local 13th-century saint, by the Florentine painter Domenico Ghirlandaio.

The Torre Grossa offers a bird's-eye view of San Gimignano and its surrounding countryside

Fresco cycles in the Collegiata

Museo Civico

After the Collegiata, turn your attention to the Museo Civico which, as well as housing the town's main museum, also provides access to the **Torre Grossa** (begun 1300), the only tower in the village open to the public – an trip in time back to the Middle Ages that is not only fascinating for children. San Gimignano's towers were built by local nobles for defensive purposes and as status symbols. Most Italian towns and villages once had similar towers. The reason so many survived here is a result of the 1348 Black Death, which so devastated the village that it was forced to abandon its independence and put itself under the protection of Florence. Thereafter, the power of the nobles was gone and their towers, which no longer offered a threat, could remain standing.

The museum is ranged across two floors, and opens with the **Sala del Consiglio**, or Sala di Dante, so called because it was here that Dante, then a Florentine diplomat, met members of San Gimignano's council to enlist their support. The room is dominated by a painting of the *Maestà* (*Madonna Enthroned*; 1317) by Lippo Memmi, a permanent fixture, unlike other displays on this floor which are often temporary.

The core of the museum lies in four rooms on the **second floor**, filled with paintings by Florentine, Umbrian and Sienese artists such as Filippino Lippi, Pinturicchio and Coppo da Marcovaldo (► 118). Some of the most appealing paintings, however, are by less well-known artists, notably those detailing the lives of saints such as St Gimignano (by Taddeo di Bartolo) and St Bartholomew and St Fina (both by Lorenzo di Niccolò).

Insider Tip

Don't miss the **14th-century works** by Memmo di Filipuccio, in the room on the left at the top of the stairs from the Sala del Consiglio – three wedding scenes include panels where a young couple cavort in bed and in a bath.

Church of Sant'Agostino

From Piazza del Duomo you should walk north towards the church of Sant'Agostino, either on Via San Matteo or on smaller side streets such as Via delle Romite. If you take the former route, notice **San Bartolo**, a pretty 13th-century Romanesque church on the right. Churches built by the Augustinian order *(Agostini)* are, as here, often near the edge of towns or villages – they were among the last of the main religious orders to build churches so the most central sites had already been occupied.

Sant'Agostino is best known for a 17-panel **fresco cycle** around the main altar on the *Life of St Augustine* (1464–65), by Benozzo Gozzoli. As in Florence's Cappella dei Magi (➤77), Gozzoli's work here is notable for its lovely incidental detail and vignettes of 15th-century life. The striking painting on the high altar is by Piero del Pollaiuolo and portrays the ***Coronation of the Virgin*** (1483), just one of several charming paintings around the walls by Florentine and Sienese artists.

The church's second major work, however, is a piece of sculpture: the **Cappella di San Bartolo**, a funerary monument immediately on the left as you enter. It contains the tomb of St Bartolo, a local 13th-century saint, and includes three reliefs (1495) of scenes from his life by Benedetto da Maiano.

Museums and Medieval Streets

From Sant'Agostino, walk east on Via Folgore da San Gimignano to look at **San Iacopo**, a 13th-century church

Detail from Gozzoli's depiction of the *Life of St Augustine*

INSIDER INFO

- San Gimignano becomes crowded with **day-trippers** from Florence or Siena Easter to October. To enjoy the village at its best, stay overnight.
- A **combined ticket** is available to the Museo Civico, Torre Grossa, Cappella di Santa Fina, Museo Ornitologico, Museo Archeologico and Museo d'Arte Sacra. Details from the tourist office (tel: 05 77 94 00 08).
- The **pilgrims' route, the Via Francigena,** from Canterbury to Rome, was first described in detail in the year 990. Some 1000 years later, the local government is now overseeing a project to restore the 15 sections of the route that pass through Tuscany, including the stretch between San-Gimignano and Siena, and for low-priced accommodation to be provided along the way.

reputedly founded by the Knights Templar. From here, walk through the Porta San Jacopo and a little way along the town wall, then through the Porta dei Fonti. After a further 150 m heading south, you will reach another 13th-century church, **San Lorenzo in Ponte** (Via Santo Stefano). West of Piazza della Cisterna and Piazza del Duomo you should wander to the **Rocca** (1353), a ruined castle at the heart of a quiet public park. You may also wish to visit the **Museo d'Arte Sacra**, a museum of religious art and archaeological exhibits, and the **Museo Ornitologico**, a collection of stuffed birds. The village has a small **Museo Archeologico-Galleria d'Arte Moderna** at Via Folgore 11.

TAKING A BREAK

A good place for lunch is the **Dulcisinfundo** (➤ 130). For something slightly more expensive try **Dorandò** (➤ 130).

---

207 F1

Collegiata and Cappella di Santa Fina
Piazza del Duomo 05 77 28 63 00 Feb, March, Nov, Dec Mon–Sat 10–4:40, Sun 12:30–4:40, April–Oct Mon–Sat 10–7:10, Sun 12:30–7:10 €4

Museo Civico and Torre Grossa
Palazzo del Popolo, Piazza del Duomo 05 77 99 03 12
April–Sept 9:30–7, Oct–March 11–5 €5. Combined ticket to musuem, tower and Palazzo Comunale: €7.50

Sant'Agostino
Piazza Sant'Agostino 05 77 90 70 12
Apr–Oct daily 7:30–noon, 3–7; Nov–March 7:30–noon, 3–6 Free

Museo d'Arte Sacra
Piazza Pecori 05 77 28 63 00 Feb, March, Nov, Dec Mon–Sat 10–4:40, Sun 12:30–4:40, April–Oct Mon–Sat 10–7:10, Sun 12:30–7:10 €3.50

Museo Ornitologico
Via Quercecchio 05 77 94 13 88 Apr–Sept daily 11–5:30; Jan–March, Oct–Dec may remain closed €1.50

30 Pinacoteca Nazionale & Chiese

By visiting the Museo Civico (➤ 99), cathedral (➤ 104), Ospedale (➤ 105) and Museo dell'Opera (➤ 108) you will already have seen many captivating paintings. The best collection of Sienese art, and the one that best enables you to follow the development of the city's distinctive school of painters, including Sassetta and Vecchietta, is housed in the city's main art gallery, the Pinacoteca Nazionale.

Pinacoteca Nazionale

Early Sienese painting owed much to Byzantine art, which was characterised by lavish use of gold backgrounds and a stylised portrayal of the Madonna and Child. Early local masters in this tradition, all of whom are represented in the gallery, were Guido da Siena, Duccio, Simone Martini and Pietro and Ambrogio Lorenzetti, brothers who died during the plague of 1348.

Later Sienese artists remained wedded to their Byzantine roots, only slowly adopting the Renaissance innovations of their Florentine rivals. The first 15th-century painters to master the new approach were Sassetta and Vecchietta, but plenty of others – notably Sano di Pietro, Giovanni di Paolo and Matteo di Giovanni – continued to remain loyal to the old conventions.

By the 16th century, Sienese art had largely had its day, with the notable exception of Domenico Beccafumi, a Mannerist artist, and Sodoma, best known for his frescoes at Monte Oliveto Maggiore (➤ 145).

The beautifully decorated interior of San Domenico in Piazza San Domenico

The Descent from the Cross **by Sodoma in the church of San Francesco**

Churches

Many of Siena's churches can be visited as you stroll between the major sights, and those that can't – notably Santa Maria dei Servi and San Francesco – are only a few minutes' walk from the city centre (➤ 188). The colossal brick outline of the Gothic 13th-century **San Domenico** (Piazza San Domenico) dominates the city's northern skyline. The church has strong associations with Siena-born St Catherine (1347–80), patron saint of the city, and with St Francis of Assisi. The Cappella di Santa Caterina midway down the right (south) aisle has a marble tabernacle containing part of her skull and frescoes (1526) by Sodoma of episodes from her life.

The less alluring and rather austere interior of the church of **San Francesco** (Piazza San Francesco) has a few patches of fresco by Sassetta and Pietro and Ambrogio Lorenzetti, but the church is worth visiting more for the

The church of San Domenico in the north of Siena

separate **Oratorio di San Bernardino**. Inside, its beautiful upstairs chamber is distinguished by Sodoma and Beccafumi's frescoes on the *Life of the Virgin* (1496–1518).

The church of **Santa Maria dei Servi** (Via dei Servi), which is about a 10-minute walk from the Campo, has several works of art and offers superb views of the city. The first altar on the right aisle contains a painting of the Madonna by Coppo da Marcovaldo (born 1225), a Florentine artist who was captured in battle by the Sienese and obliged to paint this picture as part of his ransom. There are also two grisly paintings of *The Massacre of the Innocents*: one by Matteo di Giovanni (1491); the other, painted 150 years earlier, by Pietro Lorenzetti.

Pinacoteca Nazionale
214 Palazzo Buonsignori, Via San Pietro, 29 05 77 28 61 43
Tue–Sat 8:15–7, Sun, Mon 9–1 €4

Oratorio di San Bernardino
214 Piazza San Francesco, 10 05 77 28 63 00
March–Oct 1:307; Nov–Feb by appointment only €3

INSIDER INFO

- **Most churches** close for two or three hours in the middle of the day, usually from noon.
- It is sometimes possible to visit small, individual churches and museums of Siena's ***contrade***. Enquire at the tourist office (➤ 45).
- Insider Tip **Trekking urbano** is a popular pastime in the city of Palio fame. New tours focussing on different topics are devised every year to make the city's many hidden facets better known. Some take visitors to the natural springs so vital to the city's existence, for example, or to medieval view points (www.trekkingurbano.info).

In more depth The Sienese ignored the **Fortezza Medicea** (204 A5) just outside the city walls for many a year. And for a good reason! The fortress was constructed by the Medicis right on the doorstep of the proud Republic of Siena following its defeat by the much-hated Florentine troops in 1555. But bad feelings are now a thing of the past – today joggers clock up their rounds, pensioners soak up the sun and children rush around happily.

31 Cortona

Cortona's chief beauties are its magnificent views – its hilltop site provides a vast panorama over swathes of Tuscany and Umbria – and its picture-perfect medieval streets, as well as a handful of small churches and galleries which contain treasures out of all proportion to the town's modest size.

If you are journeying to Cortona by car, the chances are you will approach the town from Camucia on the N71, which passes **Santa Maria del Calcinaio**, an unmissable Renaissance church around 2.5km (1.5mi) from the town's walls. The church takes its name from a lime-burner *(calcinaio)* who discovered a miraculous image of the Virgin Mary on the site.

Museums

Once inside the walls, the town centres on Piazza della Repubblica. From here, a short stroll to the northwest through Piazza Signorelli brings you to Piazza del Duomo. This is the setting for an unremarkable cathedral but a memorable gallery, the **Museo Diocesano**. The highlights are two masterpieces by Fra Angelico, who spent two years as a monk in the town's Dominican monastery. Angelico's paintings, an ***Annunciation*** and *Madonna and Child with Saints* (1428–30), share the gallery with paintings which would shine in any other company, notably works by Sassetta, Bartolomeo della Gatta and the Cortona-born Luca Signorelli. Don't miss the archaeological star turn, a second-century Roman **sarcophagus** carved with scenes representing Dionysus battling with the Amazons, a work much admired by the Renaissance sculptors Donatello and Filippo Brunelleschi.

Cortona's second major gallery, the **Museo dell'Accademia Etrusca e della Città Cortona**, is devoted largely to the Etruscan civilization – the town, which is considered one of the oldest in Tuscany, is thought to have been founded

Exhibits in the Museo dell'Accademia Etrusca e della Città Cortona

by the Etruscans in the eighth century BC. Exhibits include a huge fifth-century BC bronze lamp, the **Lampadario Etrusco**, some exquisite Etruscan jewellery, urns and vases, the contents of a partially reconstructed Etruscan tomb, an eclectic range of silverware, medieval paintings, Renaissance medallions and an impressive, if incongruous, collection of ancient Egyptian artefacts.

Compianto Sul Cristo Morto by Luca Signorelli is on display in the Museo Diocesano

Fortress and Churches

From the museum the only way is up, particularly if you want to enjoy the best of Cortona's views and the attractive tangle of streets in the town's northern quarters. Prepare yourself for the climb to the **Fortezza Medicea**, a ruined fortress built on the orders of Cosimo I de' Medici in 1556. Views from here are breathtaking, and on a clear day include the hazy outline of Lake Trasimeno in Umbria. Among the jumbled walls are remnants of the town's old Roman and Etruscan ramparts. Just below the fortress stands **Santa Margherita** (rebuilt in 1856), a large sanctuary that houses the tomb (1362) of St Margaret of Cortona, the town's much-revered patron saint.

Heading back down to the rest of the town, plan your route so that it takes you past **San Cristoforo**, a Romanesque chapel off Piazza della Pescaia, and to **San Nicolò** on Via San Nicolò. The former is closed to the public but pretty to look at from outside, while a custodian should be on hand at the latter to show you a double-sided high altarpiece by Luca Signorelli. Another church worth seeking out is **San Domenico**, which features a faded exterior fresco by Fra Angelico.

TAKING A BREAK

La Locanda del Loggiato (► 130) does light lunches.

---

209 F1

Museo Diocesano
Piazza del Duomo, 1 · 0 57 56 28 30
Easter–Oct daily 10–7; Nov–Easter Tue–Sun 10–5 · €5

Museo dell'Accademia Etrusca e della Città di Cortona (MAEC)
Piazza Signorelli, 19 · 05 75 63 72 35; www.cortonamaec.org
Apr–Oct daily 10–7; Nov–March Tue–Sun 10–5
€10; combined ticket with Museo Diocesano: €13

Left: A quiet side street in Cortona

INSIDER INFO

The **Capuchin Convent Le Celle,** located on a steep slope, takes about 40 minutes to reach on foot. St Francis of Assisi often came here seeking solitude. It is well-known today as a place for retreats (tel: 05 75 60 33 62; www.lecelle.it).

At Your Leisure

32 Monteriggioni

This unsullied vision of the Middle Ages comprises a ring of tower-studded walls atop a hill cloaked in olive groves that is still unmarked by modern buildings. It is 13km (8mi) south of the modern town of Poggibonsi, just west of the main Florence to Siena road, from which it is signposted. Like Colle di Val d'Elsa, the village is easily and quickly seen and well worth a short detour.

Monteriggioni was founded by the Sienese in 1203 as a defensive bastion to guard approaches to Siena from the Florentines. The walls were added between 1213 and 1219, but had to be rebuilt in 1260 (when the 14 towers were added) after they were breached by the Florentines in 1244. The defences were remarkable in their own day, and earned a mention in Dante's *Inferno,* where the towers are described as resembling giants in an abyss.

The relevant passage from the poem, Canto XXX1, 40–44, greets you on a plaque as you enter the village, which consists of little more than a church and main square (Piazza Roma), a single street (Via Maggio) and a 4-star hotel and restaurant (➤ 127).

211 D5
Visitor centre: Piazza Roma, 23
Visitor centre: 9:30–1:30, 2–7:30, closes earlier in winter

33 Colle di Val d'Elsa

Colle di Val d'Elsa sees few visitors; most people head straight to nearby San Gimignano (➤ 110). Those tempted to linger are often deterred by Colle Basso, the town's rather unattractive and modern lower suburb. Don't be put off, however, for the old part of Colle on the hill, Colle Alto, offers quiet flower-decked lanes, old churches, views and lots of pretty medieval corners.

Navigation is easy, for once you've parked at the top of the road from Colle Basso, Colle Alto is little more than a single main street, Via del Castello, that runs the length of the town's hilly ridge. Midway down, the street opens into Piazza del Duomo, where the cathedral (1603–30) on the left (north) side contains an exquisite 15th-century marble tabernacle, tentatively attributed to Mino da Fiesole.

Alongside the cathedral on the left, in the 14th-century Palazzo Pretorio, is a small **Museo Archeologico**, whose exhibits are devoted mainly to finds from local Etruscan tombs. Farther down Via del Castello lies the **Museo Civico e d'Arte Sacra** a small museum with a varied collection of silverware, sculpture and medieval and Renaissance paintings

Via del Castello becomes more medieval as you walk, with alleys darting off to either side. In its final section you pass **Santa Maria in Canonica**, a little 12th-century Romanesque church, and the **Casa-Torre di Arnolfo di Cambio**, so called because it is believed to have been the birthplace of 13th-century architect Arnolfo di Cambio.

After the tower you come to a belvedere known as the Baluardo, a vantage point which offers sweeping views over Colle Basso and the surrounding countryside.

Note that Colle is a place to shop for **glassware**. There are a number of shops on Via di Castello and a museum, the Museo del Cristallo (Via dei Fossi, 8a; tel: 05 77 92 41 35; www.cristallo.org).

208 B2

Tourist Office
Via Francesco Campana, 43
05 77 92 27 91;
www.comune.colle-di-val-d-elsa.si.it
Daily 10–12:30, 3–5

Museo Archeologico
Piazza del Duomo, 42
05 77 92 04 90
May–Sept Tue–Fri 10:30–12:30, 4:30–7:30, Sat, Sun 10:30–12:30, 3–7:30; Oct–Apr Tue–Fri 3:30–5:30, Sat, Sun 10:30–12:30, 3–4:30
€4

Left: Dante described the towers at Monteriggioni as resembling giants in an abyss

Museo Civico e d'Arte Sacra
Via del Castello, 33
05 77 92 38 88 or 05 77 92 29 54
April–Oct 10:30–12:30, 3–7:30, Nov.–March Sat, Sun 10–noon, 3:306:30
€3

34 Volterra

Volterra stands apart from the rest of Tuscany, both in its isolated position and in its rather forbidding appearance – its hilltop site is in contrast to some of the region's sunnier hill towns. Yet it is also a major historic town, founded by the Etruscans and home to plenty of fine medieval buildings, evocative old streets, two small galleries, and one of the region's most important archaeological museums. It is also full of shops selling alabaster. The **Ecomuseo dell'Alabastro** (Via dei Sarti), a small museum, plus two themed itineraries, provide background on the industry.

The town perches like an eyrie among the windswept volcanic hills between Siena and the Tuscan coast, well away from major roads and well off the normal tourist beat. As a result it sees relatively few visitors.

The town's medieval heart centres on **Piazza dei Priori**, a lovely ensemble of buildings which includes the Palazzo Pretorio, the Palazzo dei Priori, the cathedral (begun in 1120), the marble-striped 13th-century baptistry, and the Torre del Porcellino, so called because of the little boar *(porcellino)* carved alongside one of its upper windows.

The cathedral's artistic highlights are a *Desposition* (1228), a group of polychrome wooden figures (in a chapel on the right, or south, transept) and the high altarpiece's marble tabernacle and flanking angels, dating from 1471, the work of Mino da Fiesole.

Just beyond the baptistry lies the **Museo Diocesano d'Arte Sacra**, a collection of paintings, sculptures

The impressive Palazzo Pretorio on Piazza dei Priori in Volterra was built in 1208

and religious artefacts dominated by Rosso Fiorentino's painting of the *Madonna Enthroned with Saints* (1521). Fiorentino also dominates the town's art gallery and civic museum, the **Pinacoteca e Museo Civico**, where his other-worldly *Deposition* (1521) is one of the masterpieces of the Mannerist school of painting. Almost equally celebrated is *Gli Sposi (The Married Couple)*, an Etruscan tomb sculpture from the **Museo Etrusco Guarnacci**, Tuscany's most important Etruscan museum.

Further vestiges of Volterra's Etruscan – and Roman – past can be found in the **Parco Archeologico**, or in excavations to the north of the town which have uncovered a bath complex, Roman theatre and other ruins. Wander at random to soak up the medieval flavour. A good endpoint are the *balze*, dramatic eroded cliffs reached through the town's western fringes.

202 A2

Tourist Office
Piazza dei Priori, 10
0 58 88 61 50; www.provolterra.it
Daily 9–6, shorter opening times in winter

Museo Diocesano d'Arte Sacra
Via Roma, 13
0 58 88 62 90 Mid-March to early Nov daily 9–1, 3–6; early Nov to mid-March 9–1
closed for restoration at present; admission prices to be revised

Pinacoteca e Museo Civico
Palazzo Minucci-Solaini, Via dei Sarti, 1
0 58 88 75 80
Mid-March to Oct daily 9–7; Nov to mid-March 10–4:30
€10 (combined ticket with Museo Etrusco Guarnacci)

Museo Etrusco Guarnacci
Via Don Minzoni, 15
0 58 88 63 47 Mid-March to Oct daily 9–7; Nov to mid-March 10–4:30
€10 (combined ticket with Pinacoteca e Museo Civico)

Parco Archeologico
mid-March–Oct 10:30–5:30; Nov to mid-March Sat, Sun 10–4 €3.50

35 Certaldo

The diminutive walled medieval town – Rione Castello or Certaldo Alto – crowns a hilltop above the modern centre of Certaldo and can be reached on foot or by funicular (summer: 7:30am–1am; winter until 7:30pm, €1). The narrow streets and alleyways are worth exploring for their harmonious period architecture.

Look for **Palazzo Pretorio**, a 13th-century castle. There's also a **museum** dedicated to the Renaissance poet Giovanni Boccaccio, a native of the town. The **Museo d'Arte Sacra**, housed in a 400-year-old Augustinian monastery, has a small collection of religious art, including a 13th-century crucifix depicting 'Christ triumphant'.

208 B2

Tourist Office
Via Giovanni Boccaccio, 18
05 71 65 67 21
Apr–Oct 9:30–1:30, 2:30–7; Nov–March Wed–Mon 9:30–1:30, 2:30–4:30

Palazzo Pretorio
Piazzetta del Vicariato, 3
05 71 66 12 19; www.sistemamusealecertaldo.it
Apr–Sept 9:30–2, 2:30–7; Oct–March 9:30–4:30
Combined ticket with Casa Boccaccio and Museo d'Arte Sacra: €6

Casa Boccaccio
Via Boccaccio, 18
05 71 66 42 08; www.casaboccaccio.it
Apr–Oct 9:30–1:30, 2:30–7; Nov–March Wed–Mon 9:30–1:30, 2:30–4:30
Combined ticket with Palazzo Pretorio and Museo d'Arte Sacra: €6

Museo d'Arte Sacra
Piazza Santi Jacopo e Filippo, 2
05 71 66 13 10
Apr–Sept 9:30–2, 2:30–7; Oct–March 9:30–4:30
Combined ticket with Palazzo Pretoria and Casa Boccaccio: €6

36 Fiesole

Fiesole is a small hill town about 7km (4mi) northeast of central Florence. If you have an afternoon to spare in Florence, take a taxi or the No. 7 bus from outside the Santa Maria Novella railway station (► 44) for a brief glimpse of the countryside.

The town's main reward is its hilltop site, with views over Florence below. Look into the cathedral on the main square, Piazza Mino da Fiesole. From here you can climb Via San Francesco for the best views of Florence, or take a less strenuous walk to the **Museo Bandini**, a small museum of ivories, ceramics and paintings, before continuing to the **Area Archeologica** (archaeological zone), east of Piazza Mino da Fiesole. This park contains a small museum, a well-preserved first-century BC Roman theatre and sixth-century BC Etruscan ruins.

Farther south is the church of San Domenico, which has a painting by Fra Angelico of the ***Madonna and Saints with Angels*** (1430). To the west of San Domenico is the Badia Fiesolana, an ancient abbey church with a lovely Romanesque façade.

208 C4

Tourist Office
Via Portigiani 1
05 55 96 13 23; www.comune.fiesole.fi.it
Apr–Sept 10–6:30; March, Oct 10–5:30; Nov–Feb 10–1:30

Museo Bandini
Via Dupré, 1
05 55 96 12 93 Apr–Sept Fri–Sun 10–7; Nov–Feb 10–2; March, Oct 10–6
€10 (combined ticket with Area Archeologica)

Area Archeologica
Via Marini-Via Portigiani
05 55 96 12 93 Apr–Sept 10–7; Nov–Feb Wed–Mon 10–2; March, Oct 10–6
€10 (combined ticket with Museo Bandini)

Where to… Stay

Prices
Expect to pay per double room per night
€ under €125 **€€** €125–€200 **€€€** over €200

AREZZO

B&B Villa i Bossi €€€
The building is so big that you can easily get lost, the garden is a Baroque labyrinth amidst a bamboo grove – and the typically Italian sign 'privato' is not to be seen anywhere. Insider Tip Guests here are not seen as intruders but as part of the whole. And if you like, you can help in the vegetable garden, for example, instead of relaxing by the pool.
209 E2 Località Gragnone, 44
05 75 36 56 42, www.villaibossi.comcertaldo

CERTALDO

Hotel Certaldo €€
This converted mill on the outskirts of Certaldo makes a comfortable and well-priced base for exploring the town and the surrounding region. The mill has been sympathetically renovated and rooms are spacious and well furnished. Prices include a generous breakfast, but there's no restaurant in the hotel so you'll need to eat in town – about a 10-minute walk. The staff get high marks for friendliness and helpfulness and there's ample parking on site.
208 B2 Via del Molina 74
05 71 65 12 61; www.hotelcertaldo.it

CHIANTI

Castello di Spaltenna €€€
Like many towns and villages in Chianti, Gaiole is unexceptional, but in the Castello di Spaltenna it offers one of the region's best 4-star hotels. It is set in a splendid 13th-century castle on a hill on the outskirts of town. The rooms and apartments are individually furnished in a traditional style – some have fireplaces – and all have a view of the surrounding countryside. The hotel also has a first-rate restaurant (Ristorante La Pieve), fitness centre, tennis courts and swimming pool.
208 C2 Pieve di Spaltenna, Gaiole
05 77 74 94 83; www.spaltenna.it
Closed Nov to mid-March

CORTONA

Hotel Sabrina €
This 3-star property has a good central position just south of Cortona's main Via Roma. A 15th-century town house that was once the home of the sculptor Fabbrucci, it's an intimate family-run hotel now with well presented rooms which retain some period touches. It makes a comfortable base, but the price is the main selling point here: don't expect boutique luxury.
209 F1 Via Roma, 37
05 75 63 03 97; www.hotelsabrinacortona.it

Il Falconiere €€€
The 4-star Falconiere is a beautifully restored 17th-century villa located about 3km (2mi) outside the town walls, off the SR71 road for Arezzo. The rooms are furnished in period style – some even retain original frescoes and antiques. There is a pool and the

one-Michelin-star restaurant has a terrace for outdoor dining in summer and boasts a good wine list.
209 F1
Località San Martino a Bocena, 370
05 75 61 26 79; www.ilfalconiere.com
Restaurant closed Mon Nov–Feb

San Michele €/€€
This 4-star hotel is the best in town, thanks to its setting in a converted Renaissance palace. The rooms all retain many original architectural features, but one room in particular, in the old tower, stands out.
209 F1 Via Guelfa, 15
05 75 60 43 48; www.hotelsanmichele.net
Closed Nov–March

MONTERIGGIONI

Monteriggioni €€€
This stylish 4-star boutique hotel is an enticing place in its own right: the fact that it lies at the heart of one of Tuscany's finest fortified villages only makes it all the more special. Book in advance. The rooms combine modern facilities, with air-conditioning and tasteful decor. There is a garden and swimming pool, but no restaurant.
2011 D5 Via I Maggio, 4
05 77 30 50 09; www.hotelmonteriggioni.net
Closed mid-Nov to mid-March

SAN GIMIGNANO

La Cisterna €/€€
San Gimignano has several 3-star hotels within the village walls. The two that offer the best combination of location, facilities and relative value for money are on the same piazza. La Cisterna is tucked away in the eastern corner of Piazza della Cisterna. It has been open since 1919, but is thoroughly renovated inside. Rooms are well furnished with painted Tuscan furnishings, but they do vary in size. The hotel has a restaurant, Le Terrazze, which makes it a good option for a half-board stay.
208 B2 Piazza della Cisterna, 24
05 77 94 03 28; www.hotelcisterna.it
Closed for a period between Epiphany and mid-March; restaurant closed lunchtimes Tue–Wed

La Collegiata €€€
If money is no object, then this extremely smart 4-star hotel offers beautiful rooms set in a converted 16th-century convent, about 2km (1.25mi) north of the town walls. Facilities include a recommended restaurant, swimming pool, air-conditioning and lovely grounds with incomparable views of San Gimignano and its towers.
208 B2 Località Strada, 27
05 77 94 32 01; www.lacollegiata.it
Closed Nov–March

Leon Bianco €/€€
This 3-star hotel shares La Cisterna's perfect position just a stone's throw from the Collegiata and Museo Civico (➤ 112–113). The rooms and reception areas are bright and airy, with lots of vaulted ceilings, cool marble and terracotta floors: the building is medieval, with many period features preserved. There are rooms with countryside views, but those overlooking the piazza may suffer from late-night noise. There is no restaurant, but you can take breakfast or drinks on the pretty terrace.
208 B2 Piazza della Cisterna, 13
05 77 94 12 94; www.leonbianco.com
Closed for periods in Nov–Dec and Jan–Feb

SIENA

Antica Torre €€
The 3-star Antica Torre is just what its name suggests – an ancient medieval tower which in the last few years has achieved an excellent word-of-mouth reputation. You will need to book well in advance to secure one of the

eight pretty but moderately sized rooms in this restored 16th-century building. Try for rooms on the upper floor at the rear – they have the best views. The hotel lies about 600m (a quarter-mile) east of the Campo on a side street off Via di Pantaneto, close to the church of Santa Maria dei Servi. There is no restaurant, but breakfast is served in the medieval cellar.

208 C1 Via Fieravecchia, 7
05 77 22 22 55; www.anticatorresiena.it

Certosa di Maggiano €€€

This magnificent converted 14th-century abbey is one of Tuscany's finest hotels, favoured by honeymooners and other visitors prepared to splash out on cost. The hotel, with glorious, antique-filled rooms, lies within beautiful grounds 5km (3mi) east of Siena, so it is more a base for romance and self-indulgence than city sightseeing. Facilities include a heated swimming pool, tennis courts and heliport. Difficult to find – phone for directions.

208 C1 Via di Certosa, 82
05 77 28 81 80;
www.certosadimaggiano.com

B&B Antica Residenza Cicogna €/€€

Elisa Trefoloni had some initial reservations when she inherited her grandmother's huge flat in the middle of the town. In the meantime she has given up her secure job as a teacher and now devotes herself with great enthusiasm to running her B & B with its seven, delightfully restored rooms – which are incidentally often booked up many months in advance.

208 C1 Via delle Terme, 76
05 77 28 56 13,
www.anticaresidenzacicogna.it

Palazzo Ravizza €€/€€€

The 18th-century Palazzo Ravizza has been owned by the same family for more than two centuries. The hotel retains much of its period appeal, thanks to its many original features, antiques and furniture. The rooms all have satellite TVs and air-conditioning and either look over a garden to the rear or, if they are high enough, over the city and a potentially noisy road to the front. The hotel is located on the south-western fringes of Siena's old centre, about 250m (270 yards) beyond the Hotel Duomo.

2208 C1 Via Piano dei Mantellini, 34
05 77 28 04 62; www.palazzoravizza.it

Villa Scacciapensieri €€€

This tranquil hotel occupies a 19th-century hilltop villa about 3km (2mi) north of the city. A tree-lined drive sets the tone for the peaceful nature of your stay. The rooms and suites vary considerably, so ask to see a selection. Facilities include tennis courts and a pool, and there are gardens with views of the city and countryside. The restaurant offers regional specialities and home-made pastas. In summer, meals are served on the terrace under wisteria and linden trees.

208 C1 Strada di Sacciapensieri, 10
0 57 74 14 41; www.villascacciapensieri.it

VOLTERRA

Albergo Villa Nencini €

This beautiful old Tuscan mansion (plus new extension), set in gardens overlooking lovely countryside, with a pool and parking, nestled just outside the walls of old Volterra, is a typical Tuscan auberge with prices that are good value for the location. Rooms are comfortably furnished, but there is no air-conditioning, so if you find it difficult to sleep in hot conditions it may be worthwhile booking elsewhere in high summer. Some rooms have shared bathroom facilities. There's an excellent restaurant on site and an *enoteca* (wine bar).

208 A2 Borgo Santo Stefano, 55
0 58 88 63 86; www.villanencini.it

Where to ...
Eat and Drink

Prices
Expect to pay for a three-course meal for one with wine
€ under €26 **€€** €26–€52 **€€€**over €52

AREZZO

Antica Osteria L'Agania €
Arrive early at this busy, centrally located restaurant, as no reservations are accepted. The food is simple but expertly cooked by a group of women who have worked here for years. Typical Tuscan dishes include *ribollita* (vegetable soup) and tripe, plus home-made pasta. The wood-panelled dining room, complete with red and white checked tablecloths, is typically Italian. The decor is an eclectic mixture of old photographs, pictures, wine bottles and strings of garlic and peppers. The family also runs a wine bar next door.
209 E2 Via Mazzini, 10
05 75 29 53 81; www.agania.com
Tue–Sun 12–2:30, 7–10:30. Sept–June closed Mon

Buca di San Francesco €€
This central restaurant has been in business since 1929, serving simple, Tuscan staples such as thick *ribollita* (vegetable soup), *agnello* (roast lamb) and more ambitious dishes such as *pollo del Valdarno* (roast chicken flavoured with anise). The cellar dining room with its bold colours and medieval paintings is well-placed for the church of San Francesco and Piero della Francesca's fresco cycle.
209 E2 Via San Francesco, 1
0 57 52 32 71; www.bucadisanfrancesco.it
Wed–Mon 12–2:30, 7–9:30. Closed Mon evenings and Tue

Le Logge Vasari €€
There are three good reasons in favour of this restaurant in an old salt store: it retains the charm of a bygone age, it serves excellent regional dishes and you have a wonderful view of the busy comings and goings in this Tuscan town from the tables under the pergola.
209 E2 Piazza Grande, 19 05 75 29 58 94 Wed–Mon noon–3, 7:30–10:30

CERTALDO

Il Castello €/€€
As the name suggests, this restaurant is set in one of the historic fortified buildings in the historic upper town. The menu offers typically Tuscan seasonal dishes, including game such as hare and wild boar. Tables are spread through lovely vaulted dining rooms and then spill out onto a shady terrace or are totally al fresco, with views across the city rooftops. The small team here will make you most welcome.
208 B2 Via G della Rena, 6, Certaldo Alto
05 71 66 82 50; www.albergoilcastello.it
Daily 12–2:30, 7:30–9:30

CHIANTI

Osteria di Passignano €€/€€€
Two completely different worlds exist side by side behind the walls of an ancient abbey near Panzano, where a top-class restaurant rubs shoulders with Vallombrosan monks. The chef, Matia Barciulli, tempts his guests with worldly delights which taste like a Tuscan holiday – light, carefree and easy-going.

208 C2
Via Passignano, 33, Tavarnelle Val di Pesa
05 58 07 12 78; www.osteriasipassignano.com Mon–Sat 12:15–2:15, 7:30–10

L'Antica Trattoria €€/€€€

This elegant restaurant with a relaxed atmosphere is not in the medieval part of Colle di Val d'Elsa, but on the edge of a busy, modern square in the lower town. Don't let this put you off, however, for the sophisticated Tuscan food here is some of the best in the immediate region. The dining rooms are rustic in appearance and the service professional. The wine list is also outstanding.
208 C2 Piazza Arnolfo di Cambio, 23, Colle di Val d'Elsa 05 77 92 37 47
Wed–Mon 12:30–2:30, 8–10:30. Closed Tue

CORTONA

La Loggiato €€

It is hard to fault the tasteful brick-vaulted medieval interior, or the restaurant's central position just off the main square. The menu is filled with dishes typical of the region and the chef uses local seasonal produce throughout the year, where possible, so that you get a real taste of Tuscany – though the presentation is contemporary rather than country style. The wine list has a comprehensive range of Tuscan labels. If the weather is fine, aim to eat outdoors on the terrace.
209 F1 Piazza Pescheria, 3
05 75 63 05 75; www.laloggetta.com
Thu–Tue 12:30–3, 7–11

Osteria del Teatro €/€€

A definite first choice in Cortona, thanks to its central position close to the Teatro Signorelli (hence the restaurant's name), pleasing interior – the walls are lined with photographs of actors and actresses – and good food, which rarely strays from local staples. The *antipasto dell'osteria* is a good way to start, with lots of different tasters, followed by *ravioli ai fiori di zucca* (filled pasta with courgette flowers) or *pappardelle alle lepre*, a typical Tuscan dish of pasta ribbons with a hare sauce. It only seats 30 people, so be sure to book.
209 F1 Via Maffei, 2 05 75 63 05 56; www.osteria-del-teatro.it Thu–Tue 12:30–2:30, 7:30–10:30. Closed in Nov

SAN GIMIGNANO

Dorandò €€€

The aim of this restaurant is to re-create recipes from Tuscany's Etruscan and medieval past, which may sound pretentious but the results are usually first rate. The restaurant is small – just 36 people can be served in the three small dining rooms – and enjoys an elegant medieval setting. Prices, though, are high, even by San Gimignano's standards.
208 B2 Vicolo dell'Oro, 2
05 77 94 18 62; www.ristorantedorando.it
Daily 12–2:30, 7:30–9:30. Closed Dec–Jan, Mon Nov–Easter

Dulcisinfundo €€

Hidden in an alleyway behind the Piazza della Cisterna, this small restaurant serves excellent Tuscan and Italian food. The owner is a jazz aficionado, so the decor is certainly different from the normal Tuscan style, with music memorabilia covering the walls.
208 B2 Vicolo degli Innocenti, 21
05 77 94 19 19; www.dulcisinfundo.net
March–Oct and in the pre-Christmas period Thu–Tue 12–2:30, 7:15–9:30

Gelateria Dondoli € Insider Tip

This ice-cream parlour serves San Gimignano's best ice-cream, specializing in flavours which use only the best natural ingredients and no artificial additives.
208 B2 Piazza della Cisterna, 4
05 77 94 22 44; www.gelateriadipiazza.com
Mid-March to mid-Sept daily 9am–midnight; mid-Sept to mid-Nov, mid-Feb to mid-March 9–8. Closed mid-Nov to mid-Feb

Osteria delle Catene €
In a village clogged with visitors, this pleasant *osteria* has resisted the temptation to serve low-quality tourist fare. Instead, the owners Gino and Virgilio offer a variety of simple but far from boring local dishes, including *nana col cavolo nero* (duck with red cabbage) and *coniglio alla Vernaccia* (rabbit cooked with San Gimignano's Vernaccia white wine). There are also daily specials which offer good value for money.
208 B2 Via Mainardi, 18 05 77 94 19 66
Thu–Tue 12:30–2, 7:30–9:30. Closed periods Dec–Feb

SIENA

Antica Osteria da Divo €€
It's hard to imagine a more evocative series of dining rooms than those of Da Divo, just west of the cathedral and half-excavated from one of the city's ancient walls. The unique stone and vaulted rooms, dimly lit and cosy with rich, dark fabrics, date back to the early Middle Ages, and some contain Etruscan stones. The food is refined Tuscan fare and the menu features such dishes as terrine of rabbit with fresh pecorino cheese or risotto with saffron and asparagus.
208 C1 Via Franciosa, 25
05 77 28 60 54; www.osteriadadivo.it
Daily 12:30–2:30, 7:30–10:30. Closed Tue Nov–Apr, Sun May–Oct

Le Logge €€
Few Tuscan restaurants are prettier than this former medieval pharmacy just off the Campo, complete with its original wooden cabinets. The quality of the innovative food can be hit and miss: when it works, however, it's very good. Be sure to reserve a table in the downstairs dining room.
208 C1 Via del Porrione, 33
0 57 74 80 13; www.giannibrunelli.it
Mon–Sat 12:30–2:30, 7:30–10:30. Closed Jan–early Feb

Al Marsili €€
Al Marsili rivals Antica Osteria da Divo as the best of the more expensive restaurants in central Siena. The dining room still retains a few touches of its medieval decor, notably the brick vaulting. The food is a mixture of Tuscan staples and more ambitious dishes such as *cinghiale* (wild boar) or *faraona alla Medici* (guinea fowl with almonds, pine nuts and prunes).
208 C1 Via del Castoro, 3
0 57 74 71 54; www.ristorantealmarsili.it
Tue–Sun 12:30–2:30, 7:30–10:30

Osteria Castelvecchio €
Tucked away in the pretty grid of streets of the Tartuca *contrada*, west of the Pinacoteca Nazionale, this *osteria* has a more modern look and feel than many of Siena's rustic restaurants, combining medieval brick-vaulted ceilings with more contemporary pastel-coloured walls. The food is also somewhat more adventurous than usual, with regularly changing menus that offer plenty of home-made pastas, meat dishes and, unusually, several tasty options for vegetarians. The wine list is well thought out, the atmosphere pleasantly informal, and the prices fair.
208 C1
Via di Castelvecchio, 65
0 57 74 95 86
Mon–Sat 12:30–2:30, 7:30–10:30

VOLTERRA

Da Badò €
Two brothers run this popular, long-established *trattoria*, with their mother working in the kitchen. Soups such as *zuppa alla volterrana* and robust main dishes such as *cinghiale* (wild boar) are good, as are the local porcini mushrooms.
208 A2 Borgo San Lazzaro, 9
0 58 88 04 02; www.trattoriadabado.com
Thu–Tue 12:30–2:30, 7:30–10:30. Closed July and early Sept

Where to... Shop

SIENA

Food is a good buy, especially olive oil and *panforte*, a cake flavoured with cinnamon and other spices.

Antica Drogheria Manganelli 1879 (Via di Città 71–73; tel: 05 77 28 00 02) is crammed with things to eat, wines and spirits in old wooden cabinets.

The Sienese's favourite bakery is Il **Magnifico** (Via dei Pellegrini, 27) where you can find *ricciarelli* (almond biscuits), spicy *panpepato* and fruity *panforte*.

You can buy picnic provisions at **La Lizza**, Siena's main market, held Wednesday mornings north of the city beyond Piazza Matteotti and Piazza Gramsci.

For wine, head to the **Enoteca Italiana** (Fortezza Medicea; tel: 05 77 22 88 11; www.enoteca-italiana.it), where the old Medici castle's cellars hold around 750 of the best Italian wines to buy.

For gifts and household items, visit **Toscana Lovers** (Via delle Terme, 33, tel: 05 77 24 72 44) – the shop showcases Tuscan handicrafts – and **Ceramiche Santa Caterina** (Via di Città 74–76; tel: 05 77 28 30 98).

CHIANTI

In the region you can find masses of vineyards selling wine directly to the public. For a good one-stop selection visit **Enoteca del Gallo Nero** in Greve (Piazzetta Santa Croce 8; tel: 055 85 32 97; www.chianticlassico.it) which has wines by most of the Chianti Classico Gallo Nero producers plus other wines, olive oil and vinegar.

Where to... Go Out

Sleepy Siena and the Chianti hills are not places teeming with nightclubs or lively bars. Things are much livelier on the streets and squares, such as around the Piazza del Campo or on the Via Porrione.

Siena also has a range of musical associations which organise classical concerts and summer jazz and other music festivals.

Contact the **Accademia Chigiana** (tel: 0 57 72 20 91; www.chigiana.it) or the tourist office (➤ 45) for details of events, which are liable to change from year to year.

Tourist offices are also the best source of information on the plethora of small festivals devoted to food, wine, local saints and historical events across the region.

Larger events – when towns are likely to be busy and almost all accommodation full – include the **Giostra del Saraceno** in Arezzo, a medieval joust held twice a year in mid-June and the first week of September, and the **Volterra Teatro**, a festival held in the second half of July when international plays are staged.

Arezzo also has a major antiques fair on the first Sunday of each month and a well-regarded festival of choral music in August.

Cortona has an atmospheric crossbow competition, the **Giostra dell'Archidado**, and the **Festival del Sole** that draws stars from the world of classical music to Tuscany.

Southern Tuscany

Little Treats

Herbal magic

Luigi Gianelli of Hortus Mirabilis in **Bagno Vignoni** (➤ 151) relies on the power of nature for his lotions and potions.

Ruins with a view

Wonderful views of the surrounding area are to be had from the ruins and gardens around **Pienza** (➤ 138), west of Piazza Dante.

Precious crocuses

Find out why saffron is so expensive at the Azienda Agricola Brandi in **San Quirico d'Orcia** (www.crocusbrandi.it, ➤ 150).

Getting Your Bearings

Southern Tuscany is Tuscany at its best. The pastoral landscapes south of Siena are the most beautiful in the region, gentler and more varied than those of Chianti or the mountainous region to the north – and they are dotted with a succession of ancient abbeys, fascinating historic towns and tiny hill villages.

Church of Madonna di San Biagio, Montepulciano

The area to see, if time is short, lies immediately south of Siena. Here the landscape is that most often associated with Tuscany – olive groves, rustic stone farmhouses, rippling fields of wheat or sunflowers, and tranquil hills covered in vines or topped with lonely cypresses. Here, too, are some of the region's loveliest small towns and villages – Montalcino, famous for its red wine; Pienza, a tiny Renaissance jewel; and Montepulciano, a lofty historic redoubt with wonderful views. All three places make good overnight stops, with Montalcino the first choice, if only for its proximity to two wonderful abbeys – Sant'Antimo and Monte Oliveto Maggiore.

Farther south, beyond the Val d'Orcia (valley of the River Orcia), the landscape becomes higher, wilder and less inhabited. The best countryside clusters around Monte Amiata, southern Tuscany's highest point, a brooding mountain swathed in beech woods and circled by a coronet of villages and hamlets. Farther south still, however, the landscape changes again, becoming flatter and, by Tuscany's exalted standards, relatively uninspiring. Large towns near the coast such as Grosseto and Piombino are lacklustre, while little on the coast itself merits a special journey when there is so much to see inland – Castiglione della Pescaia and the Marina di Alberese, both within 20km (12mi) of Grosseto, are the best options if you want an afternoon by the sea.

TOP 10

Don't Miss

At Your Leisure

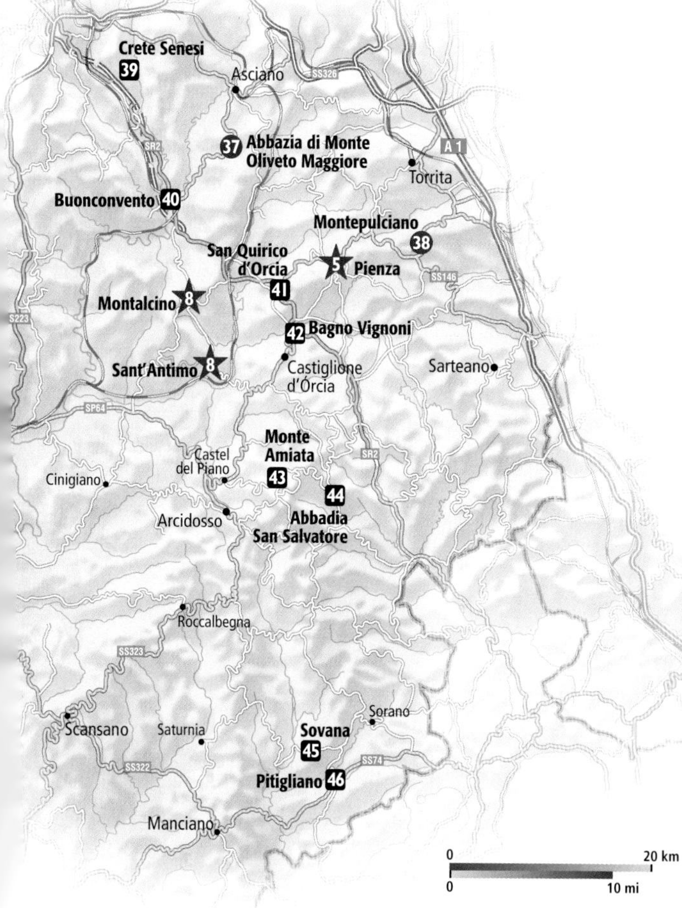

On a short visit, the historic little village of Sovana and the spectacularly situated Pitigliano are more worthwhile – but note that both will leave you a long way south and a quite a long drive from Tuscany's other highlights.

Southern Tuscany

Two Perfect Days

If you're not quite sure where to begin your travels, this itinerary recommends two practical and enjoyable days out in Southern Tuscany, taking in some of the best places to see. For more information see the main entries (➤ 138–155).

Day 1

Morning

From San Gimignano, Montalcino or Siena drive southeast, either on the main SR2 (Via Cassia) road, or the scenic SP438 from Siena through the hills of the 39 **Crete Senesi** (➤ 150) to Asciano. From the SR2 road at Buonconvento or on the minor road south from Asciano via Montecontieri, visit 37 **Abbazia di Monte Oliveto Maggiore** (➤ 145, right).

Lunch

Have lunch or a snack in the abbey café or enjoy a picnic in the open air.

Afternoon

You could spend an hour or so exploring 40 **Buonconvento**'s medieval centre (➤ 150) before driving to 5 **Pienza** (➤ 138), which should occupy two or three hours. Then drive on to 38 **Montepulciano** (➤ 147) where you can spend the night.

Day 2

Morning

Drive from Montepulciano to 42 **Bagno Vignoni** (➤ 151, left), and explore the village, along with Castiglione d'Orcia and the other villages and lovely countryside around Montalcino. Then go to 8 **Montalcino** (above) and **Sant'Antimo** (➤ 141).

Lunch

Taverna Il Grappolo Blu in Montalcino makes an ideal spot for lunch (➤ 156).

Afternoon

In the afternoon drive south to see 43 **Monte Amiata** (➤ 151) and its more rugged landscapes and villages. A longer drive takes you to the villages of 45 **Sovana** (➤ 152) and 46 **Pitigliano** (➤ 153). Sovana makes a good overnight base (➤ 158).

5 Pienza

Pienza is one of the smallest but most memorable of all Tuscany's villages, a tiny medieval and Renaissance jewel of considerable charm set at the heart of some of the region's most beautiful countryside.

A view of Pienza's cathedral from the city walls

Pienza was known as Corsignano until 1459, when Enea Silvio Piccolomini – better known as Pope Pius II – decided to turn the place of his birth into a planned Renaissance city. In the event, he died before his grandiose scheme could be realised, but not before the modest hamlet had been given a cathedral filled with artworks, a handful of palaces and a grand central piazza, Piazza Pio II. This trio of sights is complemented by some wonderful views, a small but fascinating museum and two medieval churches.

Renaissance Vision

Pienza amounts to little more than a maze of small lanes and a main street, **Corso Rossellino**, which takes its name from Bernardo Rossellino, the architect Pius commissioned to design his model city. The Corso bisects the village from east to west, passing through the Piazza Pio II, distinguished by a Renaissance well, the **Pozzo dei Cani**, complete with twin columns and a classical frieze. This sets the tone for the rest of the square, conceived as a unified whole, and offers a tantalising glimpse of what might have been had Pius lived to realise his vision.

Pius' coat of arms – a garland of fruit – adorns the **façade** (1462) of the cathedral, the piazza's grand set piece. Inside, the church boasts five prominent paintings – all individually commissioned by Pius – by five prominent Sienese painters: the most accomplished is Vecchietta's ***Assumption*** with

The Pozzo dei Cani, a Renaissance well on the Piazza Pio II

Pope Pius I and the saints Agatha, Callistus and Catherine of Siena in the chapel to the left of the choir.

To the right of the cathedral as you face its façade stands the **Palazzo Piccolomini**, Pius' papal residence inhabited by his descendants until 1962. Guided tours take you round many of its state apartments, notably the library, music room, dining salon and papal bedroom, all which are overflowing with books, manuscripts, rich carpets and other precious antiques (though not all are original to the palace). One of the most striking rooms is the **Sala d'Armi**, or armoury, which bristles with all manner of medieval weaponry. Equally memorable are the **views** from the rear loggia. On the east side of Piazza Pio II stands the Palazzo Borgia (also known as Palazzo dei Vescovi), home to the **Museo Diocesano**, a wonderfully rich and eclectic collection of paintings, sculpture, tapestries, portrait busts and other medieval and Renaissance artefacts. First among its treasures is a beautifully embroidered 14th-century English *piviale* (cape), part of Pius' personal wardrobe.

East and West Pienza

From Piazza Pio II you could explore the little lanes to the east and especially the alleys which run along the top of the village's south-facing walls behind the cathedral – the **views** towards Monte Amiata are spell-binding. To the west, Corso Rossellino brings you to **San Francesco**, a late 13th-century Gothic church which survived Pius' redevelopment. Another, the **Pieve di Corsignano**, lies about 1km (0.6mi) from Piazza Dante. This parish church dates from the 10th century. To view the interior you should contact the tourist office (tel: 0 57 87 74 90 71).

San Francesco cloisters

The panoramic views from Pienza's city walls are spectacular

TAKING A BREAK

Try popular **Falco** on Piazza Dante for good country cooking.

Duomo
211 F4 Piazza Pio II
No phone Daily 7:30–1, 2–7. Closed during services
Free

Palazzo Piccolomini
201 E4 Piazza Pio II
05 78 28 63 00; www.palazzopiccolominipienza.it
Mid-March to mid-Oct Tue–Sun 10–6:30; mid-Oct to mid-March 10–4; closed early Jan to mid-Feb €7

Museo Diocesano
201 E4 Corso Rossellino, 30
05 78 74 99 05 Mid-March to Oct Wed–Mon 10:30–1:30, 2:30–6; Nov to mid-March Sat, Sun 10–4 €4.50

INSIDER INFO

- Pienza becomes busy with day-trippers from Florence and Siena in summer, so aim to arrive early or – better still – stay overnight: the village has a good central hotel, **Il Chiostro di Pienza** (➤ 155).
- You won't be able to **park** in the centre of Pienza, but the village is so small you won't need to – leave your car outside the walls to the west near Piazza Dante or in the car park to the north on Via Mencatelli, off Largo Roma. The Largo is on Viale Enzo Mangiavacchi, the road that runs around the outside of the walls eastward from Piazza Dante.

In more depth The surrounding area is delightful. An 8-km (5mi) drive along the SS146 beyond San Quirico leads to gently undulating countryside, rising to much steeper hills in the distance. One of the most famous photo motifs in Tuscany can be seen on the left: the **Podere Belvedere**, an imposing farmhouse under a red-tiled, pagoda-style roof with the obligatory cypress trees in front.

8 Montalcino & Sant'Antimo

Montalcino is another perfect Tuscan hill town: its breezy site offers magnificent views and it is almost completely unspoilt, it sits amid beautiful countryside and its red wines – Brunello and Rosso di Montalcino – are some of Italy's finest. Its hotels and restaurants, though few in number, are first rate. It also lies close to Sant'Antimo, the region's loveliest abbey.

The town of Montalcino is one of Tuscany's most picturesque and most ancient settlements, dating back to Palaeolithic or Etruscan times. Its first mention in written records in AD814 cites it in a list of territories awarded to the abbey of Sant'Antimo by Louis the Pious, son of Charlemagne. Its finest hour came in 1555, when it was the last town in the Sienese Republic to surrender to the Florentines – Montalcino's banner still heads the procession at the Siena Palio in memory of the feat (➤ 22).

Exploring Montalcino

The town's most striking sight is the **Rocca** (or ***fortezza***), a picture-perfect, 14th-century castle on the town's southern edge. Its main keep houses a busy – albeit extremely expensive – *enoteca* (wine bar) where you can buy or sample local wine. It's well worth paying the small fee to visit the castle battlements, which offer superb views across the Crete, a region of bare hills, to one side, and the wooded slopes of the Val d'Orcia on the other.

From the castle, head northeast on Via Panfilo and then turn left on Via dell'Oca. A short walk brings you to Piazza Garibaldi and **Sant'Egidio**, a pretty old church with several

Take time to explore Montalcino's main street

fragments of medieval fresco. From the piazza walk north, passing the tiny tourist office on the left, to the **Piazza del Popolo**, the town's narrow main square, which is dominated by the Palazzo Comunale (1292), a fine civic palace, and a pretty café (► 156).

Sant'Antimo is one of Italy's finest Romanesque abbeys

To see the splendid **Museo di Montalcino Raccolta Archeologica Medievale e Moderna,** the town's main museum, walk back towards the tourist office and take the first arched alleyway on your right. Climb the steps and then continue straight on past the 14th-century **church of Sant'Agostino** on your left. Have a quick look in the church, which has several fine medieval frescoes by unknown artists, and then allow an hour or so for the adjacent museum. Among the museum's exhibits are lovely 14th and 15th-century paintings by Sano di Pietro and other Sienese artists, a pair of illuminated 12th-century bibles and a 12th-century crucifix from Sant'Antimo.

After visiting the museum you should take some time to enjoy the streets almost at random. To the north, you might take Via Spagni past the Duomo – remodelled to dull effect in 1832 – to the **Santuario della Madonna del Soccorso**, a large church with a 17th-century façade flanked by a park to the right (on Viale Roma). From here you can explore the town's northern and eastern limits, following Via Mazzini from Piazza Cavour at the bottom of Viale Roma back to Piazza del Popolo, or taking the meandering small lanes east to the Fonte Castellane, a medieval washhouse, and the nearby deconsecrated church of San Francesco.

Sant'Antimo

However long you stay in Montalcino – and the town makes an excellent base – be certain to devote a couple of hours to **Sant'Antimo**, an abbey that lies in glorious countryside just 10km (6mi) south of the town (the abbey is signposted

The ambulatory around Sant'Antimo's high altar

at the main road junction just below the Fortezza). Its beautiful situation, nestled amid a timeless pastoral landscape of olive groves and wooded hills, is reason enough to visit, but what makes the abbey still more compelling is its fascinating history and superb architecture.

Many myths surround its foundation, the most persistent being that it was created by Charlemagne, the Holy Roman Emperor, in AD781. As Charlemagne marched his army from Rome, it's said his troops were ravaged by a mysterious disease and that the emperor promised God he would build a church if he effected a cure. While camped close to the site of the present abbey, Charlemagne was reputedly told by God in a dream to feed his men a local herb mixed with wine. The cure worked and the abbey of Sant'Antimo was duly built. The story may sound unlikely, but it is known that in 781 Pope Hadrian I presented Charlemagne with the relics of St Antimo – the very relics venerated at the abbey which took the saint's name. It's also a fact that an abbey existed in 814, when Charlemagne's son, Louis the Pious, granted it lands in a charter of that year. Pious' gift and other donations over the years made the abbey one of the richest in Tuscany, a status bolstered by its position on pilgrimage and trade routes.

Parts of the ancient ninth-century church still exist, but most of the present church dates from a particularly large bequest in 1118, details of which are engraved on the

INSIDER INFO

- Do not try to **park** in the centre of Montalcino. The best place to leave your car is in the car park off Via Aldo Moro at the southern entrance to the town, below the Fortezza. From here it is a short walk to the town centre.
- If you have time, you could include the **abbey of Sant'Antimo** on a longer drive to Monte Amiata and the extreme south of the region (➤ 151) or through the tiny villages and hamlets of the Val d'Orcia: Castiglione d'Orcia, Rocca d'Orcia and Campiglia d'Orcia. It's also easily seen as part of a drive to Pienza (➤ 138) and Montepulciano to the east (➤ 147).
- After standing empty for some 500 years, Sant'Antimo now has a small community of French monks. **Services** in the abbey on Sunday morning often include beautiful plainsong chants.

In more depth The private **Sculpture Park in Seggiano**, owned by the Swiss artist Daniel Spoerri, is a good hour by car from Montalcino. The 80 works of art are by the artist himself or his contemporaries, including his compatriot, the painter and sculptor Jean Tinguely, and the Venezuelan Jesus Soto. Insider Tip

One of Tinguely's kinetic scrap metal 'machines' can be set in motion at the flick of a switch. The wind keeps Soto's sound sculpture on a small hill chiming while Eva Aeppli's eerie figures peer down sternly on visitors (tel: 05 64 95 08 05), www.danielspoerri.org, €10.

Montalcino's Fiaschetteria Italiana is an excellent place to buy wine or take a break from sightseeing

stone around the **high altar**. The abbey authorities immediately looked to the mother church of the Benedictines in Cluny, France, and to French architects, for the design of the church, which is why its layout – a basilican plan with an ambulatory (a walkway around the altar) and radiating chapels – is unique in Tuscany and only found in a handful of other Italian churches.

Both the abbey's interior and exterior are striking by any standards, a gloriously simple Romanesque building embellished with some beautiful carving; in particular, note the capital of the second column on the right of the nave, which depicts Daniel in the lions' den.

TAKING A BREAK

Fiaschetteria Italiana is a café with a lovely interior. Or, for a meal out of town, try the **Taverna dei Barbi** (➤ 156).

Tourist office
211 E4 Costa del Municipio, 8
05 77 84 93 31; www.prolocomontalcino.it Daily 10–1, 2–5:50

Fortezza
211 E4 Piazzale della Fortezza 05 77 84 92 11
Apr–Oct daily 9–8; Nov–March Tue–Sun 9–6
Castle and *enoteca*: free; battlements: €4 (combined ticket with Museo Civico)

Museo di Montalcino Raccolta Archeologica Medievale e Moderna
211 E4 Ex-convento di Sant'Agostino, Via Ricasoli 31
05 77 84 60 14 Apr–Oct Tue–Sun 10–1, 2–5:50; Nov–March 10–1, 2–5:40
€4 (combined ticket with *fortezza* battlements)

Sant'Antimo
211 E4 Near Castelnuovo dell'Abate
05 77 83 56 59; www.antimo.it
Mon–Sat 10:15–12:30, 3–6:30, Sun 9:15–10:45, 3–6 Free

37 Abbazia di Monte Oliveto Maggiore

The abbey of Monte Oliveto Maggiore sits in splendid isolation on a pretty hillside amid woods of oak, pine, cypress and olive. The beauty of its setting is matched by the charm of its ancient buildings, and by the great work of art at its heart, a Renaissance fresco cycle on the *Life of St Benedict* by Sodoma and Luca Signorelli.

The Grand Cloister at Monte Oliveto Maggiore, with frescoes by Sodoma and Luca Signorelli

The abbey of Monte Oliveto Maggiore owes its foundation to Bernardo Tolomei (1272–1348), a member of a wealthy Sienese family who renounced his worldly life after being struck blind and experiencing visions of the Virgin Mary (the Tolomei family tombs can be seen in the church of San Francesco in Siena, ➤ 117).

Bernardo retreated with two companions to the site of the present abbey – the land was then owned by his family – and within six years began work on what, in 1320, would become a Benedictine hermitage. In 1344 Pope Clement VI recognised Tolomei and his growing band of followers as Olivetans, also known as White Benedictines, an offshoot of the Benedictines whose members sought to return to the humble roots of the order. Later Olivetans made light of this ambition, for the abbey became hugely wealthy and played a vital role in the economic and agricultural life of the surrounding region.

Artistic Highlights

Monte Oliveto is still a working abbey, and large parts of its extensive monastic buildings and grounds are closed to visitors. Its main artistic highlight, however, is fully accessible: the **Choistro Grande** (Grand Cloister, 1426–43) and its fresco cycle by Sodoma and Luca Signorelli on the life of

The abbey nestles in the landscape

the Benedictines' founder, St Benedict. Sodoma, a Milanese artist, completed the majority of the cycle between 1505 and 1508 –27 panels in all – adding to the eight panels executed in 1498 by Luca Signorelli, an artist born in nearby Cortona (► 119). The cycle starts on the east wall to the right of the abbey church door. The narrative is hard to decipher unless you're well versed in the life of St Benedict, though this shouldn't spoil your enjoyment, for each of the frescoes is filled with fascinating incidental and contemporary detail. The abbey church itself, however, is disappointing, except for some breathtakingly carved and inlaid choir stalls (1503–05).

TAKING A BREAK

The abbey has a **café** for drinks, snacks and light meals, but you might also consider buying a **picnic** to eat either in the attractive abbey grounds or at a scenic spot farther along the SS451 road.

---

211 E5 Near Chiusure 05 77 70 76 11; www.monteolivetomaggiore.it
Daily 9:15–12, 3:15–6 (Oct–Apr until 5); library closed weekdays Nov–Feb
Free

INSIDER INFO

- The abbey is easily visited from Buonconvento, 9km (5.5mi) to the southwest on the SS451 road. However, you'll enjoy the **best distant view** of the abbey if you continue east on this road to the first major junction 1km (0.5mi) beyond the abbey and turn right to the hamlet of Chiusure. From here you can look down on the monastery and its lovely setting.
- The abbey **closes at noon** for three hours or so, so time your visit accordingly.

38 Montepulciano

Montepulciano is a beautiful and typically Tuscan town. From its commanding position it boasts sweeping views. Its artworks and architecture are especially worth seeing and include San Biagio, one of Italy's foremost Renaissance churches. In addition, the local *vino nobile* is one of the region's most prized wines. Despite all this, the number of visitors who make the effort to come here is still relatively low.

Montepulciano may be rewarding, but it isn't easy to explore. Built on a narrow, steep ridge, it effectively consists of one main street that climbs sharply from Piazza Sant'Agnese to Piazza Grande, the main square, before continuing up to the fortress at the top of the town – a height of some 605m (1,985ft). So be prepared for a climb at either the start or end of your travels.

Along the Corso

This itinerary starts at Piazza Sant'Agnese, which has the advantage of making Piazza Grande the culmination of your walk. In the first square look briefly at **Sant'Agnese church**, with several 14th-century paintings. Then pass through

The church of San Biagio, just outside Montepulciano

the Porta al Prato, the town's main northern gateway, which marks the start of your walk up the **Corso**, the main street that, in one guise or another, will take you to the top of the town.

In the square just inside the gate stands the **Colonna del Marzocco**, a column bearing a statue of the Marzocco, Florence's heraldic lion (➤ 70). The Florentines controlled Montepulciano from 1511, a period that saw them dispatch the architect Antonio da Sangallo the Elder to strengthen the town's defences and restore or rebuild many local palaces. This trend was continued by his nephew, Antonio da Sangallo the Younger, and later by Jacopo Vignola, one of the leading lights of early Baroque architecture. The older Sangallo was responsible for both the Porta al Prato and the Palazzo Cocconi at No. 70 on the Corso. Vignola probably designed the Palazzo Tartugi (No. 82) and Palazzo Avignonesi (No. 91). The Corso's most striking palace, however, is the **Palazzo Bucelli** at No. 73, notable for the Etruscan remains incorporated into its base (its 17th-century owner, Pietro Bucelli, was an avid collector of antiquities). A short distance past the Palazzo Cocconi, on the right, stands the 13th-century **church of Sant'Agostino** (Piazza Michelozzo), its façade remodelled around 1429 by Michelozzo, one of the Medicis' favourite architects. Opposite stands the **Torre di Pulcinella**, a medieval tower and town house – the figure of the clown, Pulcinella, strikes the hours on the clock.

The tiny figure of the clown, Pulcinella, strikes the hour on the medieval clock tower

Some 100m (110 yards) beyond this point you reach the Piazza dell' Erbe and the Renaissance Loggia del Mercato on the right. Turn right here, then take a sharp

INSIDER INFO

- While you're visiting Montepulciano, don't miss the opportunity to buy a bottle or two of its famous **Vino Nobile** red wine in one of the many wine shops (➤ 158).
- Just outside the walls of Montepulciano to the west stands the church of **San Biagio**, a masterpiece of Renaissance architecture by Antonio da Sangallo the Elder. It can be reached from Via Ricci via the Porta dei Grassi and Via di San Biagio, a steep 15-minute downhill walk. When building began in 1518 the only larger church project in Italy was St Peter's Basilica in Rome. The church's honey-coloured exterior and pretty position are enchanting; the interior with its frescos from the 16th century on the other hand is quite plain.

In more depth An international summer academy for contemporary music – the **Cantiere Internazionale d'Arte** – was founded in the wine town in 1976 by the German composer, Hans Werner Henze. Since then, high-calibre musical events are held every year in July on the Piazza Grande or in the Teatro Poliziano (www.fondazionecantiere.it).

Taddeo di Bartolo's magnificent *Assumption* forms the cathedral's high altar

left up Via di Poggiolo. As you continue you pass the church of San Francesco and then the **Museo Civico**, the town's main museum, which contains early paintings, medieval sculptures and other artistic fragments from as far back as the 13th century.

Piazza Grande and the Cathedral

Soon after, Via Ricci opens onto the glorious Piazza Grande, a large square dominated by the Duomo (cathedral) and an array of austere palaces. Among the latter is the **Palazzo Contucci**, one of several places where you can sample and buy Vino Nobile di Montepulciano (➤ 28). You can also climb the tower of the Gothic 13th-century **Palazzo Comunale**, on the square's western edge – the views are far-reaching, but the opening times can be erratic: it's generally open in the morning Monday to Saturday.

The piazza's real attraction, however, is the **Duomo**. Behind its unfinished façade is one of Tuscany's greatest altarpieces, the *Assumption* (1401) by Taddeo di Bartolo. The Baptistry is filled with reliefs, terracottas and other sculptures by an array of medieval and Renaissance artists, including Andrea della Robbia and Benedetto da Maiano. Also look at Michelozzo's dismembered tomb (1427–36) of the humanist Bartolomeo Aragazzi.

TAKING A BREAK

Caffè Poliziano (➤ 157) or **La Grotta**, just outside town, by the church of San Biagio, are both good places for lunch.

---

211 F4

Museo Civico e Pinacoteca Crociani

Palazzo Neri-Orselli, Via Ricci 10 05 78 71 73 00

March–May, Sept, Oct Tue–Sun 10–1, 3–6, June, July 10–1, 3–7, Aug 10–7, Nov–Feb Sa, So 10–1, 3–6 €5

At Your Leisure

39 Crete Senesi

'The land of the wind and the desert' is how the Tuscan poet Mario Luzi aptly described this bizarre hilly area south of Siena, taking in the settlements of Asciano, west to Monteroni d'Arbia then south to Buonconvento and east to San Giovanni d'Asso.

Crete means 'clay' in the Tuscan dialect and it is a clay substrate that gives the area its pleasing, rounded hills and rich colours of umber and terracotta. The Crete is one of the agricultural heartlands of Tuscany; for centuries it produced grain, and solid ancient granaries dotting the landscape are the cathedrals of the Crete. Today it is famed for its rare white truffles and excellent pecorino cheese and olive oil.

211 E5

40 Buonconvento

Buonconvento, 27km (16.5mi) south of Siena, has unattractive outskirts, but beyond these is a walled medieval centre – a brick-built redoubt forged by the Sienese as a part of their southern defences.

The town is easily and quickly seen, especially if you're on road SR2 en route for Montalcino or visiting Monte Oliveto Maggiore a few kilometres to the east (➤ 145). There's little to see or do save wandering the old streets lined with handsome period patrician houses, where you should devote most time to the **Museo d'Arte Sacra**, typical of Tuscany's many tiny small-town museums. Here, as elsewhere, the richness of the collection is out of all proportion to the size of the town. Highlights among the medieval Sienese paintings on display are an *Annunciation* by Andrea di Bartolo and the *Madonna del Latte* (*Madonna of the Milk*), by Luca di Tommè. The latter shows a breast-feeding Madonna, an unusual subject in Italian art but relatively common in parts of Tuscany, where several churches claimed to have reliquaries containing drops of the Virgin's milk. Also interesting is the **Museo della Mezzadria**, with varied displays devoted to the rural and social history of the region.

211 E4

Tourist Office
Museo della Mezzadria, Piazzale Garibaldi
05 77 80 71 81; www.turismobuonconvento.it
Apr–Oct Tue–Sun 10–1, 2–6; Nov–March Wed–Fri 10–1:30, Sat 10–1, 2–6

Museo d'Arte Sacra
Via Soccini, 18 05 77 80 71 90
Apr–Oct Tue–Sun 10–1, 3–6; Nov–March Sat, Sun 10–1, 3–5 €3.50

Museo della Mezzadria
La Tinaia, Piazzale Garibaldi
05 77 80 90 75; www.museomezzadria.it
Apr–Oct Tue–Sun 10–1, 2–6; Nov–March Tue–Fri 10–1:30, Sat, Sun 10–1, 2–6 €4

41 San Quirico d'Orcia

San Quirico is a mixture of the enchanting and the banal; a blend of bland modern housing and exquisite medieval churches and Renaissance gardens. It has a forlorn feel, but is worth a brief stop on a drive between Siena (44km/27mi to the north) and southern Tuscany, or between Montalcino (15km/9mi to the west) and Pienza (9.5km/6mi to the east). The partly walled village takes its name from San Quirico a Osenna, one of many churches that were built along the Via Francigena (➤ 115), an ancient pilgrimage route between Rome and northern Europe.

Today, its highlight is another church, the **Collegiata**, a 12th-century architectural gem off Piazza Chigi built on the ruins of a much older church. The carvings around the doors are exceptional, as are the interior's inlaid Renaissance choir stalls and a painting of the *Madonna and Saints*by Sano di Pietro in the north (left) transept. The choir stalls were originally from a chapel in Siena cathedral (➤ 104). On the edge of the village, near the Porta Nuova, are the **Horti Leonini** (open daily dawn–dusk; free), peaceful Renaissance gardens laid out in 1580. Walk down Via Dante Alighieri to see the house at No. 38, which is said to have once hosted St Catherine of Siena, and the lovely 11th-century church of Santa Maria Assunta.

211 E4

Tourist Office

Piazza Chigi, 2

05 77 89 97 28

April–Oct, Mon–Sat 10–1, 3:30–6:30, Nov–March Sat, Sun 10–1, 3:30–6:30

42 Bagno Vignoni

Try to arrive in Bagno Vignoni early in the morning, to enjoy one of Tuscany's more magical sights in full. The hill village's main square, Piazza delle Sorgenti, is actually not a square at all but a large pool containing a natural hot spring – when the air is cool a mist rises from the warm water, drifting over the little square and its old stone buildings in an eerie shroud. The springs were known to the Romans and enjoyed by popes and saints – St Catherine of Siena took the waters and Pius II built a 15th-century summer house (now a hotel) close to the square. Lorenzo de' Medici (➤ 64) also came here; the Medici built the arcaded loggia and **piscina** (pool) that holds the spring. You can no longer bathe in the square, but you can soak in the waters in the nearby Hotel Posta Marcucci. The village lies in the midst of some pretty countryside, and the small lanes radiating from the central square lead into the surrounding woods and fields.

211 E4

Bagno Vignoni lies 1km (0.5mi) west of the main SR2 road, from which it is signposted 5km (3mi) south of San Quirico d'Orcia

Tourist Office

Strada di Bagno Vignoni

05 77 88 89 75

May–Sept Fri–Sun 10–6

43 Monte Amiata

Stand on the ramparts of Pienza (➤ 138), or at other viewpoints in central Tuscany, and one brooding and solitary peak dominates the view: Monte Amiata (1,738m/5,702ft). The mountain's isolated position and distinctive pyramid shape – forming part of an extinct volcano – are striking. It lies too far south of Siena and Florence for a lot of tourists, but can be included

San Quirico d'Orcia's Collegiata is a 12th-century Romanesque gem

in a drive from Montalcino or Pienza, for example, to the **Parco Faunistico del Monte Amiata** near Arcidosso, where not only those from large urban areas will be captivated by the flora and fauna of southern Tuscany.

On a clear day you should drive up the mountain for some staggering views. You might also want to walk in the extensive woods that swathe the mountain's slopes – there are plenty of marked trails that start from the roads that ring the mountain. If you have time, you should also drive around the little villages that lie on the mountain's flanks – among them, Seggiano, Arcidosso, Castel del Piano and others. None, save **Abbadia San Salvatore**, have any great artistic treasures, but they all have their own distinct charm.

211 E3

44 Abbadia San Salvatore

The small town of Abbadia San Salvatore takes its name from the third of the great trio of abbeys in southern Tuscany – Monte Oliveto, Sant'Antimo and San Salvatore. In the town's medieval quarter, on Via del Monastero, you'll find the abbey, which dates from about 743, making it one of Tuscany's oldest. It was reputedly founded by a Lombard king, Ratchis, though much of the present building – built in Monte Amiata's distinctive brown trachite stone – dates either from 1036 (notably the crypt) or from restora- tion work carried out in the 13th century. The interior's **Latin cross plan**, however, is widely considered the first of its kind in Tuscany. Most of the abbey's works of art were removed to Florence after the town fell to the Medici in 1559. Only the crypt captivates, a wonderfully austere space dominated by 35 fluted and beautifully carved columns.

211 F3

The chased metal cross at the summit of Mount Amiata

Tourist Office
Via Adua, 21
05 77 24 17 60; www.terresiena.it
Mon–Fri 8:30–1, 3–6; Sat 10–1, 3–6

45 Sovana

By Tuscany's standards, the landscape south of Monte Amiata to the border of the region of Lazio, is unremark-able, with few towns and villages of note. The one exception is a pocket of countryside on Lazio's border, home to two interesting villages, Sovana, Sorano and Pitigliano. Tiny Sovana amounts to little more than a single street, Via di Mezzo. In its day, the settlement was one of the region's most important centres, as the power base of the local Aldobrandeschi nobility and the birthplace of Hildebrand, who became Pope Gregory VII in 1073. This, in part, accounts for the presence of one of Tuscany's most beautiful parish churches, the 13th-century **Santa Maria Maggiore**, on the Piazza del Pretorio. Inside, the simple interior is dominated by lovely frescoes and a carved *ciborium* (altar canopy), a rare pre-Romanesque palaeo-Christian work from the eighth or ninth century. The Aldobrandeschi's erstwhile presence also accounts for Sovana's **Cattedrale di SS Pietro e Paolo**, whose scale and splendour are out of all proportion to the size of the village. To reach it, walk down either of the two lanes that lead off Piazza del Pretorio. The building dates from different eras: many of the carvings were done in the eighth century; most of the apse and crypt date from the 10th century; the frescoes and carvings on the capitals of the nave's columns were executed from the 12th century onwards.

Sovana also lies at the heart of an area rich in Etruscan remains. Many Etruscan graves have been excavated in the region making it an interesting **place for a day trip** for the whole family (www.leviecave.it). Some of the best can be seen as you drive east to Sorano, 10km (6mi) away, where part of the road runs past small niche tombs cut into the rock. Sovana also has a couple of good hotels and restaurants (► 158).

211 E2

Pitigliano's medieval houses, perched on a volcanic ridge, make an impressive sight

46 Pitigliano

Pitigliano is an imposing sight from afar, its castle and medieval houses crowded onto a ridge of volcanic rock that rises sheer from the surrounding countryside. The Etruscans settled here around the sixth century BC, but the village prospered most in the 13th and 14th centuries, when it was owned by the powerful Orsini family who provided three popes. Until World War II it also had a thriving Jewish community – a synagogue survives on Via Zuccarelli.

Beyond Piazza Garibaldi stand a large aqueduct and fortress, both completed in the 16th century by architect Giuliano da Sangallo. Inside the fortress is the **Palazzo Orsini**, with beautifully decorated and furnished rooms. For the most part, however, Pitigliano's main rewards come from wandering its handful of streets and admiring the views of Monte Amiata.

211 F2

Pitigliano's museums have erratic opening times: for information contact the visitor centre at Piazza Garibaldi, 51 05 64 61 71 11; www.collidimaremma.it

Where to...
Stay

Prices
Expect to pay per double room per night
€ under €125 **€€** €125–€200 **€€€** over €200

BAGNO VIGNONI

Hotel Spa Adler Thermae €€€

There may be historic thermal baths at Bagno Vignoni, but facilities at the Adler Thermae could not be more up to date. Set in ample grounds, with an impressive outdoor swimming pool and natural hot springs and salt pools, the hotel offers a range of spa and wellness opportunities. In summer there's a choice of restaurants, including an *osteria* and a gourmet dining room.

Rooms are well furnished and finished in warm woods and soothing neutral tones. Family suites are also available.

211 E4
I-53072 Bagno Vignoni
05 77 88 90 01; www.adler-thermae.com
Closed early Jan–early Feb

MONTALCINO

Albergo Il Giglio €€

This 3-star hotel has been a fixture in Montalcino for many years thanks to its authentic Tuscan feel. The rooms are presented in a traditional style with period furniture. The best rooms have original frescoes and views over the countryside to the rear. There is a reasonable restaurant and plenty of good alternatives in town. Breakfast is expensive, so aim to have a *caffè* and *cornetto* in the Fiaschetteria Italiana instead (➤ 144).

211 E4
Via Soccorso Saloni, 5
05 77 84 65 77; www.gigliohotel.com
Closed for a period in Jan; restaurant closed lunchtimes and Tue

Dei Capitani €€

This 3-star converted town house is one of the most appealing hotels in Montalcino. All the rooms are comfortable and decorated in a fresh, modern style, and the rooms to the rear have wonderful views over the countryside. All have telephones, air-conditioning and TVs. In summer, the terrace, small garden and panoramic bar area are a bonus, as is the small swimming pool, on a slope behind the hotel. There is no restaurant, but breakfast is served and included in the room price. A handful of parking places are available outside the hotel. Note that there are five extra rooms in a separate *dipendenza* (annexe).

201 E4 **Via Lapini, 6**
05 77 84 72 27; www.deicapitani.it
Closed mid-Jan to Feb

MONTEPULCIANO

Duomo €/€€

This family-run, 3-star hotel is a safe choice, thanks to its friendly welcome and excellent position just a few moments' walk from the cathedral and main Piazza Grande. It has bright, modern and unelaborate rooms decorated with simple fabrics, marble or tiled floors and the occasional period detail.

211 F4 **Via San Donato, 14**
05 78 75 74 73;
www.albergoduomomontepulciano.it

Il Marzocco €

The 3-star Il Marzocco is the smartest hotel in Montepulciano, occupying a 16th-century *palazzo.* Its location, just inside the Porta al Prato at the northern end of the Corso, leaves a steep climb to Piazza Grande. The rooms are simply decorated with period furniture – the best have terraces with panoramic views. Limited private parking is available and the hotel has a reasonable restaurant.

211 F4
Piazza Girolamo Savonarola, 18
05 78 75 72 62; www.albergoilmarzocco.it
Closed mid to end Nov

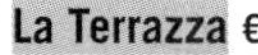

La Terrazza €

There may be cheaper private rooms in town, but this 2-star property is the best bet if you are looking for an inexpensive, clean hotel. It is centrally located on a quiet side street (with parking) that runs south from the church of San Francesco and just a few minutes' walk from Piazza Grande.

211 F4 Via Piè al Sasso, 16
05 78 75 74 40; www.laterrazzadi montepulciano.it

PIENZA

Il Chiostro di Pienza €€€

The superb 3-star hotel lies just off the main street and takes its name from the courtyard *(chiostro)* of the 15th-century convent from which it was converted. The communal areas and rooms are simple but elegant, with period furniture and tasteful fabrics. Many original features have been retained, notably wooden ceilings, brick vaults and odd patches of frescoes. Some rooms enjoy views of the countryside, and there is also a small garden area, gym, swimming pool and restaurant. Breakfast is included in the room price. You will need to book well ahead to secure one of the more lovely rooms.

211 F4
Corso Rossellino, 26 05 78 74 84 00;
www.relaisilchiostrodipienza.com

Sant'Anna in Camprena €€

Insider Tip

This *agriturismo* accommodation near Pienza is one of those places which are pure heaven on earth. There are a number of reasons for this – the former monastery itself, its wonderful location, the fantastic views from the more than 40 rooms, its magical garden, the friendly atmosphere and the cordial service. This is also what Anthony Minghella thought who shot the film *The English Patient* here.

211 F4 Località Sant'Anna in Camprena, Pienza 05 79 74 80 37, www.camprena.it

SORANO

Hotel della Fortezza €€

Beamed ceilings, tasteful antique furniture and modern bathrooms. This is how you could sum up the atmospheric hotel now to be found within the thick walls of Orsini Castle (*c.* 1550) that towers over the town since its careful restoration. The view from the windows is impressive indeed.

211 F2 Piazza Cairoli
05 64 63 20 10; www.fortezzahotel.it
Closed Jan and Feb

VAL D'ORCIA

Castello di Ripa d'Orcia €€

This hotel is built around a 13th-century *borgo* (fortified village). It also sits at the heart of some beautiful countryside, so peace and quiet are assured, and you can hike on marked trails that start right outside the walls. Rooms must be booked for two nights minimum, and the large, simply furnished apartments must be taken on a weekly basis. Meals are available. The nearest village is San Quirico d'Orcia, 7km (4mi) northeast.

211 E4 Via della Contea, 1, Ripa d'Orcia
05 77 89 73 76; www.castellodiripadorcia.it

Where to...
Eat and Drink

Prices
Expect to pay for a three-course meal for one with wine
€ under €26 **€€** €26–€52 **€€€**over €52

BAGNO VIGNONI

Restaurant La Parata €€
Housed in the annexe to the old carriage stop in the heart of the spa village, La Parata mixes traditional Tuscan ingredients with chef/owner Giancarlo Diodato's creative touches. The menu changes on a weekly basis, depending on what's in season, though local game features along with home-made pastas. The cosy dining room has a formal feel and there's a terraced garden for summer dining with views across the valley.
211 E4
Piazza del Moretto, 40
05 77 88 75 08
Thu–Tue 12:20–2:20, 7:30–9:30

CRETE SENESI

La Locanda del Castello €€
This is a delightful place to spend a long lazy lunchtime during your tour of the Crete, set in the heart of a tiny village on the southeastern flank of the area. Find an al-fresco table in the square or on the terrace at the rear and choose a few courses. The menu concentrates on local ingredients and dishes served without pretension but with care, matched with wines from Tuscan vineyards.
201 E4
San Giovanni d'Asso
05 77 80 29 39; www.lalocandadelcastello.com
Mon–Sat 12:30–3, 7:30–10, Sun 12:30–3. Closed mid-Jan to Feb

MONTALCINO

Fiaschetteria Italiana €
A local institution, this is the best café and bar in town, thanks to its fine 19th-century interior and central position on the main square (there are outside tables in summer). You can also buy local wine here by the glass or by the bottle.
211 E4 **Piazza del Popolo 6**
05 77 84 90 43; www.caffefiaschetteriaitaliana.com
Daily 7:30am–midnight. Closed Thu Nov–Feb

Taverna dei Barbi €€
This smart restaurant is annexed to a Brunello vineyard 5km (3mi) southeast of Montalcino. You can indulge in good local cooking and home-produced wines in a tasteful, rustic dining room dominated by a huge stone fireplace.
211 E4
Fattoria dei Barbi, La Croce, Località Podernovi **05 77 84 71 17; www.fattoriadeibarbi.it**
Thu–Tue 12:30–2:30, 7:30–10:30. Closed Tue linch, Wed (except Aug), Jan, and two weeks in July

Taverna Il Grappolo Blu €
The cool, stone-walled medieval interior of this informal restaurant has two small dining rooms with space for just 35 people, so be sure to book. The pasta dishes are especially good and also often innovative – watch for some fiery sauces with plenty of garlic and chillies – and the wine list is good.

Service, however, can be a bit slow at busy times, but it's usually worth the wait.
211 E4 Via Scale di Moglio, 1
05 77 84 71 50; www.grappoloblu.com
12–3, 7–10; Closed mid-Jan to mid-Feb

MONTE AMIATA

Silene €€

People come from miles around to eat at Silene, tucked away just outside Pescina, one of the tiny villages ringing the summit of Monte Amiata. The cooking makes use of local ingredients – mushrooms, asparagus, roebuck, boar, truffles, snails and much more. There's nothing rustic about the refined cooking, however, which is overseen by owner Roberto Rossi, who also produces excellent olive oils from his groves on the surrounding hills.
211 E3 Signed from Pescina, 4km (2.5mi) east of Seggiano
05 64 95 08 05; www.ilsilene.it
Tue–Sun 12:30–2:30, 7:30–9:30. Closed Sun dinner Nov–March

MONTEPULCIANO

Caffè Poliziano €

The best café in Montepulciano, with an art nouveau interior and good cakes, snacks and Vino Nobile wines by the glass. There is a more formal restaurant, Il Grifon d'Oro, for fuller meals.
211 F4
Via di Voltaia nel Corso, 27–29
05,78 75,86,15; www.caffepoliziano.it
Bar: daily 7pm–midnight; bar-restaurant: daily noon–3; restaurant: daily 7pm–10:30pm

La Chiusa €€€

The small village of Montefollonico is home to this former mill and award-winning hotel-restaurant. The meals are expensive, but outstanding. Dishes might include *crespelli ai funghi* (pancakes filled with mushrooms) or *agnello da latte al rosmarino* (tender lamb with rosemary). Booking is essential.
211 F4
Via della Madonnina, 88, Montefollonico
05 77 66 96 68; www.ristorantelachiusa.it
Daily 12:30–2:30, 7:30–10:30. Closed mid-Jan to mid-March

Osteria del Borgo €€

Located right on the Piazza Grande, the quality and service represent good value for money. Typically Tuscan dishes such as homemade *pici* pasta can be enjoyed outside on the terrace in summer.
211 F4 Via Ricci, 7
05 78 71 67 99; www.osteriadelborgo.it
Daily April–Oct; Closed Tue Nov–März

PIENZA

Latte di Luna €€

This family-run trattoria near the centre of the village has simple but appetizing food: try the daily specials or local *pici all'aglione* (pasta in garlic and tomato sauce). Be sure to book, especially in summer if you want to eat outdoors.
211 F4 Via San Carlo, 2–4
05 78 74 86 06
Wed–Mon noon–2:30, 7–9. Closed periods in Feb, early March and July

La Porta €/€€

Insider Tip

Take the road between Pienza and Montepulciano via Monticchiello for a lunch stop at this excellent *osteria*. It is small, so book ahead, especially for a table on the terrace. The cooking is regional, with staples such as *ribollita* and *zuppa di cecci* (chickpea soup), but there are more unusual dishes such as *taglioni al piccione* (fine pasta strands with pigeon) and roast meats such as *faraona* (guineafowl).
211 F4 Via del Piano, 1, Monticchiello
95 78 75 51 63; www.osterialaporta.it
Fri–Wed 12:20–2:30, 7:30–9:30. Closed early Jan–early Feb

SOVANA

Taverna Etrusca €€/€€€
A simple but beautiful interior in a 13th-century building provides the elegant setting for this restaurant. The menu concentrates on locally produced and seasonal ingredients. Presentation and service are crisp and contemporary rather than country casual and rustic, combining the best of old-world and 21st-century Tuscany.
211 E2 Piazza del Pretorio, 16
05 64 61 41 93
Thu–Tue 12:30–2:30, 7:30–10:30

Where to... Shop

MONTALCINO

Montalcino is full of wine and gourmet food shops. One of the cheapest is the Co-op supermarket off Via Ricasoli, and one of the nicest the **Fiaschetteria Italiana** (➤ 156).

One of the best-known wine producers, the **Fattoria dei Barbi** (tel: 05 77 84 11 11; www.fattoriadeibarbi.it) is open to visitors. It is situated 8 km (5mi) southeast of Montalcino.

MONTEPULCIANO

Contucci (Via del Teatro, 1; tel: 05 78 75 70 06; www.contucci.it; open daily) is a central outlet for Vino Nobile. The **Enoteca Oinochóe** (Via di Voltaia nel Corso, 82; tel: 05 78 75 75 24) sells wine by leading local producers. For olive oil, visit Piazza Pasquino 9.

PIENZA

Pienza is renowned for its ***pecorino*** (sheep's cheese) – check the label showing where it was made. One good shop is **La Cornucopia** (Piazza Martiri della Libertà 2, tel: 05 78 74 81 50; www.emporiofattorie.com), or you can visit local producers such as **Silvana Cugusi**, 10km (6mi) away off the SS146 towards Montepulciano at Via della Boccia, 8 (tel: 05 78 75 75 58; www.caseificiocugusi.it).

Where to... Go Out

MONTALCINO

The start of the hunting season is celebrated with the **Torneo dell' Apertura della Caccia** (second Sun in Aug). A similar event is the **Sagra del Tordo** (last Sun in Oct). A weekly market is held on Friday morning under the castle walls.

MONTEPULCIANO

The key festival is the **Bravio delle Botti** (last Sun in Aug), a barrel-rolling race between the town's eight districts, with processions and banquets. The **Feast of the Assumption** (14–16 Aug) is celebrated by the *Bruscello*, a series of concerts in the town's squares.

PIENZA

The **Fiera** (first Sun in Sept) is a celebration of the town's cheese and includes a medieval street market and fair.

VAL D'ORCIA

Castiglione d'Orcia, Montalcino, Pienza, Radicofani and San Quirico host the **International Festival of Montalcino and Val d'Orcia** (July–Aug).

Northern Tuscany

Little Treats

Street food *all'Italiano*

The crisp pizzas made at Da Felice (Via Buia, 12) show why fast food chains have such a tough time in **Lucca** (➤ 168).

Throw out the nets

Roll up your sleeves and help out at Mare Nostrum in **Viareggio** (➤ 178, Piazzale Don S. Politi).

Naughty but nice

Are the sweet temptations sold at the *pasticceria* Caflisch in **Carrara** (➤ 178, Via Roma, 2) *really* addictive?

Northern Tuscany

Getting Your Bearings

Northern Tuscany does not have the many small historic villages and hill towns of southern Tuscany, nor as much of the pretty pastoral countryside found elsewhere – the landscapes here are dominated by forested and marble-streaked mountains – but in Lucca and Pisa it has two cities that stand comparison with any in Italy.

Lucca is unmissable – an urbane and immediately likeable city. Pisa is far less charming, but in the Leaning Tower and its surrounding buildings it has one of the most beautiful medieval ensembles in Italy. The two cities are only a few kilometres apart, but Lucca is by far the better place to stay.

Whereas Pisa was badly bombed during World War II, leaving much of the city with a modern architectural veneer, Lucca is almost completely unspoiled. Clasped within a ring of walls, its grid of cobbled streets dating back to Roman times is thickly scattered with Romanesque churches, museums, galleries, gardens and, in the words of the American novelist Henry James, "everything that makes for ease, for plenty, for beauty, for interest and good example." Lucca is also a city in which it is a pleasure to wander at random or to join the locals and ride around by bicycle. There are several rental outlets around town.

Pisa, on the other hand, is a much larger city and one that concentrates its historic treats in one or two key areas. Chief of these is the Campo dei Miracoli a large grassy piazza that provides the stage not only for the famous Leaning Tower, but also for the less celebrated but almost equally beautiful cathedral and Baptistry. Elsewhere, the city's charms are confined to one or two galleries and isolated churches.

The imposing mountains of the Garfagnana

TOP 10

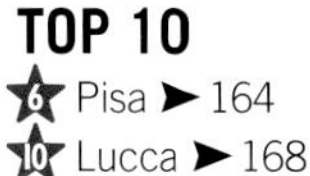

- 6 Pisa ➤ 164
- 10 Lucca ➤ 168

At Your Leisure

- 47 Viareggio ➤ 178
- 48 Carrara ➤ 178
- 49 Garfagnana ➤ 179
- 50 Ville & Giardini ➤ 180
- 51 Pistoia ➤ 182
- 52 Vinci ➤ 182

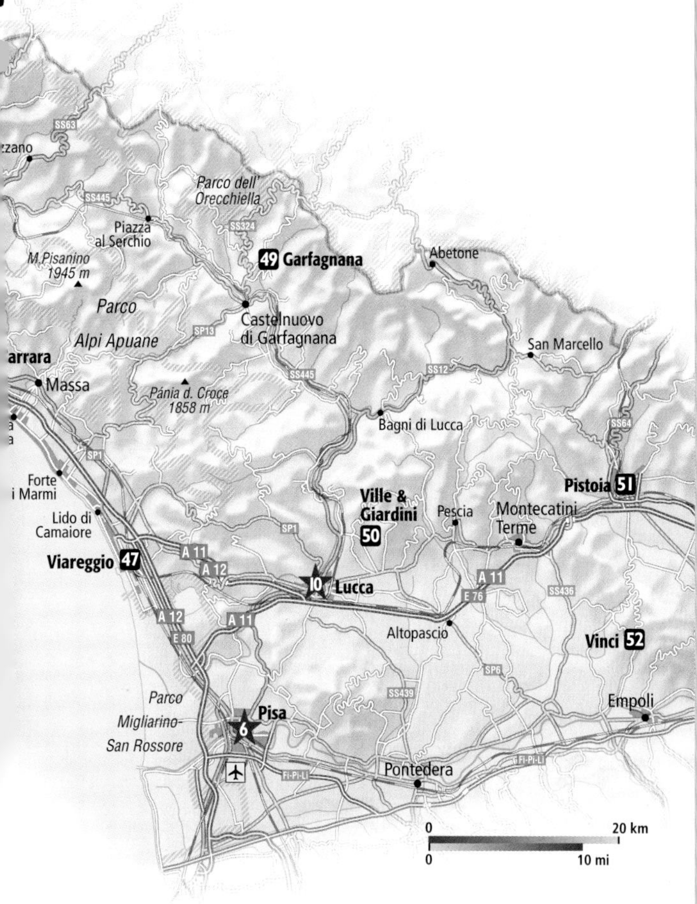

Around Lucca lies a medley of villas and gardens, while to the north is the Garfagnana region, defined by the Alpi Apuane mountains noted for Carrara marble mines, and the wild, forested slopes of the Orecchiella. For those who fancy an afternoon on a beach, Viareggio is a traditional seaside resort, and Pistoia, one of Tuscany's least-visited historic towns, offers more in the way of art and architecture, while tiny Vinci is renowned as the birthplace of Renaissance genius Leonardo da Vinci.

Three Perfect Days

If you're not quite sure where to begin your travels, this itinerary recommends three practical and enjoyable days out in Northern Tuscany, taking in some of the best places to see. For more information see the main entries (➤ 164–182) .

Day 1

Morning

Travel to – or wake up in – 10 **Lucca** (➤ 168), booking a hotel for two or three nights (➤ 183). Visit the **tourist office** (➤ 45) and then walk to Piazza San Michele to see the church of San Michele in Foro and Casa di Puccini (➤ 168). The route to the cathedral takes you past the Cioccolateria Caniparoli.

Lunch

Have lunch at Da Leo (➤ 185), or buy a picnic to eat on the town walls.

Afternoon

Continue exploring the eastern and northern parts of Lucca, visiting **Piazza del Mercato**, **Museo Nazionale di Villa Guinigi**, **Casa Guinigi** and the churches of **Santa Maria Forisportam**, **San Frediano** and **San Pietro Somaldi**. In the late afternoon, explore the shops on Via Fillungo. Have dinner at Buca di Sant'Antonio (➤ 184).

Day 2

Morning

If you didn't do so yesterday, spend part of the morning exploring Lucca's **walls** on foot or by bike. Then drive or take a train to 6 **Pisa** (➤ 164), where you should aim to spend the rest of the day. Head first for the Campo dei Miracoli to see the **Leaning Tower**, **Baptistry** (left)and **Duomo**. See the **Museo dell'Opera del Duomo,** with its renowned sculptures by Giovanni Pisano, now or after lunch. If you like markets, note that you'll need to to visit Pisa's main **Mercato Vettovaglie** (➤ 186) when you arrive, as it closes in the afternoon.

Lunch

Have lunch at Osteria in Domo (➤ 185) south of the Campo.

Afternoon

Visit the Museo dell'Opera and admire Piazza dei Cavalieri (above) before exploring the **church of Santa Maria della Spina** and one or both of Pisa's **main museums** (► 166). Break for tea, coffee or a snack in Pasticceria Salza (► 185). If you want to shop, head for Borgo Stretto (► 186) after about 4pm, when many shops re-open after the afternoon break. Return to Lucca for dinner, or for a treat stop at the Gazebo restaurant at the Locanda l'Elisa hotel on the road between the two cities.

Day 3

Spend the morning exploring more of Lucca or drive out of the city to see some of the **50 villas and gardens** in the countryside nearby (► 180). Or visit **51 Pistoia** (► 182) and **52 Vinci** (► 182), which would leave you well placed for reaching Florence or Siena. Alternatively, devote the day to the **49 Garfagnana** (► 179), driving up the Serchio valley, seeing the Orecchiella mountains before crossing the Alpi Apuane. You could even see **48 Carrara** and its marble mines (► 178) or spend an hour or two on the beach at **47 Viareggio** (► 178).

49 Garfagnana
48 Carrara
Ville & Giardini 50
Pistoia 51
Viareggio 47
10 Lucca
Vinci 52
6 Pisa

Pisa

Pisa is so closely associated with one dramatic building – the Leaning Tower – that it's all too easy to overlook the city's glorious cathedral and Baptistry, not to mention an idiosyncratic little church, an evocative medieval piazza and its trio of art-filled museums.

For centuries Pisa was one of Italy's greatest cities. An Etruscan and then a Roman colony, it prospered throughout the Middle Ages, reaching the peak of its power in the 11th to 12th centuries, when its maritime prowess yielded the riches that would help finance the Leaning Tower and many other buildings. Naval defeats and the loss of its harbour to silt then led to a waning influence and after 1406, when Florence assumed control of the city, it became little more than a centre of science and learning.

Campo dei Miracoli

Today's visitors are denied much of the city's former glory, however, for a great deal of the old city was destroyed by World War II bombing in 1944. Pisa is therefore something of an anomaly in a region famed for its medieval patina, as post-war rebuilding means that both the city's suburbs and much of what should be its historical core have a bland, modern appearance. The great exception is the **Campo dei Miracoli** (Field of Miracles), a grassy sward that survived the bombs and is home not only to the celebrated Leaning Tower, but also to the Duomo (cathedral), Baptistry and a medieval cemetery, the Camposanto.

Decisive intervention by scientists and engineers during the 1990s means that the **Torre pendente** (Leaning Tower) – which had threatened to collapse – now appears to be safe. The fame of the tower has long overshadowed the

Pisa's Duomo, flanked by the famous Leaning Tower

The building of the circular Baptistry was begun in 1152

Baptistry and Duomo, which rank among Tuscany's most outstanding medieval buildings.

The **cathedral** was begun in 1064, well before the cathedrals of Florence (1296) and Siena (1179), a hint as to the relative wealth of Pisa at the time. Its ornate marble-striped exterior, in particular the tiny columns and arcades of the façade, provided the model for similar Pisan-Romanesque churches across central Italy, notably in Lucca, Siena and Florence. The style developed in the wake of Pisa's growing trade links with the Orient, which brought the city into contact with the architecture of the Middle East and eastern Mediterranean.

Before entering the cathedral, take time to admire the **Portale di San Ranieri** (1180), a door that once provided the building's main entrance but which now lies behind the right (south) transept facing the Leaning Tower. Its bronze panels portray stories from the *New Testament,* while its architrave is made up of Roman friezes and reliefs salvaged from an earlier building dating from the second century.

Sadly, many of the cathedral's interior treasures were destroyed by fire in 1595, though at least two masterpieces survived: one, the apse mosaic of *Christ in Majesty* (1302) by Cimabue, the second, a superlative carved **pulpit** (1302–11) by Giovanni Pisano, one of several medieval Pisan artists whose work influenced Italian sculpture for centuries.

The work of Giovanni and another of these sculptors, Nicola Pisano, adorns the circular **Baptistry,** the beautiful circular building a short distance from the cathedral. Both men were responsible for much of the delicate carving that embellishes the building's exterior, added between 1270 and 1297, though it is the work of Nicola, in the shape of another breathtaking pulpit (1260), that holds centre stage inside the Baptistry's largely plain interior. A sculptor from northern Italy, Guido Bigarelli da Como,

Detail from Nicola Pisano's beautiful baptistry pulpit

was responsible for the other main highlight, an inlaid font dating from 1246.

Some idea of how close Pisa came to losing these treasures in 1944 can be gained by visiting the **Camposanto**, a medieval cemetery contained within a large Gothic cloister on the Campo's northern edge. In its day, the cloister was decorated with one of Tuscany's most important fresco cycles, but an incendiary bomb destroyed all but a handful of the precious frescoes. One or two panels survived, along with a variety of carved tombs and headstones from different eras. Various *sinopie*, the rough sketches often found beneath frescoes, were also salvaged, and are now displayed in the **Museo delle Sinopie** on the southern side of the Campo.

Pisa's Museums

Other items saved from the bombing, or otherwise removed from the buildings of the Campo, are housed in the **Museo dell'Opera del Duomo**, in the square's southeast corner.

Pisa's other principal museum, the **Museo Nazionale di San Matteo**, is 1.5km (1mi) east of Campo dei Miracoli.

INSIDER INFO

- If you are **flying** in or out of Pisa (➤ 41), consider visiting the city's sights – which can be seen in a couple of hours – on the day you arrive or depart.
- An easy to find pay-and-display car park is at Via C.S. Cammeo 51. From here it is just a 5-minute walk to the Campo dei Miracoli. One option is to visit the city from Lucca (➤ 168) by **train**. It's a 15-minute walk from the station to the Campo dei Miracoli, or you can take a taxi or city bus No. 1 (LAM red shuttle) from the station forecourt.
- To **pre-book tickets** (compulsory) to the **Leaning Tower**, visit www.opapisa.it (at least 16 days in advance) or go to the ticket office next to the tourist office. For further information call 05 04 22 91. Tickets cannot be booked by phone.

If you want to walk here, head first for Piazza dei Cavalieri, pausing in Piazza Vettovaglie, home to a lively market held every morning except Sunday. Via Dini leads from Piazza dei Cavalieri to Borgo Stretto, where you'll find Pisa's most interesting shops. A left turn at the street's southern end by the River Arno takes you along Lungarno Mediceo to Piazza San Matteo and the museum. Among its great works are a bronze bust of San Lussorio by Donatello and fine paintings by Masaccio, Simone Martini, Fra Angelico and Gentile da Fabriano. More paintings, ceramics and decorative arts are in the **Museo Nazionale di Palazzo Reale**, farther west.

Just across the river, on Lungarno Gambacorti, stands the 14th-century **Santa Maria della Spina**. It was built by a merchant who had obtained a 'thorn' *(spina)* from Christ's Crown of Thorns, hence its name.

TAKING A BREAK

Pasticceria Salza on Borgo Stretto, is ideal for lunch, or for a more formal meal try the **Osteria dei Cavalieri** (► 185).

Duomo, Baptistry, Museo dell'Opera, Camposanto
206 C2 · Campo dei Miracoli · 0 50 83 50 11; www.duomo.pisa.it; Leaning Tower visits: 0 50 56 05 47; www.opapisa.it
Tower: April–Oct daily 9–7; Nov, Feb 9:40–5:40; Dec, Jan 10–5; March 9–6. Duomo: Apr–Oct daily 10–7; Nov–Feb 10–12:45, 2–5; March 10–6. Baptistry, Camposanto, Museo dell'Opera: Apr–Sept daily 8–8; Oct 9–7; Nov–Feb 10–5; March 9–6
Tower: €18; cathedral: free; Baptistry, Camposanto, Museo dell'Opera: €5 each (combined ticket: €8)

Museo Nazionale di San Matteo
196 C2 · Piazza San Matteo
0 50 54 18 65 or 05 09 71 13 95
Tue–Sat 8:30–7:30, Sun 8:30–1
€5; Combined ticket with Palazzo Reale: €8

Museo Nazionale di Palazzo Reale
196 C2 · Piazza Carrara, Lungarno Pacinotti, 46
0 50 92 65 39 · Tue–Fri 9–2:30, Sat 9–1 (but hours may vary)
€5; Combined ticket with Museo Nazionale: €8

A fresco at the Camposanto was painted in the wake of the Black Death in 1348

10 Lucca

Lucca is the most intimate and charming of Tuscany's cities, a civilised and untroubled backwater where neither the pace of life nor the appearance of the medieval streets and squares seem to have changed over the centuries. Preserved within a redoubtable oval of walls, the city is full of exquisite churches, fascinating museums and galleries, and plenty of quiet corners and lanes bedecked with flowers.

Medieval buildings on Piazza San Michele

Piazza San Michele

Lucca's heart is Piazza San Michele, the site of the old Roman forum, or **foro**, hence the name of San Michele in Foro, the beautiful **Romanesque church** at the piazza's centre. The church was begun in 1070 but never finished, the result of a financial shortfall caused by the vast sums of money lavished on its façade. One of Italy's most dazzling church exteriors, it is an intricate medley of tiny loggias, blind arcades and countless decorated columns; the decoration and distinctive striped marble walls are repeated in churches around the city.

The architectural style was borrowed from Pisa – it is often known as Pisan-Romanesque – and developed during the course of Pisa's trading links with the Orient (➤ 165). Few of these exotic influences found their way into the church's austere interior, however: the only outstanding work of art is a late 15th-century painting by Filippino Lippi of *Saints Jerome, Sebastian, Roch and Helena* (at the end of the south nave).

A few moments' walk from Piazza San Michele is the **Casa di Puccini**, the birthplace of Giacomo Puccini (1858–1924), the composer who wrote operas such as *Tosca,*

A statue of the composer Giacomo Puccini is on display outside the Casa di Puccini

La Bohème and *Madame Butterfly*. His former home is now given over to a music academy and a small museum filled with artefacts connected with the composer. It was re-opened to the public in autumn 2012 following a thorough renovation. A couple of streets to the west, on Via San Paolino, stands the Baroque church of San Paolino, unremarkable save for the fact that Puccini served as organist here in his youth.

From Piazza San Michele you should head south on either Via Vittorio Veneto or Via Beccheria to **Piazza Napoleone**, named after Napoleon Bonaparte, who presented the city to his sister, Elisa Baciocchi, during his campaigns in Italy at the beginning of the 19th century. The large building on the square's western flank is the **Palazzo della Provincia** (1578–1728), erstwhile home of Lucca's ruling councils. Behind the palace rises San Romano, a medieval church that has been under restoration for years. A short walk east of Piazza Napoleone brings you to Piazza San Martino, the stage for Lucca's magnificent cathedral, the **Duomo di San Martino**.

The Duomo di San Martino

The cathedral was begun in 1060 on or close to the site of several earlier churches, though work on its glorious façade, a close facsimile of San Michele, was only completed around 1261. The façade's squashed appearance – the third of its three arches is decidedly smaller than its neighbours – came about because it had to be squeezed alongside the bell-tower to its right, the lower half of which (built originally as a defensive redoubt) was already in place when work on the façade began.

The Archangel Michael crowns the façade of San Michele in Foro

Duomo Santa Martino

Lucca Cathedral houses several unique masterpieces: the tomb of Ilaria del Carretto, an intricately worked marble sculpture that looks like porcelain, Tintoretto's *Last Supper* of 1592 and a cedarwood crucifix, the 'Volto Santo', that is reputed to have been made by St Nicodemus with the help of a few angels.

❶ **Portico:** In the mid 13th century Lombard sculptors decorated the portico with reliefs.

❷ ***St Martin on Horseback*:** This sculpture of around 1300 depicts the saint to whom the cathedral is dedicated, after Charlemagne's defeat of the Lombards in 774.

❸ **Interior:** Coloured marble and several artworks of importance can be seen inside the cathedral. These include Alessandro Allori's *Presentation of the Virgin in the Temple* in the right aisle.

❹ **Sacristy:** The sarcophagus of Ilaria del Carretto dei Marchesi di Savona, Paolo Guinigi's wife, who died in 1405, can be found in the sacristy accessed from the right aisle, as can Domenico Ghirlandaio's altarpiece, *Sacra Conversazione*, painted in vibrant colours.

❺ **Important altar paintings:** Federico Zuccari's *Adoration of the Magi* (1595) and Tintoretto's *Last Supper* (1592) hang over the second and third altars respectively on the right-hand side.

❻ **Tomb of Pietro da Noceto:** It is considered to be Matteo Civitali's first work, completed at the end of the 15th century after tombs in Santa Croce in Florence.

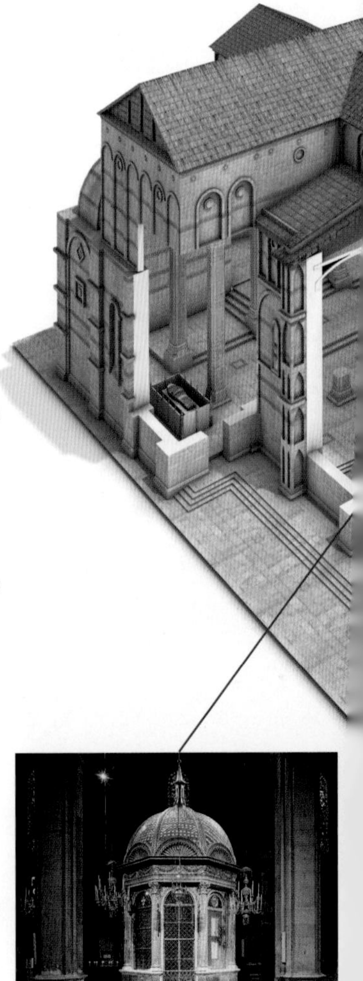

The main attraction in the cathedral is the Volto Santo *tempietto*, a marble temple in which the wooden crucifix carved by St Nicodemus is housed. According to legend the crucifix was brought to Lucca from the Orient in the 8th century.

One of the most breath-taking works of art in Lucca Cathedral: *The Annunciation* (1597) by Giovanni Battista Paggi

The exterior's most important works of art are the **13th-century reliefs** on and around the three principal doors. Noted Pisan sculptor Nicola Pisano was responsible for the carvings on the left-hand door – an *Annunciation, Nativity, Adoration of the Magi,* and for the *Deposition* in the lunette above the door. The carvings between the doors are attributed to Guidetto da Como, the architect responsible for much of the façade: they portray episodes from the Life of St Martin (San Martino) and a series of narrative scenes depicting the labours of the Twelve Months of the Year.

The cathedral's **interior** has some equally notable works of art. One of the most eye-catching is the **Tempietto** (1482–85), an octagonal chapel midway down the nave, designed by local sculptor Matteo Civitali (1436–1502) to house the *Volto Santo* (Holy Face), a cedar-wood Crucifix reputed to be an exact likeness of Christ carved by Nicodemus, an eyewitness to the Crucifixion. Scholars believe it is a 13th-century copy of an 11th-century copy of an original 8th-century statue, but pilgrims still venerate the image.

Civitali was responsible for other interesting works around the cathedral, notably the **Altare di San Regolo** (1484) or

The cathedral's distinctive façade with its rows of arches

Three panels from the *Cycle of the Months* between the cathedral's main portals

Tomb of St Regolus, an early bishop of Lucca (on the wall right of the high altar), and the Tomb of Pietro da Noceto (1472), secretary to Pope Niccolò V. The **Tomb of Illariaof del Carretto** (1407) is a sublime funerary monument by the Sienese sculptor Jacopo della Quercia, which portrays the body of Illaria, wife of Paolo Guinigi, member of a dynasty that ruled medieval Lucca for decades. The dog at her feet is a symbol of her faithfulness. The tomb is housed in the sacristy off the south aisle.

The sacristy admission also admits you to the **Museo della Cattedrale** on Piazza Antelminelli, home to a collection of paintings, sculptures and religious artefacts, and the church of **Santi Giovanni e Reparata**. Excavations in this church in the northwest corner of Piazza San Martino have uncovered remnants of Roman buildings, parts of Lucca's first medieval cathedral, and two fifth- and eighth-century baptisteries.

The Walls and East of the Town

The streets near the cathedral are a convenient point from which to climb up to Lucca's tree-lined **walls** (1544–1645), part or all of which you should walk or cycle along at some point during your visit. The walls were built to counter the threat from Florence: in the event, they never had to be defended in earnest and were converted into the present-day promenade in the 19th century.

From the cathedral you can explore Lucca's eastern fringes, which contain a small assortment of worthwhile sights. The first is **Santa Maria Forisportam** (St Mary Outside the Gates), an unfinished 13th-century Pisan-Romanesque church which takes its name from the fact that it once lay outside the limits of the Roman and medieval city.

To its southeast lies the **Giardino Botanico**, Lucca's pretty and peaceful botanical garden, while to the east on or close to Via Santa Croce and Via Elisa is a **quartet of small churches**: SS Trinità, San Ponziano, San Gervasio and San

Michelotto. The last stands close to the entrance of the Villa Bottini, also known as the Villa Buonvisi, whose Italianate gardens are worth a visit.

North of the villa is the **Museo Nazionale di Villa Guinigi**, a major city museum housed in a palace built for the Guinigi family in 1413. It has a large collection of paintings, sculpture, textiles, Roman and Etruscan archaeological displays, silverware and works by the painter Fra Bartolommeo and the sculptor Matteo Civitali. Look out, too, for the lovely cathedral choir stalls (1529) decorated with inlaid wood images of Lucca. A few steps west of the entrance to the museum on Via della Quarquonia lies **San Francesco**, a huge 13th-century church noteworthy only for a few frescoes.

A more captivating church lies a little farther west, the Romanesque **San Pietro Somaldi**. It dates from the 12th century, but was built over a Lombard chapel raised as early as AD763. Walk south from here and pick up Via Guinigi, one of Lucca's most evocative old streets, and less than 200m (220 yards) from San Pietro stands the **Casa Guinigi**, another rambling palace built for the Guinigi family. Its key feature is a medieval tower, the 44.25m (145ft) **Torre Guinigi**, unmistakable by virtue of the holm oaks growing from its battlements. It is well worth climbing the tower for some wonderful views over the medieval rooftops. In Lucca there were once 250 such towers.

Piazza Anfiteatro to San Frediano

Retrace your steps north on Via Guinigi and turn left on Via Antonio Mordini and then first right on the little alley that leads into **Piazza Anfiteatro**. The piazza's oval

Piazza Anfiteatro is built over an old Roman amphitheatre

The fine 12th-century mosaic of the Ascension at San Frediano

shape corresponds exactly to the outline of the Roman amphitheatre which once stood here. Much of the stone from the arena was ransacked in the 12th century to build Lucca's churches and palaces, but fragments of the structure stillexist embedded in the piazza's buildings.

From the square's northern edge it is just a few steps across Lucca's main street, Via Fillungo, to **San Frediano** (1112–47), the third most important church in town after San Michele and San Martino. The façade is unusual for its 13th-century mosaic of the Ascension, while the interior is distinguished by a 12th-century carved font, the **Fontale Lustrale**. Behind these is a chapel containing the uncorrupted body of St Zita, a 13th-century Lucca-born maid who became the patron saint of servants. Also admire the fine frescoes (1508–09) on a variety of subjects by the little-known Amico Aspertini in the **Cappella di Sant'Agostino**.

Via Fillungo takes you south from San Frediano back to Lucca's heart, but by following a more circuitous route you can take in other sights around the north and west. The closest of these to San Frediano is **Palazzo Pfanner** (1660), where the residence and 18th-century gardens are open to the public.

Almost alongside are the 14th-century church of Sant' Agostino and the chapel of San Salvatore in Muro. Farther west is the **Museo e Pinacoteca Nazionale di Palazzo Mansi**, a rambling museum which makes up for a lack of genuine masterpieces by the richness and variety of its tapestries, fabrics, carpets, *objets d'art* and fine furniture.

The Fontale Lustrale, the 12th-century font, in San Frediano

TAKING A BREAK

People are happy to queue down the street for **Amedeo Giusti's** pastries and *focaccia* (Via Santa Lucia, 18).

San Michele

207 D3 Piazza San Michele No phone
Mid-March to Oct daily 9–noon, 3–6; Nov to mid-March 9–noon, 3–5. Closed during services Free

Casa di Puccini

207 D3 Corte San Lorenzo, 9, Via di Poggio, 30
05 83 58 40 28 April–Oct Tue–Sun 10–6, Nov–March 11–5 €7

INSIDER INFO

- The best way to visit Lucca is by **train** – the station is a short walk from the city walls. If you arrive by car, you may find a parking space at Piazzale Giuseppe Verdi. Otherwise, park outside the walls and walk to the centre.
- Insider Tip: It's worth **renting a bike** in Lucca: unusually for Italy, which is devoted to the motor car, locals largely get around on bicycles and you can follow suit, to explore the town and to ride around the ramparts. There are several rental outlets around the city, including the visitor centre and Piazza Santa Maria.
- The oldest **comic festival** in Europe is held in Lucca in October. The **Museo Nazionale del Fumetto** with which it is associated is open all year (Piazza San Romano, 4; www.museonazionaledelfumetto.com; Tue–Sun 10–6; €4).

Duomo di San Martino

207 D3 Piazza San Martino 05 83 49 05 30
Cathedral: mid-March to Oct Mon–Fri 9:30–5:45, Sat 9:30–6:45, Sun 9:30–10:45, 2–6; Nov to mid-March Mon–Fri 9:30–4:45, Sat 9:30–6:45, Sun 9:30–10:45, 2–5
Cathedral: free; Sacristy: €3; Combined ticket with Museo della Cattedrale, Sacristy and Santi Giovanni e Reparata: €7

Museo della Cattedrale

207 D3 Piazza Antelminelli, 5 05 83 49 05 30
Mid-March to Oct daily 10–6; Nov to mid-March Mon–Fri 10–2, Sat, Sun 10–5 (same hours for Santi Giovanni e Reparata) €4

Museo Nazionale di Villa Guinigi

207 D3 Via della Quarquonia 05 83 49 60 33 Tue–Sat 8:30–7:30, Sun 8:30–1:30 €4; Combined ticket with Palazzo Mansi: €6.50

Torre Guinigi

207 D3 Via Sant'Andrea 05 83 58 30 86 June–Sept daily 9:30–7:30; Apr–May 9:30–6:30; March, Oct 9:30–5:30; Nov–Feb 9:30–4:30 €4

San Frediano

207 D3 Piazza San Frediano Mid-March to Oct daily 9–noon, 3–6; Nov to mid-March 9–12, 3–5. Closed during services

Palazzo Pfanner

207 D3 Via degli Asili, 33 05 83 95 40 29 Apr–Oct daily 10–6
Palazzo or gardens: €4 each. Combined ticket: €6

Museo e Pinacoteca Nazionale di Palazzo Mansi

207 D3 Via Galli Tassi, 43 C0 58 35 55 70 DTue–Sat 8:30–7, Sun 8:30–2
€4; Combined ticket with Villa Guinigi: €6.50

Statues line the steps of the elaborate gardens of Palazzo Pfanner

At Your Leisure

47 Viareggio

The coastal town of Viareggio does have things to see – a handful of art nouveau buildings on the palm-lined seafront for a start – but virtually no one comes here for the sights. Rather they are here for the **beach**, which is one of the best on a tract of coast known as the Riviera di Versilia that stretches north to the Ligurian border. Much of this coastline is lacklustre or worse – the chic resort of Forte dei Marmi is an honourable exception – which is why the ordered, late 19th-century elegance of Viareggio is so attractive. Many of the visitors here are Florentines escaping the city for a day or two – the resort is a little over an hour by road or rail from Tuscany's landlocked capital. There is plenty of sand on the long, broad beach, but it is divided up between *stabilimenti bagnari* (bathing concessions), which means you have to pay to use the beach. This means that the sand is groomed daily and kept clean, and it also allows you to use sunloungers, showers, changing rooms and other useful facilities. Viareggio is also crammed with inexpensive hotels, as well as numerous pizzerias, fish restaurants, shops and nightlife.

206 C3

The art deco Bagno Balena in Viareggio was built in 1928

Tourist Office
Viale Carducci, 10
05 84 96 22 33; www.luccaturismo.it
Mon, Fri, Sat 9–2, Tue, Thu 9–2, 3–7, closed Sun

48 Carrara

Carrara has long been synonymous with one thing – marble. The town's distinctive ivory- and milky-grey coloured stone has been quarried from the nearby Alpi Apuane for thousands of years, and been prized by sculptors from Michelangelo – the stone for the statue of *David* came from here – to Henry Moore.

It is well worth driving the short distance from the town to see some of the quarries and the staggering scale of the mining operation. Platforms at the roadside enable you to watch operations during working hours.

Some of the most accessible quarries are at **Colonnata**, 8km (5mi) east of the town, but those at **Fantiscritti** (5km/3mi to the north-east on a twisting road via Miseglia) are more impressive. Another twisting road, the 446d to the north, offers sensational views, particularly where the road cuts eastward to climb to Campo Cecina at over 1,500m (4,920ft).

Unlike its near neighbour to the south, **Massa**, another marble town, Carrara is an attractive place in its own right. At its hill-encircled heart is **Piazza Alberica**, a gracious

Whole hillsides of marble have been taken from quarries near Carrara

square flanked by pretty coloured medieval houses; the 11th- to 14th-century Pisan-Romanesque Duomo is a few moments' walk to the northeast in Piazza del Duomo.
206 B4

Tourist Office
Via le XX Settembre, Loc. Stadio Carrara
05 85 84 41 36; www.aptmassacarrara.it
Daily 9–4

49 The Garfagnana

The Garfagnana is the name given to a region to the north of Lucca. It centres on the valley of the River Serchio, which divides two beautiful sets of mountains: to its west rise the Alpi Apuane, a rugged and spectacular range of upland meadows, fast-flowing rivers and jagged peaks (the highest point is Pania di Croce at 1,858m/6,094ft). To the east lie the forested and more rounded slopes of the Orecchiella – less spectacular to look at, but still no less wild, beautiful or lofty (the highest point is Monte Prato at 2,053m/6,733ft). Both areas are protected nature parks *(parchi naturali)*.

The valley and the mountains are well worth exploring if you have a car. If you don't have transport, then a quaint railway runs from Lucca up the valley and through the mountains to Aulla (connections to La Spezia) near the Tuscan border with Liguria. You could sit back on the train and admire the scenery as far as Piazza al Serchio, then catch a return train to Lucca. **Insider Tip**

If you're driving up the valley, it's as well to know that the first 20km (12.5mi) or so from Lucca are fairly uninspiring – only beyond the village of Borgo a Mozzano does the scenery begin to improve. You might detour slightly to visit Bagni di Lucca, a quiet but elegant 19th-century spa 27km (16.5mi) from Lucca that has played host to visitors such as Lord Byron, Shelley and Robert and Elizabeth Barrett Browning. The best detour, however, is to Barga, a pretty hill village 5km (3mi) from the valley road that has a wonderful 10th-century cathedral.

Castelnuovo di Garfagnana, 14km (8.5mi) farther up the valley, is the region's largest town, and is best used as a departure point for drives into the mountains to the

The thermal springs found at Bagni di Lucca were well known in Etruscan and Roman times

east and west. If you have time, almost any minor road has its scenic rewards, but a good loop into the Orecchiella takes you on the minor road to the north (with sensational views en route) to the hamlet of San Pellegrino in Alpe (1,524m/5,000ft), where there is an excellent folk museum, the **Museo Etnografico Provinciale**. From here the road climbs to 1,529m (5,016ft) at Foce dei Radici and then curves back to Castelnuovo via Castiglione di Garfagnana (a total round-trip of 50km/31mi). To enjoy a scenic taste of the Alpi Apuane, take the minor road west over the mountains, either to Massa or Seravezza.

Both the Alpi Apuane and Orecchiella are laced with marked hiking trails, though you should note that many of the better walks in the Apuane start from trailheads in villages such as Levigliani on the western side of the mountains.

Unlike much of Tuscany, there are also plenty of large-scale maps for walking available locally. For more information, contact the tourist office in Lucca (► 45) or park centres in Castelnuovo for the Alpi Apuane (Piazza delle Erbe, 1; tel: 05 83 64 42 42) or, for the Orecchiella, the isolated centre 7km (4mi) north of the hamlet of Corfino on the minor road to Sillano (tel: 05 83 61 90 98 or 05 83 61 90 02).

207 D4

Museo Etnografico Provinciale
Via del Voltone, 14 · 05 83 64 90 72
April–May Tue–Sun 10–1, 2–4:30, June–Sept Tue–Sun 10–1, 2–6:30, Oct–March Tue–Fri 9:30–1, Sat, Sun 9:30–1, 2–4:30 · €2.50

50 Ville & Giardini

Insider Tip

The countryside around Lucca has many houses and grounds open to the public. The partly 16th-century villa, much altered since the 1850s, plays host to a number of musical performances during the summer months, held in the outdoor Box Hedge Theatre.

One of the most sumptuous is the **Villa Reale**, a 14th-century villa about 14km (8.5mi) northeast of Lucca. Only the gardens are open to the public. The grounds were mostly laid out in the 17th century, but modified later in the 19th century by Elisa Baciocchi, the sister of Napoleon Bonaparte.

Just 200m (220 yards) away is a lesser but still charming villa, the **Villa Grabau**, where both the grounds and ground floor of the building are open to the public. Of more note is the **Villa Torrigiani**, or **Villa Camigliano**, about 8km (5mi) east of Marlia, a 16th-century villa with Baroque and Rococo gardens dating from a later period, created for the then owner, the Luccan ambassador to France who was influenced by Le Notre, designer of the gardens at Versailles.

Just 2km (1.5mi) away is the **Villa Mansi**, 11km (7mi) northeast of Lucca. The 16th-century villa is distinguished by a statue-covered façade, which was added by the Mansi family when they bought the property in the early 1700s, while the grounds are a combination of English-style parkland and Italianate gardens. For more information: www.villeepalazzilucchesi.it.

The Baroque gardens of Villa Torrigiani

207 D3

Villa Reale
Via Fraga Atta, Marlia
0 58 33 01 08 or 0 53 83 00 09
March–Nov Tue–Sun, guided hourly visits at 10, 11, 12, 3, 4, 5, 6; Dec–Feb by appointment only €6

Villa Grabau
Via di Matraia, 269, Marlia 05 83 40 60 98 April–July, Sept, Oct daily daily 10–1, 2–6, July, Aug 10–1, 2–7, Nov–March Sun 11–1, 12:30–5:30 Uhr €7

Villa Torrigiani
Via del Gomberaio, 3, Camigliano, off the SS435
05 83 92 80 41 March–Oct daily 10–1, 3–7; rest of year by appointment €10

Villa Mansi
Via delle Selvette, 242, Segromigno in Monte
05 83 92 02 34 April–Oct daily 10–1, 3–6, Nov–March 10–1, 3–5 €10

51 Pistoia

Pistoia would be a must-see historic town in almost any region other than Tuscany, where there are so many outstanding towns and villages. However, push past Pistoia's built-up and uninspiring outskirts, and you'll find a fine medieval and Renaissance heart. The **Piazza del Duomo**, the stage for a magnificent Campanile (bell-tower), 14th-century Gothic Baptistry and art-filled Duomo San Zeno, is not to be missed.

Highlights in the latter include the *Dossale di San Jacopo* (1287–1456), a stunning silver altarpiece that weighs more than a tonne and contains 628 individual figures.

Three churches in the town are also worth visiting: San Bartolomeo in Pantano, San Giovanni Forcivitas and Sant'Andrea, largely for their 13th- and early 14th-century carved pulpits; the best is Giovanni Pisano's pulpit (1301) in Sant'Andrea.

Try to see the **Chiesa del Tau,** famed for its 14th-century frescoes by local artists, and the **Ospedale del Ceppo**, a 13th-century hospital which is noted for its 16th-century Della Robbia frieze of coloured and glazed terracotta.

197 E3

Tourist Office
Piazza del Duomo, 4
0 57 32 16 22; www.comune.pistoia.it
Daily 9–1, 3–6

52 Vinci

This tiny unassuming Tuscan village would certainly have been a backwater were it not for one event which did little to change Vinci but undoubtedly changed the world. In 1452 a child was born who would grow up to be one of history's geniuses, a true man of the Renaissance – none other than Leonardo da Vinci. Leonardo left Vinci at the age of 14 to take up an apprenticeship in Florence. The simple **stone farmhouse** where he spent his childhood stands in a small hamlet 3km (2mi) from the town at Anchiano. However, though the landscape is much as it was during his childhood, there are few exhibits with links to the great man.

The castle in Vinci plays host to the **Museo Leonardiano di Vinci**, which has a display of life-size models of the many amazing machines that Leonardo designed – including a helicopter, human-sized wings for flight, and an underwater breathing apparatus.

Insider Tip

207 E2

Pistoia's superb medieval Cattedrale di San Zeno contains some stunning artworks by Della Robbia

Tourist Office
Via del Torre, 11
05 71 56 80 12; www.comune.vinci.it
March–Oct daily 10–7; Nov–Feb Mon–Fri 10–3, Sat 10–6

Casa Natale di Leonardo da Vinci
Anchiano 0 57 15 65 19
March–Oct daily 10–7; Nov–Feb10–5
€2; Combined ticket with Museo Leonardiano di Vinci €8

Museo Leonardiano di Vinci
Castello dei Conti Guidi
0 57 15 6055; www.museoleonardiano.it
March Oct daily 9:30–7, Nov–Feb 9:30–6
€7; Combined ticket with Casa Natale di Leonardo da Vinci €8

Where to...
Stay

Prices
Expect to pay per double room per night
€ under €125 **€€** €125–€200 **€€€** over €200

GARFAGNANA

Hotel Ristorante Ludovico Ariosto €

Most accommodation in the Garfagnana region is run along *agriturismo* lines. Those who prefer staying indoors should head for the Ludovico Ariosta, a neat and tidy 19th-century town house set in the heart of Castelnuovo, with a more modern extension added at the rear. The rooms are clean and fresh, even if some of the furnishings are a little lacking in contemporary style. There's a very modern restaurant on site serving typical Tuscan country dishes, and a choice of other places lies within a few minutes' walk.

207 D4
Via Francisco Azzi, 28, Castelnuovo
0 58 36 23 69; www.hotelludovicoariosto.it

LUCCA

La Luna €€

This family-run 3-star hotel has rooms arranged in two 17th-century palaces that face each other across a sleepy courtyard in the heart of the old town. All rooms have TVs, and there is a wide variety of styles, with some larger suites and apartment-type rooms available. There is no restaurant, but a buffet breakfast is included in the room rate.

207 D3
Via Fillungo, Corte Compagni, 12
05 83 49 36 34; www.hotellaluna.com
Closed Jan

Noblesse €€€

The Noblesse is the most luxurious option in the heart of Lucca and is ideally situated just west of Piazza Bernardini between the Duomo and Torre Guinigi. A converted 18th-century palace, its rooms and grand public spaces retain many fine period details, and are decorated with precious antiques, oriental rugs and sumptuous fabrics. It's a boutique hotel, so the atmosphere is intimate and exclusive. Dinner on the terrace is an experience not to be missed.

207 D3
Via Sant'Anastasia, 23
05 83 44 02 75; www.hotelnoblesse.it

Piccolo Hotel Puccini €

This charming, small 3-star hotel, just a few minutes from Piazza San Michele, occupies a peaceful 15th-century Renaissance palace. The hotel is capably and enthusiastically run and the cosy rooms, some of which have views of the small square and Puccini statue outside, are bright and tasteful. Limited private parking is available, but must be requested in advance. There is no restaurant, but a continental breakfast is available.

207 D3
Via di Poggio, 9
0 58 35 54 21; www.hotelpuccini.com

La Cappella €€

The selection of comfortable and low-priced accommodation in Lucca is not big. But if you look further afield you will have more choice. The advantage of staying at the Villa La Cappella, for example, lets you combine a town holiday with country air – and a cosy atmosphere with a wonderful view, well looked after by your host, Emilio.

207 D3
Via dei Tognetti, La Cappella, Ponte del Giglio
05 83 39 43 47, www.relaislacappella.com

PISA

Relais dell'Orologio €€€

This 5-star boutique hotel makes a luxurious retreat right in the heart of the city. Set in a converted 14th-century medieval tower and its neighbouring town house, no expense has been spared in the decor, with superb period details, elegant drapes and quality furnishings throughout. Rooms are individually furnished and many have frescoes on the walls or ceilings, but all are extremely comfortable. The hotel has a classy restaurant and there's a pretty courtyard and garden for al-fresco dining and relaxing.

206 C2 **Via della Faggiola, 12–14**
050 83 03 61; www.hotelrelaisorologio.com
Restaurant closed early Jan–Feb

Verdi €

The Verdi is conveniently located on the east side of the old centre, close to the river, the Museo Nazionale di San Matteo and the Palazzo di Giustizia. The 32 rooms are comfortable and tastefully decorated, but there's no restaurant.

196 C2
Piazza della Repubblica, 5–6
050 59 89 47; www.verdihotel.it

VIAREGGIO

Hotel Tirennia €/€€

This small, 3-star hotel is a good value option and is just a short distance from the resort beach – where it has a special rate for sunbeds on the private strand. Modern and funky, the whole place is a riot of sunny and pastel colours that gives it a warm atmosphere. There's a bar and breakfast area but no restaurant; garage facilities are available at an extra cost. Book in advance during the summer.

206 C3 **Via San Martino, 23**
0 58 44 96 41; www.tirreniahotel.com

Where to... Eat and Drink

Prices
Expect to pay for a three-course meal for one with wine
€ under €26 **€€** €26–€52 **€€€**over €52

LUCCA

Buca di Sant'Antonio €€

The Buca di Sant'Antonio, founded in 1787, has long been the best of the city's central restaurants. The service is formal and the cooking is based on Lucchese traditions. Dishes might include *tordelli lucchesi* (pasta filled with borage, beef, pork and nutmeg); *zuppa di farro* (vegetable soup made with a wheat-like grain); *capretto allo spiedo* (spit-roasted kid goat) and *semifreddo Buccellatto*, a mixture of cream and wild berries.

207 D4 **Via della Cervia, 3**
0 58 35 58 81 **Tue–Sun 12:30–2:30, 7:30–10:30. Closed Sun evening, one week in early Jan and a period in July**

Caffè Ristretto €€

This is Lucca without its medieval flair. Soak in your impressions of the town over a cup of coffee and a slice of cake, a glass of wine or a Hugo cocktail. Savour the finger food along with your apéritif in the evening accompanied – sometimes – by live music.

207 D3
Via San Giorgio, 8
05 83 95 56 52
Mon–Sat 7:30–midnight

Da Leo €

The family-run Da Leo is not the place to come for a quiet and intimate dinner. It is a lively and informal Italian restaurant with just two dining rooms (one large, one tiny) which are invariably crammed with voluble locals tucking into simple and fairly priced Tuscan food, such as home-made pasta, grilled meats, soups and stews. The building is medieval, but the decor has the post-war period look of the type of restaurant you might once have found across Italy in the 1950s. Little English is spoken, but the staff are helpful and welcoming. No credit cards are accepted.

207 D3 Via Tegrimi, 1
05 83 49 22 36; www.trattoriadaleo.it
Mon–Sat 12:30–2:30, 7:30–10:30. Closed Sun

La Mora €€€

Michelin inspectors have rewarded La Mora's sublime Lucchese and Garfagnana cooking with a coveted star, but to sample dishes such as pigeon or rare local specialities such as *anguilla* (eel) you need to travel 8km (5mi) northwest of Lucca to the hamlet of Ponte a Moriano. Booking is advised.

207 D3
Via Sesto di Ponte a Moriano, 1748
05 83 40 64 02; www.ristorantelamora.com
Thu–Tue 12:30–2:30, 7:30–10:30. Closed periods in Jan and June

PISA

Osteria dei Cavalieri €€

The two dining rooms of this long-established *osteria* occupy part of a medieval tower and town house. A wide range of Tuscan food at reasonable prices is available, including à la carte options such as *manzo con fagioli e funghi* (beef with beans and mushrooms), plus set meals based on fish, meat or vegetables. The restaurant is close to the main Piazza dei Cavalieri.

206 C2 Via San Frediano, 16
0 50 58 08 58; www.osteriacavalieri.pisa.it
Mon–Fri 12:30–2, 7:45–10, Sat 7:45–10. Closed Aug

Osteria in Domo €

This welcoming eatery with its minimalistic décor is the stellar place to be in the town centre at the moment. The philosophy behind the success story is slow food – seasonal and regional dishes made with locally sourced organic produce. And on top of this the price is right too.

206 C2 Via Santa Maria, 129
0 5055 55 42 Tue–Sun 11:30–11:30, Sun 6:30pm–11:30pm

Pasticceria Salza €

This is the most celebrated and frequented of Pisa's smart cafés. It has been in the same family since the 1920s and is ideal for coffee, *panini* (more than 40 varieties), cakes, snacks or an evening apéritif. Hot sandwiches and a few simple pasta dishes are available at lunch in a separate waiter-service room to the rear. No credit cards.

206 C2 Borgo Stretto, 46 0 50 58 01 44; www.salza.it Tue–Sun 7:45am–8:30pm

Pistoia

La BotteGaia €€

The press has been making quite a stir of this relative newcomer. Elegant, uncomplicated service,

seasonal ingredients, Tuscan dishes and a good wine list speak for themselves. The dining room combines minimalist modern style with a touch of the traditional *osteria,* and there's a lovely terrace with a view of the Duomo.
207 E3 Via del Lastrone, 17
05 73 36 56 02; www.labottegaia.it
Tue–Sat noon–3, 7–11.
Closed Sun lunch and Mon

Where to… Shop

LUCCA

The best shopping streets for shoes, clothes, china and other goods are Via Fillungo and Via del Battistero.

Olive oil from Lucca is some of the best in Italy. Find it in food stores and supermarkets. **Taddeucci** (Piazza San Michele, 34; tel: 05 83 49 49 33) is a good bakery; try local specialities such as *buccellato,* flavoured with aniseed and raisins. For chocolates visit **Caniparoli** (Via San Paolino, 96; tel: 0 58 35 34 65) and for quality shoes, bags and clothes, visit **Cuoieria Fiorentina** (Via Fillungo 155; tel: 05 83 49 11 39). For wine go to **Enoteca Vanni** (Piazza del Salvatore, 7; tel: 05 83 49 19 02). A large antiques market takes place in Piazza Antelminelli and in Piazza San Giusto over the third weekend of the month.

PISA

Most of the upmarket stores cluster on Borgo Stretto and Corso Italia. There's a food market, **Mercato Vettovaglie**, in Piazza delle Vettovaglie (Mon–Sat 8am–5:30pm), and an antiques market off Borgo Stretto (second weekend of each month). For chocolates, seek out **De Bondt** (Lungarno Pacinotti, 5; tel: 05 02 20 02 85). For cheeses, oils and wines, visit **Gastronomia a Cesqui** (Piazza delle Vettovaglie, 38; tel: 0 50 58 02 69).

Where to… Go Out

GARFAGNANA

Barga (www.barganews.com) holds several festivals and events during the year, including jazz and opera festivals (early July) and also a chocolate festival (early Dec).

LUCCA

Lucca's major festival is the **Luminara di Santa Croce**, a torchlit procession bearing the Volto Santo – the city's most sacred relic – around the streets (13 Sept). This takes place in conjunction with the **Settembre Lucchese**, a series of classical music and other events at various venues in the city (Sept–Oct). **Luminaria di San Paolino** (11–12 July) commemorates Lucca's patron saint.

PISA

Pisa's main festival is the **Festa di San Ranieri** (16–17 June), with candlelit processions. The next day there's a rowing regatta in medieval dress to celebrate Pisa's patron saint, then the **Gioco del Ponte**, a tug-of-war in medieval costume on the Ponte di Mezzo (last Sun June).

PISTOIA

The **Pistoia Blues** series of concerts runs for several days in early July at various venues in the city (www.pistoiablues.com).

Walks & Tours

1 SIENA

Walk

DISTANCE 2km (1.2mi) **TIME** 2–3 hours
START POINT Piazza San Domenico 214
END POINT Piazza del Duomo 214

This walk takes you through the heart of old Siena, starting in the north of the city and wending its way south past medieval churches and palaces to the Campo, one of Italy's finest squares. It then winds its way through the less-visited southern quarters of the city, to end in the spectacular piazza containing the cathedral and Ospedale di Santa Maria della Scala.

1–2

Start your walk in **Piazza San Domenico**, home to the church of the same name, which you should visit to see frescoes by Sodoma (► 117). With your back to the church, take Via della Sapienza east from the piazza (note the view of the Duomo to the right). A further 100m (110 yards) on the right is the **Biblioteca Comunale degli Intronati**, a library founded in 1759 in what was probably a 13th-century hospital. It contains more than 500,000 books and other documents, including precious letters by St Catherine of Siena and many noted medieval Sienese painters and architects. Just beyond, at the next minor crossroads, is the **church of San Pellegrino alla Sapienza,** built in 1767 over the site of a much older chapel.

2–3

Continue straight on at the church to emerge on Banchi di Sopra, a major street that follows the course of the Via Francigena in the city, an ancient pilgrimage route between Rome and northern Europe. Ahead is **Piazza Salimbeni**, home to a trio of fine palaces: **Palazzo Tantucci** (1548) on the left, the 13th-century **Palazzo Salimbeni** to the rear, and the **Palazzo Spannocchi** (1470) to the right. The Salimbeni family were important bankers and traders in silk and grain, while Ambrogio Spannocchi was the treasurer to the Sienese Pope Pius II. A 75m (82-yard) diversion left on Banchi di Sopra brings you to the **church of Santa Maria delle Nevi** (erratic opening hours), known for its wonderful high altarpiece, the *Madonna della Neve* (1477), by Matteo di Giovanni.

3–4

Retrace your steps (south) on Banchi di Sopra. After 175m (190 yards) look for the **church of San Cristoforo** on the left. Romanesque in origin, it was rebuilt in the late 18th century after earthquake damage. Opposite is the **Palazzo Tolomei**, part of the original fortress home of the Tolomei, one of the most powerful of Siena's medieval dynasties of merchants. It is the oldest surviving private residence in the city, dating to at least 1205. Continue south to the junction with Banchi di Sotto and Via di Città and the **Loggia della Mercanzia** (1428–45), an attractive Gothic three-arched loggia. Little alleys to either side take you into **Piazza del Campo** (► 98).

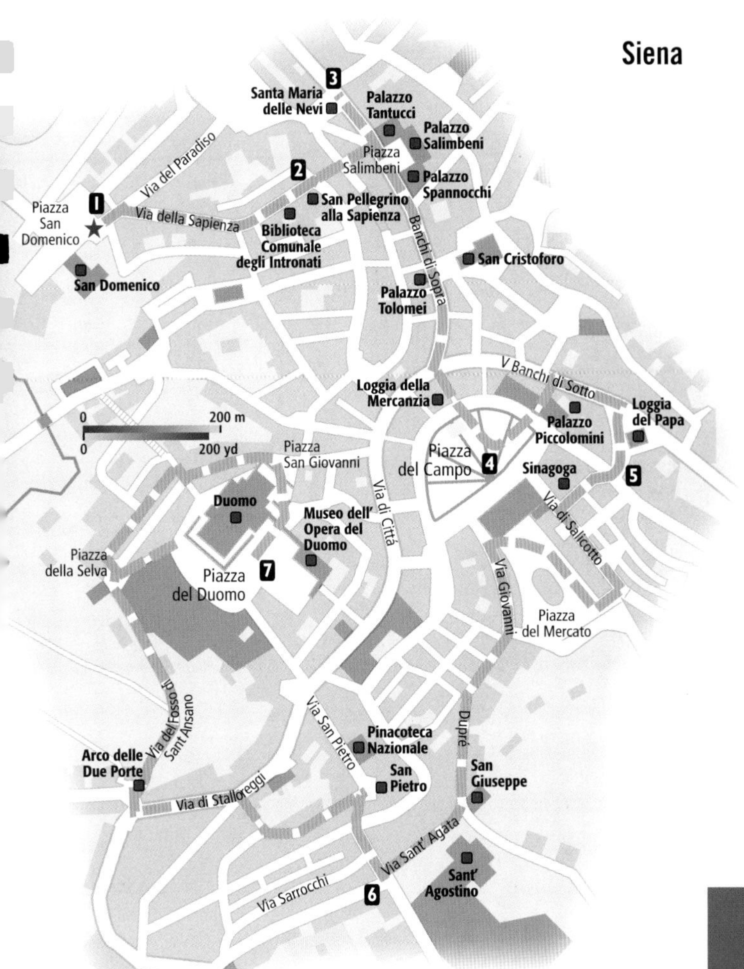

4–5

Admire the Campo, possibly from one of its many cafés, then walk to its east side to exit either by Vicolo dei Pollaiuoli or Via dei Rinaldini. Both bring you to Banchi di Sotto, where you should turn right. Immediately on your right stands the **Palazzo Piccolomini**, a majestic palace begun in 1469. Inside, on an upper floor, is the Archivio di Stato (State Archive), open to the public and full of fascinating works of art (➤ 118). Beyond the palace is the **Loggia del Papa** (Loggia of the Pope), built in 1462 on the orders of the Tuscan-born Pope Pius II (Enea Silvio Piccolomini).

TAKING A BREAK

Caffè Fiorella at Via di Città 13 can be recommended for a welcome break. **Orti dei Tolomei** behind Sant'Agostino Church is a perfect place for a picnic (entrance on Via Pier Andrea Mattioli).

Looking down one of Siena's labyrinthine streets lit by the evening sun

Take the right fork in front of the loggia and follow it to the junction with Via del Porrione, named after the Latin *emporium* ('place of the market'), as Roman markets once stood nearby.

5–6

Cross Via del Porrione and walk through the arch down Vicolo delle Scotte, passing Siena's **Sinagoga** (synagogue) on the right, the heart of the city's Jewish ghetto, created in 1571 by Cosimo I de' Medici. Turn left on Via di Salicotto, then first right to emerge on the Piazza del Mercato. Cross the square and bear right to pick up Via del Mercato and then turn left almost immediately to follow Via Giovanni Dupré. Note the many evocative alleys leading off this street. At the church of San Giuseppe on the left take Via Sant'Agata straight onto a gravel area on your left and the 13th-century **church of Sant'Agostino**, with paintings by Sodoma and Ambrogio Lorenzetti.

6–7

Head through the arch to Via San Pietro and the church of San Pietro (set back on your right) and the red-brick **Pinacoteca Nazionale** beyond (➤ 116). Just before the church turn sharp left on Via di Castelvecchio (an easily missed alley) and bear right to Via di Stalloreggi. Turn left to the Arco delle Due Porte, an arch that formed part of the city's 11th-century walls, passing a house on the left (Nos 91–93) where Duccio painted his famous *Maestà* (➤ 109). Turn right after the arch and follow the peaceful Via del Fosso di Sant Ansano to Piazza della Selva, where either Via Franciosa or Via Girolamo lead to Piazza del Duomo or Piazza San Giovanni. In the latter you can see the Battistero di San Giovanni (Baptistry) and then walk up the steps to your right to see the **Duomo Santa Maria della Scal** and **Museo dell'Opera del Duomo** (➤ 108).

2 CHIANTI

Tour

DISTANCE 110km (68mi)
TIME 1 day
START/END POINT Siena 211 D5

This drive takes you through the heart of Chianti, the name given to much of the region between Florence and Siena. An often wild landscape, it is characterised by rolling hills, rich farmland, heavily wooded slopes, isolated villas and numerous vineyards. Many minor and often circuitous roads run across the region. A good way of getting to Siena from Florence is to follow the Chiantigiana (the SR222), a designated scenic wine route that runs for 65km (40mi) between the two cities.

1–2

Begin your tour in Siena by driving to the start of the SR222 (Chiantigiana) road; follow the main road west from Siena's railway station for about 2km (1.2mi) and you will see signs for the SR222 and **Castellina in Chianti** – apart from the 4-laned dual-carriageway between Siena and Florence, the SR222 is the most important road through the Chianti region. Within just a few minutes of picking up the Chiantigiana the scenery begins to improve, setting the tone for much of the drive, where the beauty and variety of

Chianti is best known for its hills, but the towns are also part of the experience.

the landscape takes precedence over historic towns and other sights. After 6.5km (4mi) you pass through the hamlet of Quercegrossa (literally 'large oak') followed by 7.5km (4.5mi) of undulating road which brings you to another tiny hamlet, **Fonterutoli**.

SLOWLY BUT SURELY

Distances may not look great on a map, but Chianti's roads are winding and slow, so allow more time than might seem necessary when exploring the region.

2–3

From here it's about 4km (2.5mi) to **Castellina in Chianti**. Castellina's name – which means the 'little castle' – offers a clue to its former strategic importance. For many

Chianti's grapevines cover the region's landscape

centuries the town stood at the border between the territories of Siena and Florence, hence the presence of the town's fortress. Castellina was also the head-quarters of the Chianti League, a military alliance of Chianti's three main towns – Gaiole in Chianti, Castellina in Chianti and Radda in Chianti – set up by Florence at the beginning of the 13th century. Its symbol was the *Gallo Nero* (Black Cockerel), now used by one of the leading consortia of local wine producers. Stop to look at the town's Via delle Volte, an unusual vaulted street that runs around the old town walls. From the northern edge of Castellina take the SR429 road for **Radda in Chianti** (10km/6mi), ignoring the left fork for Greve in Chianti after about 1km (0.5mi). Take a detour 2km (1.2mi) south on a minor road from the centre of the village, to San Giusto in Salcio.

3–4

San Giusto in Salcio, documented in 1018, is one of Chianti's oldest places of worship. Return to Radda and follow the main road east out of the village, taking a right turn at the major junction after 3.5km (2mi). Drive for 6km (4mi) down this road to a junction of five roads, where a turn to the left takes you to the 11th-century abbey, **Badia a Coltibuono** (1km/0.5mi).

TAKING A BREAK

Chianti has only a few towns suitable for refreshment breaks, so a picnic can be a good idea. Passengers will be able to sample wine at a variety of the region's many estates, all of which are well signposted from the road (► 28).

- The **Antica Trattoria La Torre** on Piazza del Comune, 15 in Castellina in Chianti (tel: 05 77 74 02 36; www.anticatrattorialatorre.com; closed Fri and 1–15 Sept) is a simple and popular trattoria run by the Stiaccini family since 1860.
- **Radda in Chianti** has an elegant restaurant for lunch: Il Vignale at Via XX Settembre, 23 (tel: 05 77 73 80 94; www.vignale.it; closed Dec–Feb).
- **San Regolo** has a relaxed, little restaurant for a late lunch, Il Carlino d'Oro (tel: 05 77 74 71 36; closed Mon). Insider Tip
- **Castelnuovo** has a nice wine bar, Bengodi (Via della Società Operai, 11; tel: 05 77 35 51 16; www.enotecabengodi.it; closed Mon; inexpensive for light meals).

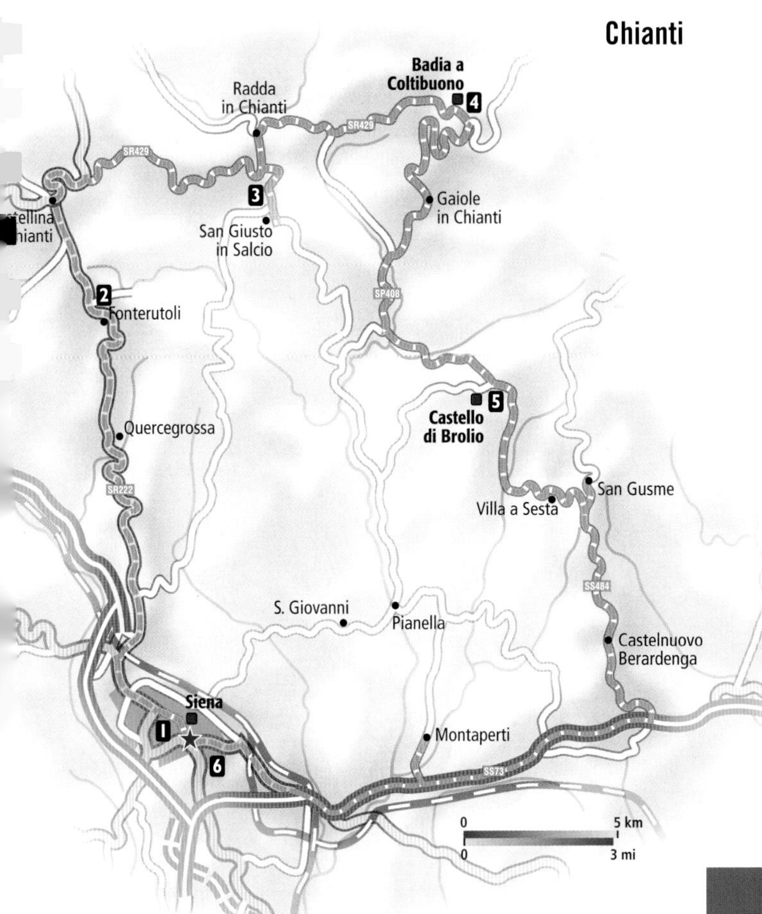

4–5
Return to the five-road junction and turn right to follow the main road south to **Gaiole in Chianti**. Continue south through the town on the main road (3km/2mi) to the junction with the SP408 to Radda, then turn left and drive for another 3km (2mi) to the next major junction. Turn left towards San Regolo and after 5km (3mi) you come to a junction with signs for the 12th-century **Castello di Brolio** (tel: 05 77 73 19 19; www.ricasoli.it; open daily in summer), one of Chianti's oldest wine estates. Whether or not you buy anything, the views from here are breathtaking.

5–6
From the junction below the Castello di Brolio take the SS484 road south. After 7.5km (4.5mi) you come to a crossroads, where a left turn takes you to the medieval hamlet **San Gusme**. Return to the junction and continue south to **Castelnuovo Berardenga** (4.5km/3mi), Chianti's most southerly village. Turn right on the SP73 towards Siena (17km/10.5mi), perhaps making a detour to **Montaperti**, the site of Siena's great victories over Florence in 1260.

3 SOUTHERN TUSCANY

Tour

DISTANCE 175km (108mi) **TIME** 2 days
START POINT Siena 211 D5
END POINT Pienza 211 F4

This drive takes you through the historic small towns and villages south of Siena and some of the richest and most archetypal landscapes in Tuscany.

1–2

Start in **Siena**, taking the ring road (SS326) to the eastern side of the city. About 5km (3mi) from the centre, take the SS438 road. This runs for about 21km (13mi) to **Asciano** through the Crete (➤ 150), an area of bare clay hills that in summer are full of wheat, flax and sunflowers. Asciano has several churches and small museums, the best of which is the Museo d'Arte Sacra (Palazzo Corboli; tel: 05 77 71 95 24; www.palazzocorboli.it; open Apr–Oct Tue–Sun 10–1, 3–7), home to some important medieval paintings.

Sant'Antimo Abbey in the region of Montalcino is a medieval gem

2–3

From Asciano take the minor road southeast signed to San Giovanni d'Asso. After 8km (5mi) turn right at Montefresco and follow another scenic minor road for 3km (2mi) through Chiusure to the junction with the SS451. Turn left and after 1km (0.5mi) turn left again to the **Abbazia di Monte Oliveto Maggiore** (➤ 145). Stop to admire the frescoes by Sodoma and Signorelli in the main cloister and perhaps take a break in the abbey café. Return to the SS451, turn left and drive 9km (5mi) to **Buonconvento** (➤ 150).

3–4

In Buonconvento turn south on the SR2, the Via Cassia, and after 2km (1.2mi) take the right fork signed to **Montalcino** (14km/9mi). At the four-road junction at the southern side of the town under the walls of the fortress, take the central road signed for Castelnuovo dell'Abate and the **abbey of Sant'Antimo** (➤ 142). The abbey is set in stunning countryside, but is closed 12:30–3 and 10:45–3 on Sunday. Continue southeast beyond Castelnuovo for 9km (5.5mi) to the junction at **Ansidonia**. If time is short, a left turn here takes you via

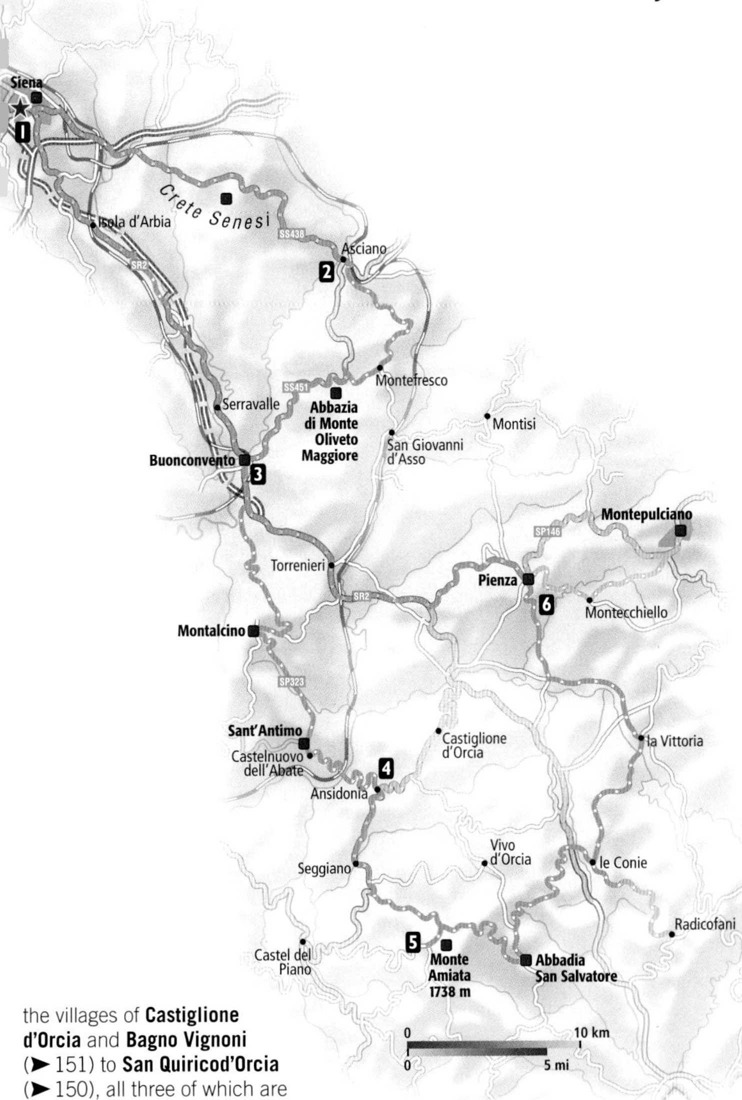

the villages of **Castiglione d'Orcia** and **Bagno Vignoni** (➤ 151) to **San Quiricod'Orcia** (➤ 150), all three of which are worth at least a half-hour exploration. From San Quirico you can return to Siena on the SR2. If you have time, however, take the SP146 east to **Pienza** (➤ 138). From here it is 13.5km (8mi) along the SP146 to Montepulciano, but you might consider the pretty (and part gravel) road from the east of Pienza to Montepulciano via **Monticchiello**.

TAKING A BREAK

The café at the **Abbazia di Monte Oliveto Maggiore** (➤ 146) is a good place for a snack break. **Fiaschetteria Italiana** wine bar or **Taverna Il Grappolo Blu restaurant** in Montalcino (➤ 156) are recommended places for lunch.

The seemingly empty countryside around Buonconvento is typical of southern Tuscany

4–5

From Ansidonia, a right turn on the SP323 leads to Seggiano (6km/4mi), beyond which you should turn left for Pescina. After another 5km (3mi) – and the start of glorious beech and other woods that flank the slopes of Monte Amiata – you come to a junction where you should turn left. About 2km (1.2mi) beyond is another junction, where a right turn leads after 5km (3mi) almost to the summit of **Monte Amiata** itself (1,738m/5,702ft) (► 151), the highest point in southern Tuscany. The views on a clear day are breathtaking.

5–6

Backtrack from the summit, take a downhill right turn and drive to **Abbadia San Salvatore** (► 152). See the abbey here then drive on the only road north from the town towards Zaccaria, beyond which a left fork leads to the SR2 (7.5km/4.5mi) via the small spa village of **Bagni San Filippo**. To the south-east towers the fortress village of **Radicofani**, visible from much of the immediate region. Be sure to drive the 9.5km (6mi) to see the village if you have time – to reach it turn right on the SR2 and then almost immediately left.

The medieval village has two simple **churches**, San Pietro and Sant'Agata, at its heart. From here, return towards the SR2, which takes you to **San Quirico d'Orcia** (► 150), or follow prettier minor roads from Le Conie. These head north past Contignano and La Vittoria to Pienza.

UNDERGROUND Insider Tip

There is an interesting  **mining museum** in Abbadia San Salvatore (Piazzale Rossaro, 6, www.museominerario.it) – tools and machines give a good impression of the hard work underground.

Practicalities

Practicalities

BEFORE YOU GO

WHAT YOU NEED

● Required
○ Suggested
▲ Not required

Some countries require a passport to remain valid for a minimum period beyond the date of entry – contact their consulate or embassy for details

	UK	USA	Canada	Australia	Germany	Ireland	Netherlands	Spain
Passport/National Identity Card	●	●	●	●	●	●	●	▲
Visa	▲	▲	▲	▲	▲	▲	▲	▲
Onward or Return Ticket	○	●	●	●	○	○	○	○
Health Inoculations	▲	▲	▲	▲	▲	▲	▲	▲
Health Documentation (► 200, Health)	●	▲	▲	▲	●	●	●	●
Travel Insurance	○	○	○	○	○	○	○	○
Driving Licence (national)	●	●	●	●	●	●	●	●
Car Insurance Certificate	●	●	●	●	●	●	●	●
Car Registration Document	●	●	●	●	●	●	●	●

WHEN TO GO

Florence

High season (May–Sep) · Low season (Jan–Apr, Oct–Dec)

JAN	FEB	MAR	APRIL	MAY	JUNE	JULY	AUG	SEP	OCT	NOV	DEC
6°C	6°C	10°C	13°C	17°C	22°C	25°C	25°C	21°C	16°C	11°C	6°C
42°F	42°F	50°F	55°F	63°F	72°F	77°F	77°F	70°F	61°F	52°F	42°F
Cloudy	Cloudy	Cloudy	Wet	Sun	Sun	Sun	Sun	Sun	Wet	Wet	Wet

Sun · Cloudy · Sunshine & showers · Wet

Temperatures shown above are the **average daily maximum** for each month. The best times of the year for good weather are May, June, July, August and September. July and August can be extremely hot and uncomfortable in the cities, although temperatures are lower and more bearable in the Tuscan countryside. Thunderstorms are possible in summer and through September and October. Winters (January–February) are short and cold, and snow is possible on higher ground, particularly the mountainous region of northern Tuscany. Spring starts in March (later in the mountains), but March and April can be humid and sometimes very rainy. Autumn weather is mixed, but often produces crisp or warm days with clear skies.

GETTING ADVANCE INFORMATION

Websites

- Official Tuscany website: www.turismo.toscana.it
- Official Florence website: www.firenzeturismo.it
- Official Siena website: www.terresiena.it
- Alitalia: www.alitalia.it
- Italian Arts and Culture Ministry: www.beniculturali.it
- Italian state railways: www.trenitalia.it
- Florence – local news: www.fionline.it

Florence Tourist Offices

Via Cavour 1r
☎ 055 29 08 32/833
Borgo Santa Croce 29r
☎ 055 2 34 04 44
Piazza della Stazion 4a
☎ 055 21 22 45

GETTING THERE

By Air Tuscany is served by two airports: Pisa's Galileo Galilei airport (▶ 37) and the smaller Amerigo Vespucci (Peretola) airport just outside Florence (▶ 37). Most European carriers fly to Pisa, but only small jets can use Peretola. Flights to Bologna's Guglielmo Marconi airport can also be useful for Florence and northern Tuscany (▶ 38).
From the UK British Airways and several charter companies, including the no-frills airlines, fly to Pisa. Meridiana flies to Florence. The flight time from London to Pisa is two hours.
From the US There are no year-round direct non-stop flights to Pisa or Florence from the US, though Delta operates seasonal flights in the past from New York. US carriers fly either to Milan (Malpensa) or Rome (Fiumicino): there are connecting flights from both airports to Pisa, bit it is easier to take a train or drive from Rome. Flying time to Rome is 8–10 hours from east coast USA, 11 hours from the west coast.
From Australia and New Zealand Qantas and Air New Zealand fly to Rome or Milan (see "From the US" above). Flying time from Australia's east coast is 21 hours, and 24 hours from New Zealand.
By Rail Numerous fast and overnight services operate to Florence and Pisa from most European capitals. The Italian state railway, Trenitalia (still often referred to by its old name, the Ferrovie dello Stato), offers high-speed trains between major Italian cities, and connecting services from both Florence and Pisa to the other major towns in Tuscany. Ticket prices are usually the same or more than equivalent air fares.

TIME

Italy is on GMT+1, making it one hour ahead of the UK, six hours ahead of New York and nine hours ahead of Los Angeles from November to March. Daylight Saving Time adds one hour to these figures between April and October.

CURRENCY AND FOREIGN EXCHANGE

Currency The euro is the legal currency of Italy. Euro notes are issued in denominations of 5, 10, 20, 50, 100, 200 and 500. Coins are denominations of 1, 2 and 5 euro cents and 10, 20 and 50 gold-coloured euro cents. In addition there is a 1 euro coin with a silver centre and gold surround and 2 euro coin with a gold centre and silver surround. Euro coins carry a common European face, and each member state decorates the reverse of the coins with their own motif. All coins and notes are accepted in all member states.
Exchange Most major travellers' cheques – the best way to carry money – can be changed at exchange kiosks *(cambio)* at the airports, Santa Maria Novella railway station in Florence and in exchange offices near major tourist sights. Many banks also have exchange desks, though lines can be long. Most major credit cards *(carta di credito)* are accepted in larger hotels, restaurants and shops, but cash is often preferred in smaller establishments. Most cities and main towns have ATM machines which accept foreign-issued cards.

In the UK
ENIT
1 Princes Street
London
W1R 2AY
☎ (020) 74 08 12 54

In the US
ENIT
630 Fifth Avenue
Suite 1565, New York
NY 10111
☎ (212) 2 45 56 18

In Australia
Italian Consulate
Fourth Floor
46 Market Street, Sydney NSW
2000
☎ (02) 9 22 16 66

Practicalities

WHEN YOU ARE THERE

NATIONAL HOLIDAYS

1 Jan	New Year's Day
6 Jan	Epiphany
Mar/Apr	Easter Monday
25 April	Liberation Day
1 May	Labour Day
2 June	Republic Day
15 Aug	Assumption
1 Nov	All Saints' Day
8 Dec	Immaculate Conception
25/26 Dec	Christmas Day/St Stephen's Day

Some towns and cities have special saints' days.

ELECTRICITY

Current is 220 volts AC (50 cycles). Plugs are two-round-pin Continental types; UK, North American and Australasian visitors will need an adaptor. North American visitors should check whether 10/120-volt AC appliances require a voltage transformer.

OPENING HOURS

○ Shops
● Offices
● Banks
● Post offices
● Pharmacies
● Museums/Monuments

8am 9am 10am noon 1pm 2pm 4pm 5pm 7pm

Day Midday Evening

Shops Many stores in major cities open all day.
Banks Some open Sat and longer weekday hours.
Post offices Mon–Fri 8:15–2 or 7, Sat 8:15–noon or 2.
Museums Varies but often Tue–Sat 9–7, Sun 9–1.
Pharmacies Mon–Sat. In Florence, the station's pharmacy and Molteni (Via dei Calzaiuoli 7r), are generally open 24 hours.

TIPS/GRATUITIES

Tipping is not expected for all services and rates are lower than in other countries. As a general guide:

Pizzerias	Nearest €2.50 or €5
Trattorias	Nearest €2.50 or €5
Smart restaurant	10–15% or discretion
Bar service	Discretion
Tour guides	Discretion
Taxis	To the nearest €0.50
Porters	€0.50 to €1 per bag
Chambermaids	€0.50 to €1 per day

TRAM SYSTEM

Since 2010, a city-operated tram system has been running in Florence that is going to be extended. To date, only Line 1 has been completed, linking the main station with Scandicci. If and when other lines are to be constructed remains uncertain (see: www.ataf.net)

TIME DIFFERENCES

Florence (CET)
12 noon

London (GMT)
11am

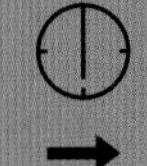

New York (EST)
6am

Los Angeles (PST)
3am

Sydney (AEST)
9pm

STAYING IN TOUCH

Post Florence's central post office is at Via Pellicceria 3. Stamps *(francobolli)* can be bought from post offices and *tabacchi* (tobacconists) Mail boxes are red or blue with two slots: one for city mail *(Per La Città)* and one for all destinations *(Altre Destinazioni).*

Public telephones Telecom Italia (TI) payphones are on streets and in bars, tobacconists and restaurants. Most take coins or a phone card *(scheda telefonica)*, available from post offices, shops and bars. Tear the corner off the card first. To dial another number in Florence while there, dial the area code then the number. Cheap rate is Mon–Sat 10pm– 8am. Hotels usually add a surcharge to calls from rooms. Dial 170 to make reverse charge calls. Dial 12 for the operator or directory enquiries.

International Dialling Codes: Dial 00 followed by

UK:	**44**
USA/Canada:	**1**
Irish Republic:	**353**
Australia:	**61**

Mobile providers and services In addition to Telecom Italia, the main mobile network providers are Tiscali, Tele2, Infostrada/Wind and BT Italy. Ask your home provider about the cost of international roaming charges for Italy. American visitors should make sure that their phone is a tri-band unit.

WiFi and internet In the major areas of population, speed and quality of service of broadband internet is good, though the most remote or rural areas may not have high-speed services. An increasing number of hotels have WiFi capability. There are generally internet cafes in all major cities and resorts, where access is charged per half or whole hour, or multiples of one hour. Costs vary, but in cities expect to pay around €3–€5 per hour.

PERSONAL SAFETY

Tuscany is generally safe – pickpockets are the main worry in Florence or busy tourist areas – but it's still wise to always take commonsense precautions:

- Carry money and valuables in a belt or pouch.
- Close bags and hold them across your front.
- Wear your camera – never put it down on a cafe table.
- Leave valuables and jewellery in the hotel safe.
- Never leave luggage or other possessions in parked cars.
- Guard against pickpockets, especially in buses, markets and busy shopping or tourist areas.
- Avoid walking in parks late at night.
- Muggings by motorcyclists or scooter riders are a fact of Italian life. These scippatori operate by riding up close behind their chosen victim, then the bike passenger grabs a bag or camera by the straps as they pass. Be aware of two-wheeled traffic around you, even in pedestrian-only areas.

Police assistance:
112/113 from any phone

EMERGENCY 113
POLICE 113 (POLIZIA DI STATO) OR 112 (CARABINIERI)
FIRE 113 OR 115
AMBULANCE 113 OR 118

Practicalities

HEALTH

Insurance It's essential to take out full travel insurance cover when visiting Tuscany. Nationals of EU countries can obtain medical treatment at reduced cost with the EHIC (European Health Insurance card). However, it is advisable to take out private insurance.

Doctors Ask at your hotel for details of English-speaking doctors.

Dental Services Travel insurance should also cover dental treatment, which is readily available in Italy but expensive.

Weather Minor health worries in Tuscany include too much sun, dehydration or mosquito bites: drink plenty of fluids and wear sunscreen and a hat in high summer. Insect repellent may be useful if you have to sleep in rooms with windows open in summer. Tuscany does have poisonous snakes *(vipere)*, although bites are generally only fatal if you have an allergic reaction.

Drugs Prescriptions and other medicines are available from pharmacies *(farmacie)*, indicated by a large green cross.

Safe Water All tap water is safe. So, too, is water from public drinking fountains unless marked *"Acqua Non Potabile"*. Mineral water is cheap and widely available.

CONCESIONS

Senior Citizens (over 65) are entitled to free entrance into state museums and galleries if they are residents of a European Union country.

Students under 18 are also entitled to free entrance into state museums.

For both concessions, you will need to carry some form of identification, such as a passport, as proof of age and nationality.

TRAVELLING WITH A DISABILITY

Medieval centres are difficult for those using wheelchairs, but many pavements now have dropped kerbs and many areas are traffic-free. In Florence, newer buses are wheel-chair accessible, as is the D electric bus. Many museums have dedicated ramps, lifts and toilets. Tourist offices have information on accessibility in the region.

CHILDREN

Most hotels, restaurants and bars welcome children, but few have baby-changing facilities. In this guide special attractions for children are indicated by the icon above.

TOILETS

Few Tuscan towns have public toilets. Men's toilets = *Signori*, women's = *Signore*.

CUSTOMS

Travellers arriving from non-EU countries can bring into Italy the following items duty-free: 400 cigarettes, 500g (1.1lb) of smoking tobacco, 2 bottles of wine, 1 bottle of liquor and 500ml of perfume.

CONSULATES AND EMBASSIES

UK
☎ 055 28 41 33 or 06 42 20 00 01

USA
☎ 055 26 69 51 or 06 467 41

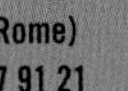

Ireland (Rome)
☎ 06 6 97 91 21

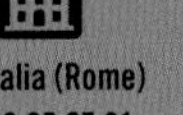

Australia (Rome)
☎ 06 85 27 21

Canada (Rome)
☎ 06 85 44 41

SURVIVAL PHRASES

yes/no **sì/non**
please **per favore**
thank you **grazie**
You're welcome **Di niente/prego**
I'm sorry **Mi dispiace**
Goodbye **Arrivederci**
Good morning **Buongiorno**
Goodnight **Buona sera**
How are you? **Come sta?**
How much? **Quanto costa?**
I would like... **Vorrei...**
open **aperto**
closed **chiuso**
today **oggi**
tomorrow **domani**
Monday **lunedì**
Tuesday **martedì**
Wednesday **mercoledì**
Thursday **giovedì**
Friday **venerdì**
Saturday **sabato**
Sunday **domenica**

DIRECTIONS

I'm lost **Mi sono perso/a**
Where is...? **Dove si trova...?**
the station **la stazione**
the telephone **il telefono**
the bank **la banca**
the toilet **il bagno**
Turn left **Volti a sinistra**
Turn right **Volti a destra**
Go straight on **Vada dritto**
At the corner **All'angolo**
the street **la strada**
the building **il edificio**
the traffic light **il semaforo**
the crossroads **l'incrocio**
the signs for... **le indicazione per...**

IF YOU NEED HELP

Help! **Aiuto!**
Could you help me, please?
Mi potrebbe aiutare?
Do you speak English? **Parla inglese?**
I don't understand **Non capisco**
Please could you call a doctor quickly?
Mi chiami presto un medico, per favore

RESTAURANT

I'd like to book a table
Vorrei prenotare un tavolo
A table for two please
Un tavolo per due, per favore
Could we see the menu, please?
Ci porta la lista, per favore?
What's this? **Cosa è questo?**
A bottle of/a glass of...
Un bottiglia di/un bicchiere di...
Could I have the bill?
Ci porta il conto

ACCOMMODATION

Do you have a single/double room?
Ha una camera singola/doppia?
with/without bath/toilet/shower
con/senza vasca/gabinetto/doccia
Does that include breakfast?
E'inclusa la prima colazione?
Does that include dinner?
E'inclusa la cena?
Do you have room service?
C'è il servizio in camera?
Could I see the room?
E' possibile vedere la camera?
I'll take this room
Prendo questa
Thanks for your hospitality
Grazie per l'ospitalità

NUMBERS

0 **zero**
1 **uno**
2 **due**
3 **tre**
4 **quattro**
5 **cinque**
6 **sei**
7 **sette**
8 **otto**
9 **nove**
10 **dieci**
11 **undici**
12 **dodici**
13 **tredici**
14 **quattordici**
15 **quindici**
16 **sedici**
17 **diciassette**
18 **diciotto**
19 **diciannove**
20 **venti**
21 **ventuno**
22 **ventidue**
30 **trenta**
40 **quaranta**
50 **cinquanta**
60 **sessanta**
70 **settanta**
80 **ottanta**
90 **novanta**
100 **cento**
101 **cento uno**
110 **centodieci**
120 **centoventi**
200 **duecento**
300 **trecento**
400 **quattrocento**
500 **cinquecento**
600 **seicento**
700 **settecento**
800 **ottocento**
900 **novecento**
1000 **mille**
2000 **duemila**
10,000 **diecimila**

MENU READER

acciuga anchovy
acqua water
affettati sliced cured meats
affumicato smoked
aglio garlic
agnello lamb
anatra duck
antipasti hors d'oeuvres
arista roast pork
arrosto roast
asparagi asparagus
birra beer
bistecca steak
bollito boiled meat
braciola minute steak
brasato braised
brodo broth
bruschetta toasted bread with garlic or tomato topping
budino pudding
burro butter
cacciagione game
cacciatore, alla rich tomato sauce with mushrooms
caffè corretto/ macchiato coffee with liqueur/ spirit, or with a drop of milk
caffè freddo iced coffee
caffè lungo weak coffee
caffè latte milky coffee
caffè ristretto strong coffee
calamaro squid
cappero caper
carciofo artichoke
carota carrot
carne meat
carpa carp
casalingho home-made
cassata Sicilian fruit ice cream
cavolfiore cauliflower
cavolo cabbage
ceci chickpeas
cervello brains
cervo venison
cetriolino gherkin
cetriolo cucumber
cicoria chicory
cinghiale boar
cioccolata chocolate
cipolla onion
coda di bue oxtail
coniglio rabbit
contorni vegetables
coperto cover charge
cornetto croissant
coscia leg of meat
cotolette cutlets
cozze mussels
crema custard
crostini canapé with savoury toppings or croutons
crudo raw
digestivo after-dinner liqueur
dolci cakes/desserts
erbe aromatiche herbs
fagioli beans
fagiolini green beans
faraona guinea fowl
farcito stuffed
fegato liver
finocchio fennel
formaggio cheese
forno, al baked
frittata omelette
fritto fried
frizzante fizzy
frulatto whisked
frutti di mare seafood
frutta fruit
funghi mushrooms
gamberetto shrimp
gelato ice cream
ghiaccio ice
gnocchi potato dumplings
granchio crab
gran(o)turco corn
griglia, alla grilled
imbottito stuffed
insalata salad
IVA VAT
latte milk
lepre hare
lumache snails
manzo beef
merluzzo cod
miele honey
minestra soup
molluschi shellfish
olio oil
oliva olive
ostrica oyster
pancetta bacon
pane bread
panna cream
parmigiano Parmesan
passata sieved or creamed
pastasciutta dried pasta
pasta sfoglia puff pastry
patate fritte chips
pecora mutton
pecorino sheep's milk cheese
peperoncino chilli
peperone red/green pepper
pesce fish
petto breast
piccione pigeon
piselli peas
pollame fowl
pollo chicken
polpetta meatball
porto port wine
prezzemolo parsley
primo piatto first course
prosciutto cured ham
ragù meat sauce
ripieno stuffed
riso rice
salsa sauce
salsiccia sausage
saltimbocca veal with prosciutto and sage
secco dry
secondo piatto main course
senape mustard
servizio compreso service charge included
sogliola sole
spuntini snacks
succo di frutta fruit juice
sugo sauce
tonno tuna
uova strapazzate scambled egg
uovo affogato/in carnica poached egg
uovo al tegamo/fritto fried egg
uovo alla coque soft-boiled egg
uovo alla sodo hard-boiled egg
vino bianco white wine
vino rosso red wine
vino rosato rosé wine
verdure vegetables
vitello veal
zucchero sugar
zucchino courgette
zuppa soup

Road Atlas

For chapters: see inside front cover

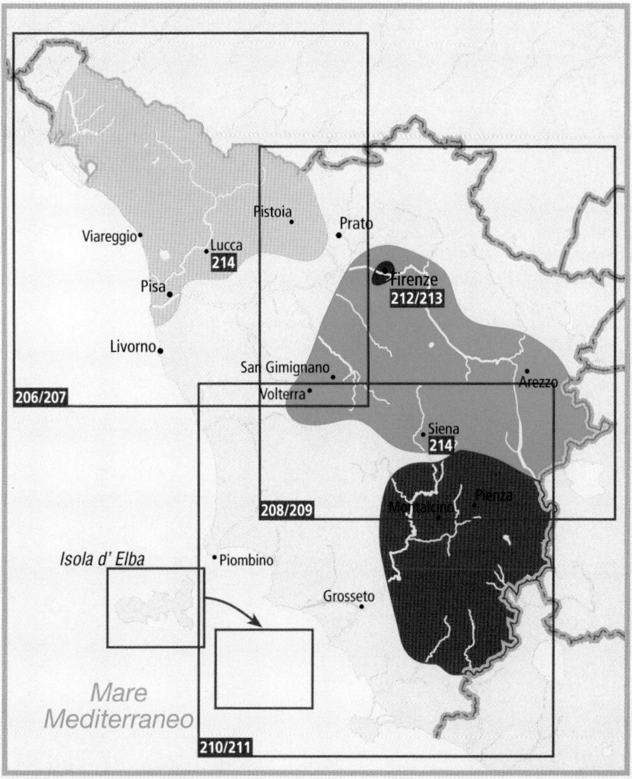

206/207
208/209
210/211
212/213
214

Viareggio
Lucca
Pisa
Livorno
Pistoia
Prato
Firenze
San Gimignano
Volterra
Arezzo
Siena
Montalcino
Pienza
Isola d' Elba
Piombino
Grosseto
Mare Mediterraneo

Key to Road Atlas

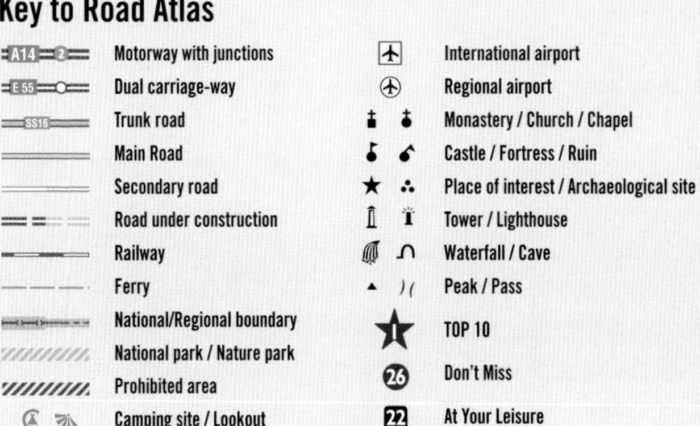

A
B
C
5
4
3
2
1
Passo del Brattello 953 m
Bratto
San Vincenzo
Boschetto
Monti
Montelungo
Gróndola
Montegroppo
Casalina
Monte Marmagna 1852 m
Parco Nazionale
Pontremoli
Adelano
Patigno
Técchia
Pontrémoli
Cáprio
Monte Sillara 1861 m
Lago Verde
Rossano
Arzelato
Filattiera
Mulazzo
Sasseta
Monteréggio
Gróppoli
Parana
Casoni
Bagnone
Villafranca
Tresana
Licciana
Cálice al Cornoviglio
Brugnato-Borghetto
Brugnato
Novegígola
Podenzana
Aulla
Brunella
Fivizzano
Cavanella Vara
Oltre Vara
Bolano
Riccò del Golfo di Spézia
M.Cárbolo 657 m
Foce il Cuccu 514 m
Fosdinovo
Foce
Stagnoni
Baccano
Romito
LA SPÉZIA
Sarzana
Castelnuovo Magra
Ortonovo
Carrara
Duomo
Bedizzano
Colonnata
Forno
Marola
Lérici
Tellaro
Portovénere
Terrizzo
Ísola Palmária
Montemarcello
Parco Naturale Cinque Terre
48
Marina di Carrara
Massa
Montignoso
Marina di Massa
Marina dei Ronchi
Strettóia
Seravezza
Forte dei Marmi
Marina di Pietrasanta
Versilia
Pietrasanta
Valdicastello
Riviera della Versilia
Lido di Camaiore
Viareggio-Camaiore
Viareggio
47
Camaiore
Stiava
Massarosa
Lago di Massaciúccoli
Macchia di Migliarino
Pisa-Nord
Migliarino
Nodica
Vecchiano
Parco di Migliarino, San Rossore, Massaciúccoli
Cascine Vecchie
Gombo
PISA
La Torre pendente
Tenuta di San Rossore
Pisa Centro
Arno
San Piero a Grado
Marina di Pisa
Tenuta di Tombolo
Tirrénia
Calambrone
Livorno
Torre della Melória
LIVORNO
Salviano
Parco delle Colline Livornesi
Montenero
Nibbiáia
Quercianella
Castiglioncello
Ranzano
Trevignano
Palanzano
Gázzolo
Castelnovo ne'Monti
Vecciatica
Mónchio
Ramiseto
Vairo
Nirone
Pietra Bismantova 1047 m
M. Fiorino 1017 m
Lago Calamone
Busana
Villa Minozzo
Succiso
M.Scalúcchia 1411 m
Collagna
Acquabona
Cerrè
M.Casarola 1978 m
Lago Paduli
dell'Appennino
M.Prampa 1699 m
Passo del Cerreto 1261 m
Cerreto dell'Alpi
Ligonchio
Camporághena
Comano
Sassalbo
Passo di Pradarena 1579 m
M.Cusna 2120 m
M.Prato 2053 m
Sillano
Casola in Lunigiana
Giuncugnano
Parco dell'Orecchiella
Piazza al Sérchio
San Romano in Garfagnana
49
Minucciano
Gramolazzo
Camporgiano
Póggio
Pieve Fosciana
M.Pisanino 1945 m
Gorfigliano
M.Umbriano 1229 m
Vinca
Antisciana
Careggine
Vagli Sopra
Lago di Vagli
Castelnuovo di Garfagnana
Parco Naturale Alpi Apuane
Sassi
Canevara
Molazzana
Pánia d. Croce 1858 m
Levigliani
Grotta del Vento
Trassilico
Stazzema
Vallécchia
Mulina
Pescaglia
Fiano
Torcigliano
Nocchi
Gombitelli
Valpromaro
Piazzano
Nozzano
Castello
Ospedaletto
Tenuta di Coltano
Palazzi

Pietre
Cigarello
Carpi
D
San Vitale
Magonfia
M.Fósala
987 m
Casteldaldo
Lugo
Montardone
E
Prignano sulla Sécchia
Serramazzoni
Levizzano Rangone
Marano s. Panaro
F
Oliveto
Ospitalette
Guiglia
Ponzano
Vologno
Carniana
Massa
P.te di Gómbola
la Berzigala
Montecorona
Monte Ombraro
5
Montepastore
Villa Minozzo
Montefiorino
Montebonello
Zocca
Vitriola
Savoniero
Polinago
Pavullo nel Frignano
Tolé
Marzabotto
la Verna
Coriano
M.Prampa
1699 m
E M I L I A R O
M.Modino
1414 m
Palagano
Lama Mocogno
Castello del Montecuccolo
Chiesa Carolingia
Pieve Roffeno
Vergato
Asta
Frassinoro
M.d.Penna
964 m
Villa d'Aiano
Castel d'Aiano
Tosco-Emiliano
Montese
Castelnuovo
Grizzana
Montecreto
Monteacuto Ragazza
Piandelagotti
Riolunato
M.Cervarola
1623 m
Sèstola
Rocchetta Mattei
Pso. delle Radici
1529 m
Pievepelago
M.Cimone
2165 m
Fanano
Gaggio Montano
Querciola
San Pellegrino in Alpe
49
Parco dell'Alto Appennino Modenese
Fiumalbo
M.Albano
1694 m
M.Láncio
1540 m
Vidiciático
Villagio Europa
Lizzano in Belvedere
Camugnano
Libro Aperto
1937 m
Porretta Terme
4
Castiglione di Garfagnana
Abetone
M.Giovo
1991 m
Monteacuto d'Alpi
Baigno
Castiglione dei Pépoli
Sillico
Pianosinatico
Granaglione
Lupináia
Cutigliano
Sambuca Pistoiese
M.Calvi
1283 m
Foce a Giovo
Sommocolonia 1674 m
Piano degli Ontani
Vizzaneta
Parco del Corno alle Scale
Castelvécchio Páscoli
Lagacci
Tréppio
Parco dei Laghi
Gallicano
Barga
Teréglio
Montefegatesi
Limano
Vico
San Marcello
Gavinana
Prácchia
Piano di Coreglia
Popiglio
Pontepetri
Passo d. Collina
932 m
Trassilico
Vitiana
Ghivizzano
Fábbriche
Lima
Pitéglio
Savaiana
Vállico
Bagni di Lucca
Casabasciana
M.Bucciana
1223 m
Motrone
Benábbio
Prunetta
Piastre
Pitéccio
Villa di Bággio
Fabbriche di Vállico
Borgo a Mozzano
Ponte della Maddalena
M.Battifolle
1105 m
Castelvécchio
Gello
Tobbiana
Fognano
Vaiano
Diécimo
M.Barbona
1026 m
San Quirico
Svizzera Pesciatina
Valdottavo
Pieve di Bráncoli
Villa Basilica
Marliana
51
PISTOIA
Montale
Montemurlo
3
San Donato
Aquilea
Massa
Serravalle Pistoiese
Pistóia
Agliana
Villa Torrigiani
Villa Reale
50
Collodi
San Gennaro
Villa Mansi
Péscia
PRATO
Piazzano
Márlia
Gragnano
Buggiano
Monsummano Terme
Cantagrillo
Prato Ovest
Lámmari
Montecatini Terme
Olmi
Prato Est
San Macario in Piano
Teatro Romano
Montecarlo
Chiesina Uzzanese
Casini
Iolo
Lucca
San Donato
10
Capannori
Quarrata
Villa d. Póggio a Caiano
Santa Maria
Settimello
Porcari
Ponte Buggianese
Pazzere
Larciano
Lucca
Capannori
Chiesina Uzzanese
Campi
Lamporécchio
Póggio a Caiano
Altopáscio
Anchione
San Rocco
Carmignano
Comeana
San Mauro
Altopáscio
Orentano
Ponte di Masino
Lazzeretto
52
Vinci
Signa
Monte Pisano
Galleno
Toiano
Artimino
Lastra a Signa
Colle di Cómpito
Cerreto Guidi
Sant' Ansano
San Giuliano
Ruota
Staffoli
Ponte a Cappiano
Castellina
Scandicci
Asciano
le Cerbáie
Certosa di Pisa (di Calci)
Montelupo Fiorentino
PISA
Mezzana
Calci
Buti
Cascine
Santa Croce sull'Arno
Fucécchio
Émpoli
Campo
Biéntina
Marcignana
Villanova
Ginestra
Riglione
Vicopisáno
Santa Maria a Monte
Castelfranco
Ponte a Égola
San Vincenzo a Torri
Casenuove
Cerbaia
Cáscina
Calcináia
Catena
San Miniato al Tedesco
Monterappoli
San Casciano in Val di Pesa
Ospedaletto
Sottili
San Lorenzo a Pagnático
Pontedera
Montópoli in Val d'Arno
Case Nuove
Montespertoli
Martí
Castelnuovo
Cambiano
Gello
Montecastello
Vallécchio
Ortimino
San Pancrazio
Balconevisi
Ponsacco
Vicarello
Paláia
Castel Fiorentino
Villa Saletta
Guasticce
Collesalvetti
Capánnoli
Montefóscoli
Toiano
Fiano
Petrazzi
Mura
Cévoli
Faúglia
Lari
San Pietro Belvedere
Légoli
Varna
Marcialla
Torretta
Créspina
Catignano
Montaione
Certaldo
35
Castelfalfi
Spicchio
Usigliano
Lorenzana
Péccioli
Luciana
Ghizzano
Gambassi Terme
S.Filippo
Montécchio
San Vivaldo
Terricciola
Crocino
Casciana Terme
Iano
Vico d'Elsa
Pieve Vécchia
Orciano Pisano
Larniano
Villamagna
San Gimignano
7
Poggibonsi
Santa Luce
Chianni
Pieve di Santa Luce
Laiático
Pástina
Spedaletto
Montauto
Castiglioni
Orciático
San Cipriano
Sensano
Colle di Val d'Elsa
207
33
Rosignano Marittima
Póggio di Mela
654 m
210
Colle-Sud
Castellma Marittima
Volterra
34
D
E
F
Miemo
Rosignano Solvay
Montecatini
Quartáia
Rosignano-

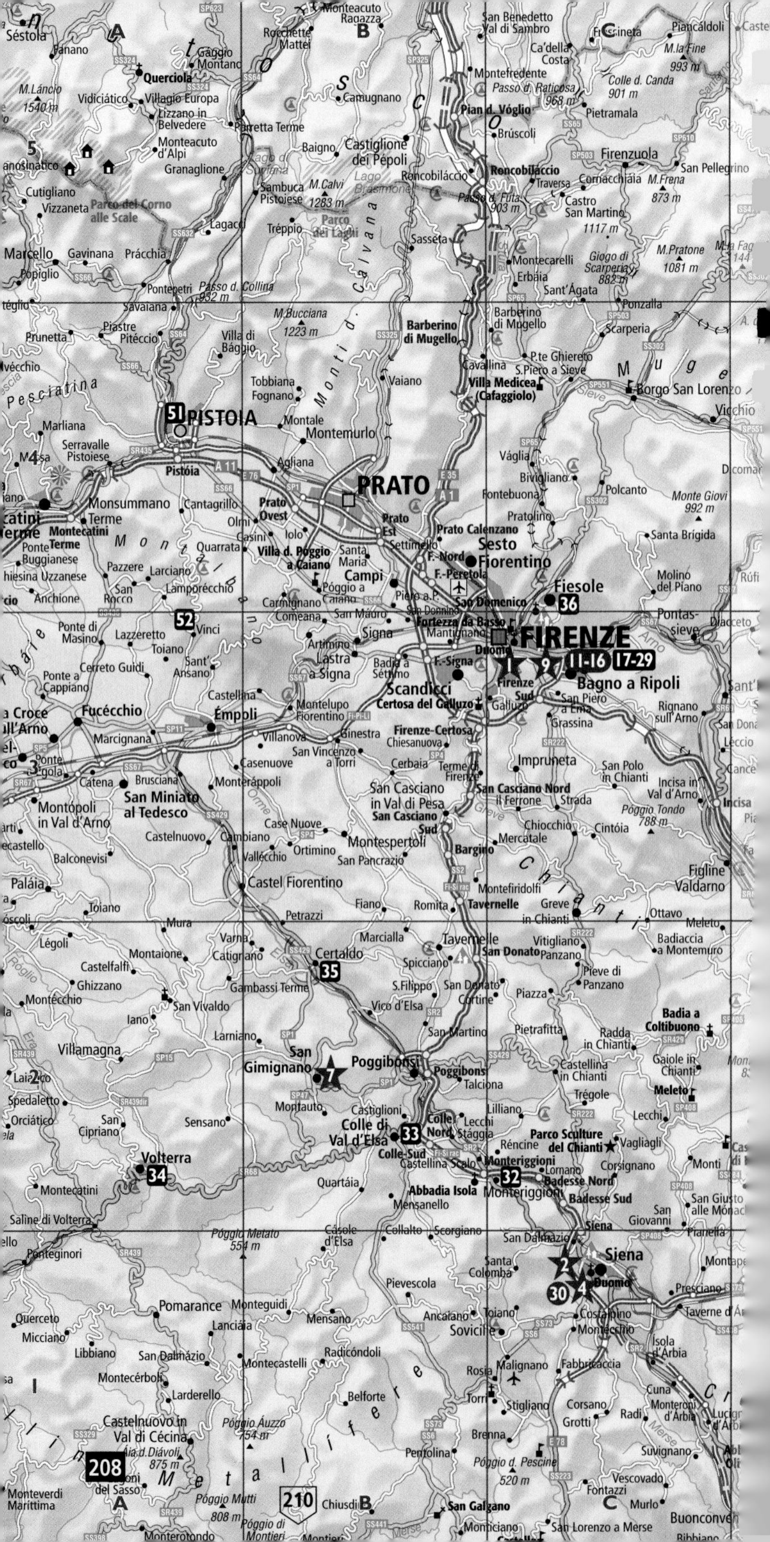

A
B
C
Séstola
Fanano
Querciola
Gaggio Montano
M.Láncio 1540 m
Vidiciático
Villagio Europa
Lizzano in Belvedere
Porretta Terme
Monteacuto d'Alpi
Granaglione
Cutigliano
Vizzaneta
Parco del Corno alle Scale
Sambuca Pistoiese
Lagacci
Tréppio
Parco dei Laghi
M.Calvi 1283 m
Lago Brasimone
Marcello
Gavinana
Prácchia
Popiglio
Pontepetri
Passo d. Collina 932 m
Savaiana
Rocchette Mattei
Monteacuto Ragazza
Camugnano
Baigno
Castiglione dei Pépoli
Roncobiláccio
San Benedetto Val di Sambro
Ca'della Costa
Montefredente
Passo d. Raticosa 968 m
Pian d. Vóglio
Brúscoli
Fiorenzuola
Piancáldoli
M.la Fine 993 m
Colle d. Canda 901 m
Pietramala
Firenzuola
San Pellegrino
Traversa
Cornacchiáia
M.Frena 873 m
Passo d. Futa 903 m
Castro San Martino 1117 m
Sasseta
Montecarelli
Erbáia
Giogo di Scarperia 882 m
M.Pratone 1081 m
Sant'Ágata
Ponzalla
Calvana
Monti d. Calvana
Prunetta
Piastre
Pitéccio
Villa di Bággio
M.Bucciana 1223 m
Barberino di Mugello
Scarperia
Tobbiana
Fognano
Vaiano
Cavallina
Villa Medicea (Cafaggiolo)
P.te Ghiereto
S.Piero a Sieve
Borgo San Lorenzo
Mugello
Vicchio
Pesciatina
PISTOIA
51
Marliana
Serravalle Pistoiese
Montale
Montemurlo
Váglia
Massa
Pistóia
Agliana
PRATO
Bivigliano
Polcanto
Dicomano
Monsummano Terme
Cantagrillo
Prato Ovest
Fontebuona
Monte Giovi 992 m
Montecatini Terme
Olmi
Iolo
Prato Est
Prato Calenzano
Pratolino
Ponte Buggianese
Quarrata
Casini
Villa d. Poggio a Caiano
Settimello
Sesto Fiorentino
Santa Brígida
Chiesina Uzzanese
Pazzere
Larciano
Santa Maria
Campi
F.-Nord
F.-Peretola
Fiesole
36
Molino del Piano
Anchione
San Rocco
Lamporécchio
Póggio a Caiano
Carmignano
Piero a P.
San Doménico
Montalbano
Comeana
San Mauro
San Donnino
Fortezza da Basso
Pontassieve
Diacceto
52
Vinci
Ponte di Masino
Lazzeretto
Toiano
Artimino
Signa
Mantignano
FIRENZE
Duomo
1
9
11-16
17-29
Sant' Ansano
Cerreto Guidi
Lastra a Signa
Badia a Séttimo
F.-Signa
Scandicci
Firenze Sud
Bagno a Ripoli
Ponte a Cappiano
Castellina
Certosa del Galluzzo
Galluzzo
San Piero a Ema
Rignano sull'Arno
Santa Croce sull'Arno
Fucécchio
Montelupo Fiorentino
Émpoli
Grassina
Marcignana
Villanova
Ginestra
Firenze-Certosa
Chiesanuova
San Vincenzo a Torri
Ponte a Egola
Casenuove
Cerbaia
Terme di Firenze
Impruneta
San Polo in Chianti
Incisa in Val d'Arno
Catena
Brusciana
San Miniato al Tedesco
Monteráppoli
San Casciano in Val di Pesa
San Casciano Nord
Il Ferrone
Strada
Incisa
Montópoli in Val d'Arno
San Casciano Sud
Chiocchio
Póggio Tondo 788 m
Castelnuovo
Cambiano
Case Nuove
Montespertoli
Mercatale
Cintóia
Balconevisi
Vallécchio
Ortimino
San Pancrazio
Bargino
Chianti
Paláia
Castel Fiorentino
Montefiridolfi
Figline Valdarno
Toiano
Fiano
Romita
Tavernelle
Greve in Chianti
Ottavo
Meleto
Petrazzi
Mura
Varna
Catignano
Certaldo
35
Marcialla
Tavernelle
San Donato
Vitigliano
Panzano
Badiaccia a Montemuro
Légoli
Montaione
Castelfalfi
Spicciano
Pieve di Panzano
Ghizzano
Gambassi Terme
S.Filippo
San Donato
Montécchio
San Vivaldo
Vico d'Elsa
Cortine
Piazza
Badia a Coltibuono
Iano
Larniano
San Martino
Pietrafitta
Radda in Chianti
Villamagna
San Gimignano
7
Poggibonsi
Poggibonsi
Castellina in Chianti
Gaiole in Chianti
Talciona
Meleto
Spedaletto
Montauto
Castiglioni
Lilliano
Trégole
Orciático
San Cipriano
Sensano
Colle di Val d'Elsa
33
Colle Nord
Lecchi
Stággia
Lecchi
Réncine
Parco Sculture del Chianti
Vagliagli
Volterra
34
Colle-Sud
Castellina Scalo
Monteriggioni
Lornano
Corsignano
Monti
Montecatini
Quartáia
Abbadia Isola
32
Monteriggioni
Badesse Nord
Badesse Sud
San Giusto alle Monache
Mensanello
Saline di Volterra
Póggio Metato 554 m
Cásole d'Elsa
Collalto
Scorgiano
San Dalmazio
Siena
San Giovanni
Pianella
Ponteginori
Santa Colomba
2
Siena
30
4
Duomo
Pievescola
Presciano
Taverne d'Arbia
Pomarance
Monteguidi
Mensano
Ancaiano
Toiano
Sovicille
Costalpino
Montecchio
Querceto
Micciano
Lanciáia
Radicóndoli
Isola d'Arbia
Libbiano
San Dalmázio
Montecastelli
Malignano
Fabbricaccia
Rosia
Montecérboli
Larderello
Belforte
Torri
Stigliano
Corsano
Cuna
Monteroni d'Arbia
Radi
Grotti
Castelnuovo in Val di Cécina
Póggio Áuzzo 754 m
Brenna
Colline Metallifere
Merse
Suvignano
208
M.ta d.Diávoli 875 m
Pentolina
Póggio d. Pescine 520 m
Sasso
del Sasso
Vescovado
Fontazzi
Monteverdi Maríttima
Póggio Mutti 808 m
210
Chiusdino
San Galgano
Murlo
Buonconvento
Póggio di Montieri
Montieri
Monterotondo
Monticiano
San Lorenzo a Merse
Bibbiano

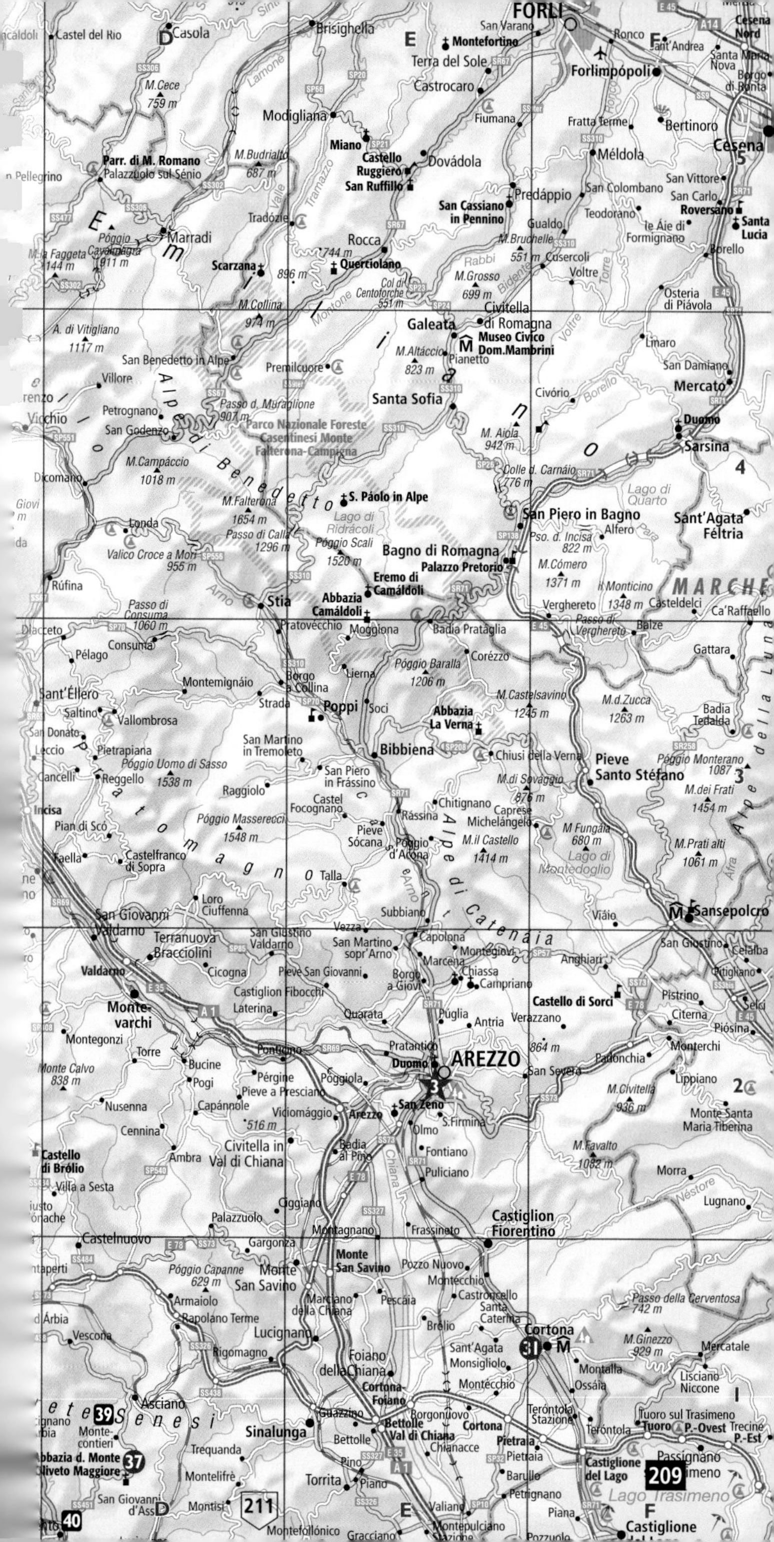

Castel del Rio
Casola
Brisighella
E
Montefortino
FORLÌ
San Varano
Ronco
F
Sant'Andrea
Cesena Nord
A14
E 45
Terra del Sole
Castrocaro
Forlimpópoli
Santa Maria Nova
Borgo di Ronta
M.Cece 759 m
Lamone
Modigliana
Fiumana
Fratta Terme
Bertinoro
Cesena
Miano
Castello Ruggiero
San Ruffillo
Dovádola
Méldola
5
Parr. di M. Romano
Palazzuolo sul Sénio
M.Budrialto 687 m
Predáppio
San Colombano
San Vittore
San Carlo
Roversano
Santa Lucia
Marradi
Tradózio
San Cassiano in Pennino
Teodorano
le Áie di Formignano
Póggio Cavallara 911 m
M.la Faggeta 1144 m
Rocca
Quertiolano
Scarzana
896 m
Gualdo
M.Bruchelle 551 m
Cusercoli
Borello
Voltre
Col di Centoforche 551 m
M.Grosso 699 m
Osteria di Piávola
M.Collina 974 m
Civitella di Romagna
Galeata
Museo Civico Dom.Mambrini
A. di Vitigliano 1117 m
M.Altáccio 823 m
Pianetto
Linaro
San Benedetto in Alpe
Premilcuore
San Damiano
Villore
Mercato
Santa Sofia
Civório
Petrognano
Passo d. Muraglione 907 m
Parco Nazionale Foreste Casentinesi Monte Falterona-Campigna
Vicchio
San Godenzo
Duomo
M. Aiola 942 m
Sarsina
M.Campáccio 1018 m
Dicomano
Colle d. Carnáio 776 m
4
Lago di Quarto
M.Falterona 1654 m
S. Páolo in Alpe
San Piero in Bagno
Sant'Agata Féltria
Lago di Ridrácoli
Londa
Alfero
Passo di Calla 1296 m
Póggio Scali 1520 m
Pso. d. Incisa 822 m
Bagno di Romagna
Palazzo Pretorio
Valico Croce a Mori 955 m
M.Cómero 1371 m
MARCHE
Eremo di Camáldoli
Rúfina
Il Monticino 1348 m
Abbazia Camáldoli
Stia
Verghereto
Casteldelci
Ca'Raffaello
Passo di Consuma 1060 m
Passo di Verghereto
Diacceto
Pratovécchio
Moggiona
Badia Prataglia
Balze
Consuma
Pélago
Gattara
Póggio Baralla 1206 m
Corézzo
Lierna
Montemignáio
Borgo a Collina
Sant'Éllero
M.Castelsavino 1245 m
M.d.Zucca 1263 m
Strada
Poppi
Soci
Saltino
Vallombrosa
Abbazia La Verna
Badia Tedalda
San Donato
San Martino in Tremoleto
Leccio
Pietrapiana
Bibbiena
Chiusi della Verna
Pieve Santo Stéfano
Póggio Monterano 1087 m
Póggio Uomo di Sasso 1538 m
San Piero in Frássino
Cancelli
Reggello
M.di Sovággio 876 m
3
M.dei Frati 1454 m
Raggiolo
Chitignano
Castel Focognano
Caprese Michelángelo
Incisa
Rássina
Póggio Masserecci 1548 m
M Fungáia 680 m
Pian di Scó
Pieve Sócana
Póggio d'Acona
M.il Castello 1414 m
M.Prati alti 1061 m
Faella
Castelfranco di Sopra
Lago di Montedoglio
Talla
Alpe della Luna
Pratomagno
Alpe di Catenaia
Loro Ciuffenna
Sansepolcro
Viáio
San Giovanni Valdarno
Subbiano
Vezza
Capolona
San Giustino Valdarno
San Martino sopr'Arno
Terranuova Bracciolini
Montegiovi
Anghiari
San Giustino
Celalba
Valdarno
Cicogna
Marcena
Chiassa
Pitigliano
Pieve San Giovanni
Borgo a Giovi
Campriano
Castiglion Fibocchi
Pistrino
Monte-varchi
Laterina
Castello di Sorci
Selci
Púglia
Citerna
A 1
Antria
Verazzano
Quarata
Montegonzi
Piósina
864 m
Torre
Pontíno
Pratantico
Monterchi
Duomo
AREZZO
Padonchia
Bucine
Monte Calvo 838 m
Pérgine
Póggiola
San Severo
Lippiano
Pogi
Pieve a Presciano
2
San Zeno
Nusenna
Capánnole
M.Civitella 936 m
Vicioméggio
Arezzo
S.Firmina
516 m
Monte Santa Maria Tiberina
Cennina
Olmo
Castello di Brólio
Civitella in Val di Chiana
Badia al Pino
Fontiano
M.Favalto 1082 m
Ambra
Puliciano
Villa a Sesta
Morra
Nèstore
Ciggiano
Lugnano
Chiana
Palazzuolo
Castiglion Fiorentino
Castelnuovo
Montagnano
Frassineto
Gargonza
Monte San Savino
Pozzo Nuovo
Póggio Capanne 629 m
Monte San Savino
Montecchio
Castroncello
Armaiolo
Marciano della Chiana
Pescáia
Santa Caterina
Passo della Cerventosa 742 m
Rapolano Terme
Vescona
Lucignano
Brólio
Cortona
M
M.Ginezzo 929 m
Mercatale
Rigomagno
Sant'Agata
Foiano della Chiana
Monsigliolo
Montalla
Lisciano Niccone
Ossáia
Asciano
Cortona-Foiano
Montecchio
Crete Senesi
39
Guazzino
Borgonuovo
Teróntola Stazione
Tuoro sul Trasimeno
Teróntola
Tuoro
P.-Ovest
Trecine
P.-Est
Monte-contieri
Sinalunga
Bettolle Val di Chiana
Cortona
Pietraia
Bettolle
Chianacce
Castiglione del Lago
Passignano
37
Trequanda
Abbazia d. Monte Oliveto Maggiore
Pino
Pietraia
Montelifrè
Torrita
Barullo
Piano
Lago Trasimeno
Petrignano
San Giovanni d'Asso
D
Montisi
211
E
Valiano
Piana
F
Castiglione
40
Montefollónico
Gracciano
Montepulciano

207
A
B
C
5
4
3
2
1
Rosignano Solvay
Rosignano Maríttimo
Riparbella
Montecatini
Saline di Volterra
Quartáia
Abbadia Isola
Mensanello
Collemezzano
Gello
Ponteginori
Póggio Metato 554 m
Cásole d'Elsa
Collalto
Scorgiano
Cécina
Montescudáio
Guardistallo
Casale Maríttima
M. Pozzácchera 382 m
Querceto
Micciano
Pomarance
Monteguidi
Lanciáia
Mensano
Pievescola
Ancaiano
Sovicille
la Califórnia
Bibbona
Sassa
Libbiano
San Dalmázio
Montecérboli
Montecastelli
Radicóndoli
Marina di Bibbona
Bólgheri
Larderello
Belforte
Maremma Pisana
Colline Metallífere
Castelnuovo in Val di Cécina
Áia d. Diávoli 875 m
Póggio Áuzzo 754 m
Pentolina
Castagneto-Donorático
Donorático
Castagneto Carducci
Monteverdi Maríttima
Lagoni del Sasso
Póggio Mutti 808 m
Chiusdino
Póggio di Montieri 1051 m
Montieri
Póggio Fogari 726 m
Monterotondo Maríttimo
Sassetta
Fontalcinaldo
San Carlo
M. Calvi 646 m
San Vincenzo
Suvereto
M. Arsenti 561 m
Prata
Boccheggiano
TOS
Campíglia Maríttima
Massa Maríttima
Rimigliano
Cafággio
Venturina
Casalappi
Parco di Montioni
Tatti
Roccatederighi
Sassofortino
Montioni
Valpiana
Póggio al Chiecco 308 m
Lago d. Accesa
Montemassi
Golfo di Baratti
Tombe etrusche
Populónia
Riotorto
Vignale
Ribolla
Monte Lattáia
Piombino
Prato Ranieri
Rondelli
Follónica
Gavorrano
Póggio d. Quercione 239 m
Stocciano Scalo
Sticciano
Canale di Piombino
Scarlino
Ravi
M. d'Alma 559 m
Caldana
Montepescali
Batignano
Golfo di Follónica
I. d. Topi
I. Palmaiola
I. Cérboli
Vetulónia
Tirli
Buriano
Póggio Ballone 630 m
Póggio di Moscona 317 m
Rio Marina
Punta Hidalgo
Punta Ala
Inset
Punta delle Cannelle
Póggio di Petriccio
Pineta del Tómbolo
Canale Diversivo
Grosseto
Castiglione della Pescáia
Porto Azzurro
Grancia
Marina di Grosseto
Ríspéscia
Principina a Mare
Punta dei Ripalti
Mar Tirreno
Spergoláia
Alberese
Marina di Alberese
Torre di Collelungo
Monti dell'Uccellina
San Rabano
Ísola d'Elba
Piombino
C. Vita
Cavo
I. d. Topi
I. Palmaiola
M. Serra 422 m
Golfo di Prócchio
Capo d'Enfola
Portoferráio
Rio nell'Elba
Bagnáia
Rio Marina
Marciana Marina
Sant'Andrea
Biódola
Madonna del Monte
Marciana
Spartáia
Villa Napoleone
Monte Capanne 1019 m
Póggio
Prócchio
Punta delle Cannelle
La Pila
San Ilário in Campo
Porto Azzurro
Parco Naturale della Maremma
Talamone
Pomonte
Lacona
Fetováia
San Piero in Campo
Marina di Campo
Golfo di Lacona
Golfo Stella
Capoliveri
Tómbolo di Giannella
P. di Fetováia
C. di Poro
Punta dei Ripalti
Parco Nazionale dell'Arcipelago Toscano
Golfo di Campo
Porto Santo Stéfano
P. Cala Grande
Ísola del Gíglio
P. d. Fenáio
Gíglio Castello
Arenella
Gíglio Campese
Gíglio Porto
Póggio della Pagana 496 m
P. d. Capel Rosso
Parco Nazionale dell'Arcipelago Toscano
C. d'Uomo
I. Rossa
P. di Torre Ciana

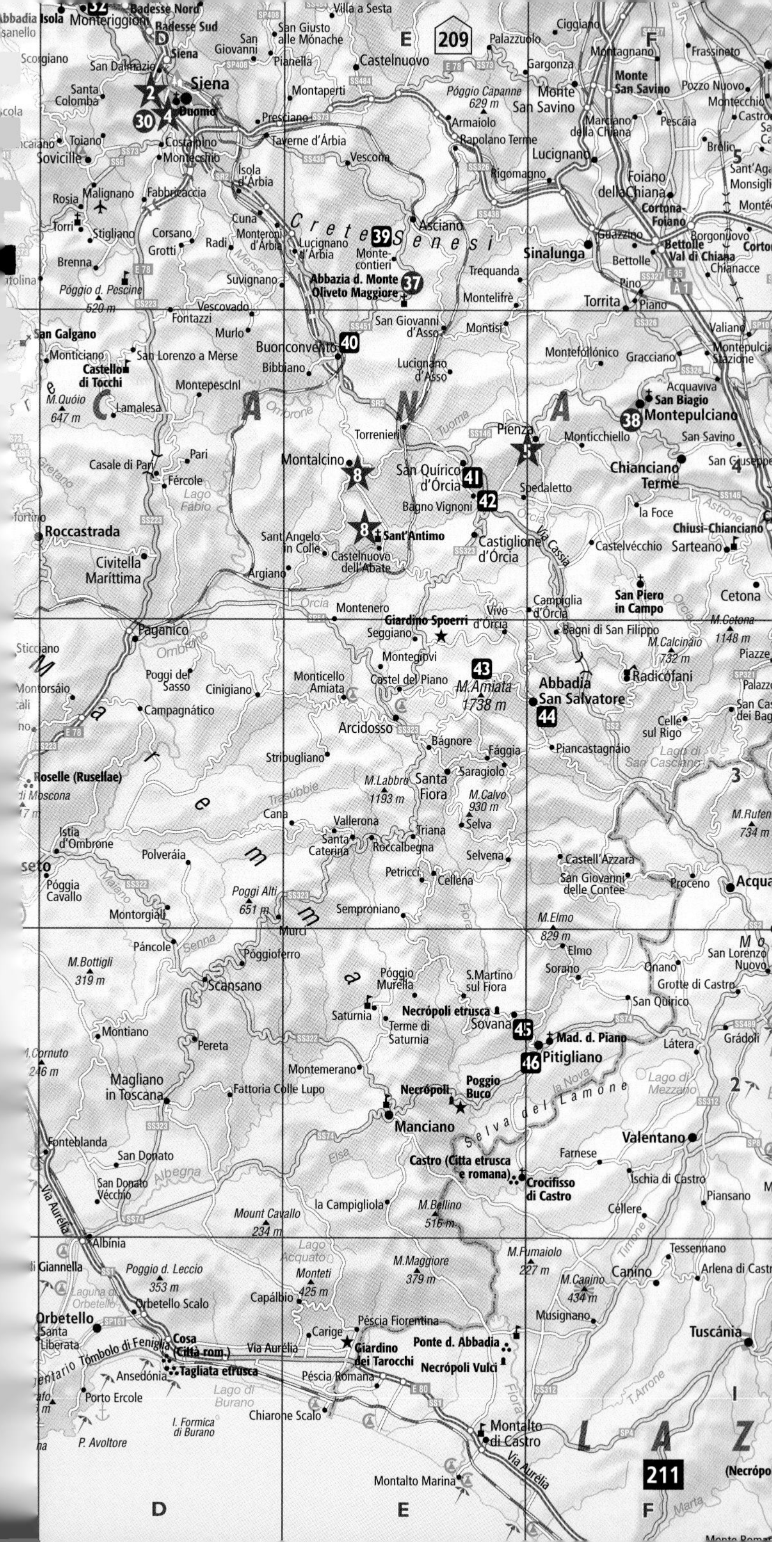

Badesse Nord
Monteriggioni
Badesse Sud
Villa a Sesta
San Giusto alle Mònache
San Giovanni
Pianella
E
209
Palazzuolo
Ciggiano
F
Montagnano
Frassineto
Scorgiano
San Dalmazio
Siena
Castelnuovo
Gargonza
Monte San Savino
Pozzo Nuovo
Santa Colomba
Duomo
Montaperti
Póggio Capanne 629 m
Monte San Savino
Montecchio
Prescìano
Armaiolo
Marciano della Chiana
Pescàia
Castro
Toiano
Costalpino
Taverne d'Àrbia
Rapolano Terme
Brolio
Sovicille
Montecchio
Vescona
Lucignano
Rigomagno
Foiano della Chiana
Monsigli
Rosia
Malignano
Fabbricaccia
Isola d'Àrbia
Cortona-Foiano
Torri
Stigliano
Corsano
Cuna
Monteroni d'Àrbia
Crete Senesi
39
Asciano
Guazzino
Borgonuovo
Cortona
Grotti
Radi
Lucignano d'Àrbia
Monte-contieri
Sinalunga
Bettolle
Val di Chiana
Bettolle
Chianacce
Brenna
Merse
Suvignano
Abbazia d. Monte Oliveto Maggiore
37
Trequanda
Pino
Póggio d. Pescine 520 m
Montelifrè
Torrita
Piano
Vescovado
Fontazzi
Murlo
San Giovanni d'Asso
Montisi
Valiano
San Galgano
Buonconvento
40
Montefollónico
Gracciano
Montepulciano Stazione
Monticiano
San Lorenzo a Merse
Castello di Tocchi
Bibbiano
Lucignano d'Asso
Acquaviva
San Biagio
Montepescini
Montepulciano
38
M. Quóio 647 m
Lamalesa
Ombrone
Torrenieri
Pienza
Monticchiello
San Savino
Tuoma
Pari
Casale di Pari
Montalcino
8
San Quírico d'Órcia
41
5
Chianciano Terme
San Giuseppe
Fércole
Lago Fábio
Bagno Vignoni
42
Spedaletto
la Foce
Roccastrada
Sant'Angelo in Colle
8
Sant'Antimo
Castiglione d'Órcia
Chiusi-Chianciano
Castelvécchio
Sarteano
Civitella Maríttima
Castelnuovo dell'Abate
Argiano
Via Cassia
San Piero in Campo
Campiglia d'Órcia
Cetona
Montenero
Giardino Spoerri
Vivo d'Órcia
M. Cetona 1148 m
Paganico
Seggiano
Bagni di San Filippo
Sticciano
M. Calcinàio 732 m
Montegiovi
43
Piazze
Poggi del Sasso
Monticello Amiata
Castel del Piano
M. Amiata 1738 m
Abbadia San Salvatore
Radicófani
Montorsáio
Cinigiano
44
Campagnático
Arcidosso
Celle sul Rigo
San Casciano dei Bagni
Bagnore
Fággia
Piancastagnáio
Stribugliano
Lago di San Casciano
Roselle (Rusellae)
Santa Fiora
Saragiolo
M. Labbro 1193 m
M. Calvo 930 m
Trasúbbie
3
Cana
M. Rufeno 734 m
Selva
Vallerona
Istia d'Ombrone
Santa Caterina
Roccalbegna
Triana
Selvena
Polveráia
Castell'Azzara
Petricci
Cellena
San Giovanni delle Contee
Proceno
Acquapendente
Póggia Cavallo
Poggi Alti 651 m
Maremma
Semproniano
Montorgiali
Fiora
M. Elmo 829 m
Murci
Páncole
Senna
Póggioferro
Elmo
San Lorenzo Nuovo
M. Bottigli 319 m
Sorano
Onano
Póggio Murella
S. Martino sul Fiora
Grotte di Castro
Scansano
San Quírico
Saturnia
Necrópoli etrusca
Sovana
45
Mad. d. Piano
Terme di Saturnia
Grádoli
Montiano
Pereta
Látera
46
Pitigliano
M. Cornuto 246 m
Montemerano
Lago di Mezzano
Magliano in Toscana
Fattoria Colle Lupo
Necrópoli
Poggio Buco
Selva del Lamone
la Nova
2
Manciano
Valentano
Fonteblanda
Farnese
San Donato
Castro (Città etrusca e romana)
Crocifisso di Castro
Ischia di Castro
San Donato Vecchio
Albegna
Elsa
Piansano
Via Aurélia
la Campigliola
M. Bellino 516 m
Mount Cavallo 234 m
Céllere
Albínia
Lago Acquato
M. Fumaiolo 227 m
Tessennano
Giannella
Poggio d. Leccio 353 m
Monteti 425 m
M. Maggiore 379 m
Timone
Canino
Arlena di Castro
Laguna di Orbetello
Orbetello Scalo
Capálbio
M. Canino 434 m
Musignano
Orbetello
Santa Liberata
Péscia Fiorentina
Tuscánia
Cosa (Città rom.)
Carige
Giardino dei Tarocchi
Ponte d. Abbadia
Tómbolo di Feniglia
Via Aurélia
Necrópoli Vulci
Ansedónia
Tagliata etrusca
Péscia Romana
Lago di Burano
T. Arrone
Porto Ercole
I. Formica di Burano
Chiarone Scalo
Montalto di Castro
P. Avoltore
Lazio
Montalto Marina
211
D
E
F
Marta

Firenze
Stazione Santa Maria Novella
Terminal
Museo di Storia della Fotografia Alinari
Piazza della Stazione
SITA
V. S. Caterina da Siena
Via Luigi Alamanni
Via Nazionale
S. Jacopino in Campo Carbolini
Piazza del Mercato Centrale
19
Via Rosina
Via dell'Ariento
Palazzo Bandinelli
Borgo la Noce
Pal. Ginori
SAN GIOVANNI
Pal. da Montauto
V. Sant'Antonino
Via Faenza
Via del Canto dei Nelli
Cappelle Medicee
12
18
S. Lorenzo
Biblioteca Laurenziana
B. S. Lorenzo
Pal. d. Cartelloni
Piazza dell'Unità Italiana
Via d. Melarancio
S. Maria Novella
13
Via d. Panzani
Via del Giglio
Via dei Conti
Via d. Avelli
Palazzo Ginori Venturi
Via degli Orti Oricellari
Via Palazzuolo
Via dell'Albero
Via di S. Lucia
Via della Scala
Il Prato
Via M. Finiguerra
Via Montebello
Borgo Ognissanti
S. Francesco d. Vanchetoni
Ognissanti
Museo Naz. Alinari della Fotografia
Piazza Santa Maria Novella
Via dei Banchi
P. S. Maria Maggiore
Via d. Cerretani
Piazza San Giovanni
Battistero
Piazza dell'Olio
Pal. Orlandini
Via d. Pecori
S. Paolino
Via del Porcellana
Ospedale S. Giovanni di Dio
Piazza d. Ottaviani
Via del Moro
Via del Trebbio
Pal. Antinori
San Gaetano
Via delle Belle Donne
Museo Marino Marini (S. Pancrazio)
Via dei Tosinghi
Via Roma
Loggia d. Bigallo
Lungarno Amerigo Vespucci
Pescaia S. Rosa
Via della Spada
Pal. Rucellai
V. dei Fossi
V. Palchetti
Via d. Tornabuoni
Via d. Pescioni
Palazzo Corsi
Palazzo Vecchietti
Piazza della Repubblica
Via d. Speziali
Via dei Calzaiuoli
Via d. Strozzi
Palazzo Strozzi
Piazza Strozzi
Piazza Goldoni
Via della Vigna Nuova
SANTA MARIA NOVELLA
Palazzo Corsini
Via d. Parione
Via d. Anselmi
Pal. dell' Arte d. Lana
Poste e Telegrafi
Via Pellicceria
Palazzo Strozzino
22
Or San Michele
Lungarno Soderini
Piazza di Cestello
S. Frediano in Cestello
Ponte alla Carraia
Lungarno Corsini
Santa Trinità
Pal. Bartolini
Pza. d. Davanzati
Pal. Davanzati
23
Via Porta Rossa
24
Via d. Terme
Mercato Nuovo
Palazzo Fenzi
Pal. Canacci
Pal. di Parte Guelfa
Puppentheater Sala Vanni
Borgo San Frediano
Piazza N. Sauro
Chiesa Scozzese
Mus. S. Ferragamo
Pal. Ferroni
Borgo Santi Apostoli
S. S. Apostoli
Via Por S. Maria
Via Vacchereccia
Lungarno Acciaioli
Fiume Arno
Lungarno Guicciardini
Via Santo Spirito
Palazzo Guicciardini
Ponte S. Trinità
Piazza del Carmine
Borgo Stella
V. d. Ardiglione
Via dei Serragli
Via Maffia
SANTO SPIRITO
Pal. Frescobaldi
S. Stefano
Galleria degli Uffizi
Lug. Archibusieri
Cappella Brancacci
26
Santa Maria del Carmine
Via S. Monaca
Santo Spirito
Via d. Presto di S. Martino
Via Maggio
S. Jacopo sopr'Arno
Borgo Sant' Jacopo
25
Ponte Vecchio
Via de'Bardi
Via d'Ardiglione
Via Sant'Agostino
Piazza Santo Spirito
Casa di Bianca
Palazzo R. Firidolfi
Via dello Sprone
Via Toscanella
Via Guicciardini
Pza. S. Felicita
Pza. S. Maria sopr'Arno
Via d. Michelozzi
Palazzo Ridolfi
S. Felicità
Palazzo Guadagni
Borgo Tegolaio
Sdr. de'Pitti
Grotta del Buontalenti
Costa di San Giorgio
C. de'Magnoli
Via della Chiesa
Palazzo Corsini
Piazza de'Pitti
Bacchus-brunnen
San Girolamo
Via d. Caldaie
Via Mazzetta
San Felice
Piazza San Felice
28
Palazzo Pitti
Santo Spirito
Via del Campuccio
Via Romana
Museo Zoologico (la Spècola)
Anfiteatro
Caffè
Forte di Belvedere
Via Serumido
Fontana di Nettuno
Porta S.
27
Giardino di Bóboli
Museo delle Porcellane
Isolotto
Via di San Leonardo
Via Madonna della Pace
Istituto d'Arte (ex Scuderie Reali)
Via del Mascherino
Via del Bobolino
A
B
C
1
2
3
4
5

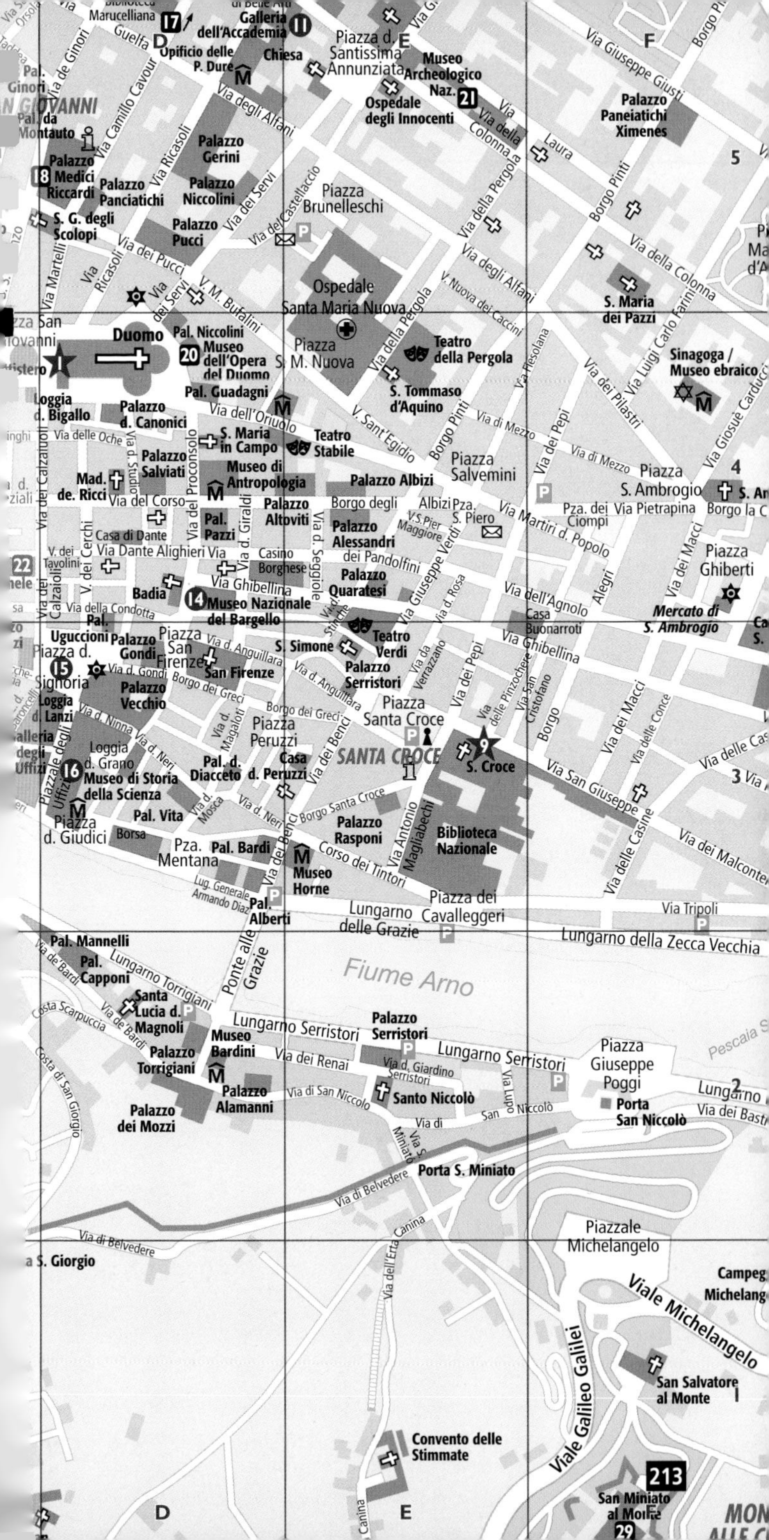

Marucelliana
Galleria dell'Accademia
Opificio delle P. Dure
Chiesa
Piazza d. Santissima Annunziata
Museo Archeologico Naz.
Ospedale degli Innocenti
Palazzo Paneiatichi Ximenes
Pal. da Montauto
Palazzo Medici Riccardi
Palazzo Panciatichi
Palazzo Gerini
Palazzo Niccolini
Piazza Brunelleschi
S. G. degli Scolopi
Palazzo Pucci
Ospedale Santa Maria Nuova
S. Maria dei Pazzi
Duomo
Pal. Niccolini
Museo dell'Opera del Duomo
Piazza S. M. Nuova
Teatro della Pergola
Sinagoga / Museo ebraico
S. Tommaso d'Aquino
Pal. Guadagni
Loggia d. Bigallo
Palazzo d. Canonici
S. Maria in Campo
Teatro Stabile
Palazzo Salviati
Museo di Antropologia
Palazzo Albizi
Piazza Salvemini
Piazza S. Ambrogio
Mad. de. Ricci
Pal. Pazzi
Palazzo Altoviti
Palazzo Alessandri
Casa di Dante
Casino Borghese
Palazzo Quaratesi
Piazza Ghiberti
Badia
Museo Nazionale del Bargello
Casa Buonarroti
Mercato di S. Ambrogio
Pal. Uguccioni
Palazzo Gondi
Piazza San Firenze
San Firenze
S. Simone
Teatro Verdi
Palazzo Serristori
Piazza d. Signoria
Palazzo Vecchio
Loggia d. Lanzi
Piazza Santa Croce
Piazza Peruzzi
SANTA CROCE
S. Croce
Galleria degli Uffizi
Loggia d. Grano
Museo di Storia della Scienza
Pal. d. Diacceto
Casa d. Peruzzi
Palazzo Rasponi
Biblioteca Nazionale
Piazza d. Giudici
Pal. Vita
Borsa
Pza. Mentana
Pal. Bardi
Museo Horne
Pal. Alberti
Piazza dei Cavalleggeri
Lungarno delle Grazie
Lungarno della Zecca Vecchia
Pal. Mannelli
Pal. Capponi
Lungarno Torrigiani
Ponte alle Grazie
Fiume Arno
Santa Lucia d. Magnoli
Museo Bardini
Palazzo Torrigiani
Palazzo Serristori
Lungarno Serristori
Piazza Giuseppe Poggi
Palazzo Alamanni
Palazzo dei Mozzi
Santo Niccolò
Porta San Niccolò
Porta S. Miniato
Via di Belvedere
Piazzale Michelangelo
Viale Michelangelo
Viale Galileo Galilei
San Salvatore al Monte
Convento delle Stimmate
San Miniato al Monte
213

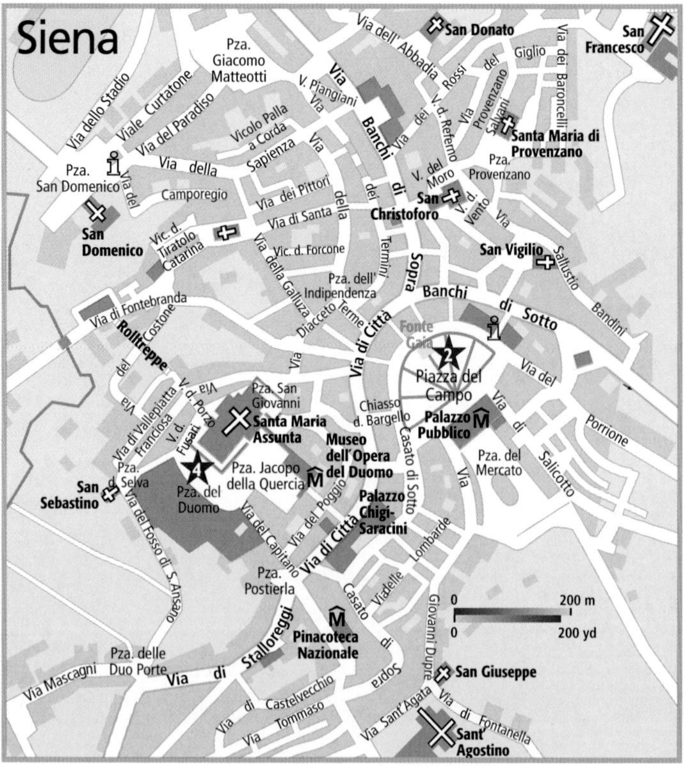

Siena
Pza. Giacomo Matteotti
Via dell' Abbadia
San Donato
Via dei Baroncelli
San Francesco
Via dello Stadio
Viale Curtatone
Via del Paradiso
V. Piangiani
Via Banchi di Christoforo
Rossi
Giglio
Vicolo Palla a Corda
Sapienza
Via dei Rossi
V. d. Referno
Via Provenzano Salvani
Santa Maria di Provenzano
Pza. San Domenico
Via della Camporegio
Via dei Pittori
V. del Moro
Pza. Provenzano
San Cristoforo
V. d. Vento
San Domenico
Vic. d. Tiratolo Catarina
Via di Santa
Via della Galluza
Vic. d. Forcone
Pza. dell' Indipendenza
Via dei Termini
Sopra
San Vigilio
Sallustio
Bandini
Via di Fontebranda
Costone
Rolltreppe
Diacceto
Terme
Banchi di Sotto
Fonte Gaia
Piazza del Campo
Via di Città
Via del Porrione
V. d. Porzo
Pza. San Giovanni
Santa Maria Assunta
Chiasso d. Bargello
Palazzo Pubblico
Via di Vallepiatta
Franciosa
V. d. Fusari
Museo dell'Opera del Duomo
Casato di Sotto
Pza. del Mercato
Via di Salicotto
Pza. d. Selva
Pza. Jacopo della Quercia
San Sebastino
Pza. del Duomo
Via del Poggio
Palazzo Chigi-Saracini
Via del Fosso di S. Ansano
Via del Capitano
Lombarde
Pza. Postierla
Viadelle
Giovanni Dupré
0 200 m
0 200 yd
Pinacoteca Nazionale
Casato di Sopra
Pza. delle Duo Porte
Via di Stalloreggi
Via Mascagni
San Giuseppe
Via di Castelvecchio
Via Tommaso
Via Sant'Agata
Via di Fontanella
Sant' Agostino

Porta S. Donata
0 200 m
0 200 yd
Piazzale Verdi
Via Tassi
Via della Stuta
Pza. S. Agostino
San Frediano
Pza S. Maria
S. M. Corte-orlandini
C. Battisti
Via San Frediano
Fillungo
Via S. Gemma Galigani
Via S. Giustina
Galli
Palazzo Orsetti
Via d. Angeli
C. Compagni
Pza. Anfiteatro
Via dell'Anfiteatro
San Salvatore
Via S. Giorgio
Via Crocefisso
S. Paolino
Pza. Cittadella
Via Calderia
San Michele in Foro
Antonio
Pza. S. Pietro Somaldi
Via del Carmine
Mordini
Via Cervia
Torre delle Ore
Vittorio Emanuele
Via Burlamacchi
Palazzo Pretorio
Pza. San Michele
Via Veneto
S. Andrea
Guinigi
Torre Guinigi
Via dell'Angelo Custode
S. Nicolao
Fosso
Via d. Tabacchi
Via Beccheria
Via Roma
Pza. S. Romana
Palazzo d. Provincia
Pza. Napoleone
Via S. Croce
Corso
Via del Battistero
Pza. d. Giglio
Via del Duomo
Pza. S. Martino
Via dell'Arcivescovado
Via della Rosa
Passeggiata Mura
V. d. Dogana
Garibaldi
Duomo
Via Francesco Carrara
Lucca

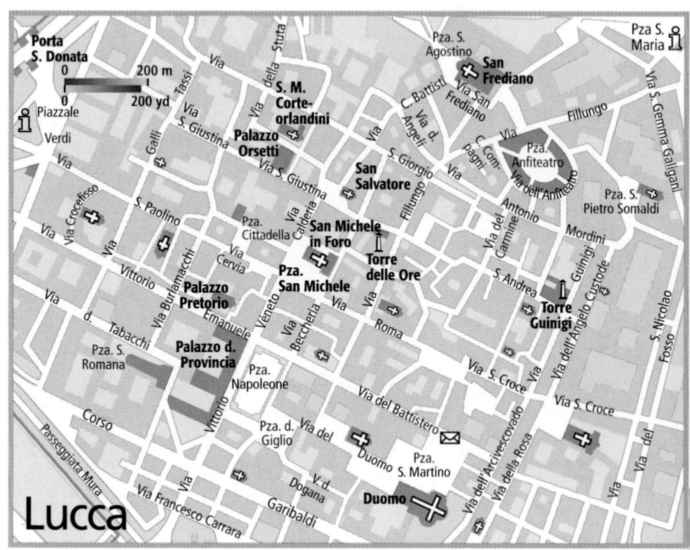

Index

Picture Credits

AA/J. Edmanson: 10, 163

AA/T. Harris: 17 (left), 57, 64, 65, 66, 97, 99, 104, 105, 108, 109, 116, 118, 121, 144, 146, 164, 165, 166, 167, 174, 178, 180, 190

AA/R. Ireland: 169 (top), 191

AA/M. Jourdan: 201

AA/S. McBride: 21, 55, 56, 58, 59, 63, 75, 76, 78, 79, 96 (bottom), 98, 112, 136, 137, 138, 139, 140, 141, 142, 143, 145, 147, 148, 151, 194, 196

AA/K. Paterson: 29, 32, 35, 36/37, 38, 67, 95, 96 (top), 110/111, 152, 153, 177, 179, 192

AA/C. Sawyer: 61, 70, 71, 73, 81, 101, 113, 134, 149, 160, 162, 168, 169 (bottom), 172, 173, 175, 176, 181

AA/J. Tims: 17 (right), 60, 68, 69, 80, 102, 119, 120, 182

akg-images: 11, album 24, Rabatti-Domingie 100 and 117

DuMont Bildarchiv/Christina Anzenberger-Fink, Toni Anzenberger: 7

getty images: SuperStock 12, Peter Zelei 15, De Agostini Picture Library/G. Nimatallah 20, 22/23, Imagno 25, 26, Laura Lezza 27, Adam Jones 122, Mondadori Portfolio 170, De Agostini Picture Library/G. Nimatallah 171

GlowImages: 19

laif: Berthold Steinhilber 4, Gamma-Rapho/Tripelon/Jarry 107, hemis.fr/Rene Mattes 124

LOOK-foto: Jürgen Richter 8

mauritius images/United Archives: 13, 30, 74, 114

On the cover: huber-images: Tom Mackie (top), Matteo Carassale (bottom), Getty Images/DNY59 (background)

1st Edition 2015

Worldwide Distribution: Marco Polo Travel Publishing Ltd
Pinewood, Chineham Business Park
Crockford Lane, Chineham
Basingstoke, Hampshire RG24 8AL, United Kingdom.

Authors: Tim Jepson, Lindsay Bennett, Christiane Büld Campetti
Editor: Frank Müller, Anja Schlatterer, Anette Vogt (red.sign, Stuttgart)
Revised editing and translation: Christopher Wynne
Program supervisor: Birgit Borowski
Chief editor: Rainer Eisenschmid

Cartography: © MAIRDUMONT GmbH & Co. KG, Ostfildern
3D-illustrations: jangled nerves, Stuttgart

Printed in China

Despite all of our authors' thorough research, errors can creep in. The publishers do not accept any liability for this. Whether you want to praise, alert us to errors or give us a personal tip – please don't hesitate to email or post:

MARCO POLO Travel Publishing Ltd
Pinewood, Chineham Business Park
Crockford Lane, Chineham
Basingstoke, Hampshire RG24 8AL
United Kingdom
Email: sales@marcopolouk.com

FSC®
www.fsc.org
MIX
Paper from responsible sources
FSC® C020056

10 REASONS
TO COME BACK AGAIN

1. Often imitated, but nothing ever compares to the **original**.
2. **2450 museums, 3500 churches** and lots more – how can a fortnight ever be long enough?
3. You only discovered that Tuscany has a **fantastic coast** just before leaving...
4. Culture or the countryside, crowds or peace and quiet – Tuscany has so many different **facets**.
5. Herbs, mushrooms, native asparagus – getting to know the light **Tuscan cuisine** takes time.
6. The many excellent **vineyards** produce wonderful wine, year in, year out.
7. You missed out on the superb **hikes and cycling tours** because of all the culture.
8. **Olive groves**, **vineyards** and roads lined with **cypresses** makes you crave for more.
9. You simply can't forget the **warm light** and **intensive colours**.
10. Your yearning for the aesthetic has by no means reached saturation point considering all the **beautiful things** to see.